A Performer's Guide to Transcribing, Editing, and Arranging Early Music

A Performer's Guide to Transcribing, Editing, and Arranging Early Music

ALON SCHAB

OXFORD

UNIVERSITY PRESS

OXFORD
UNIVERSITY PRESS

Oxford University Press is a department of the University of Oxford. It furthers
the University's objective of excellence in research, scholarship, and education
by publishing worldwide. Oxford is a registered trade mark of Oxford University
Press in the UK and certain other countries.

Published in the United States of America by Oxford University Press
198 Madison Avenue, New York, NY 10016, United States of America.

CIP data is on file at the Library of Congress
ISBN 978–0–19–760066–5 (pbk.)
ISBN 978–0–19–760065–8 (hbk.)

DOI: 10.1093/oso/9780197600658.001.0001

9 8 7 6 5 4 3 2 1

Paperback printed by Sheridan Books, Inc., United States of America
Hardback printed by Bridgeport National Bindery, Inc., United States of America

Contents

Acknowledgments

Christopher Hogwood, one of the most prominent figures in the early music revival for almost half a century, once said in a lecture:

Usually, if a journalist asks me how I spend my time, I will say that I'm 50% a performer and 50% a musicologist, and it's not strictly true, though. If one had more time to expand on that, I suppose one should say that one is 100% both of those, because there is no way you can switch off your academic musicological interest when you're performing, and no way of suspending all notions of performance when you're sitting in the dusty library. So, although I would aim to be a performing monkey for half the year and a dusty academic for the other half of the year, the two necessarily mingle and my ideal, I think, is to keep them both and juggle them so that they are both in the air and available all the time.[1]

I share Hogwood's ideal completely. The sense of inability to separate scholarship and hands-on musicianship is, for many, a defining characteristic of early music performers (indeed, I usually find the broader definition "early music people" far more practical than exclusive definitions like "early music performers" or "early music scholars"). What I find truly beautiful about the early music movement is that, for each musician, the exact balance between these two elements is unique and that balance manifests itself immediately in one's music making. Inspired by the legacy of the first generations of the early music revival (or at least by what I perceive to be those generations' legacy), I aim in this book to contribute something of my own scholarship-performance blend for the benefit of early music performers who might share with me the enthusiasm for creativity in making (early) music.

A long list of colleagues and friends helped me tremendously while working on this book. I had countless inspiring debates with my teachers Yitzhak Sadaï z"l, Ruth Apel, and Martin Adams, and with my friends Yoel Greenberg, Eran Shalev, Ayelet Even Ezra, David Rees, Yuval Shaked, Yuval Nov, and Abigail Wood. My fellow Purcellians—Rebecca Herissone, Andrew Pinnock, Bruce Wood, Alan Howard, Peter Holman, and Katherina Lindekens—are for me a lasting source of inspiration and encouragement. My friend Elam Rotem, in our hundreds of email correspondences and WhatsApp chats, reflected with me on matters of both performance and research and gave me valuable a firsthand account of what things look like in the premiere league of historically informed performance (HIP). My deepest thanks to all those who gave advice, answered queries, helped me to obtain scans, and, in general, shared their thoughts with me: Mark Kroll, Bill Hunt, Robert Rawson, Jed Wentz, David Shemer, Susie Napper, David A. Wells, Michael Hell, Jochai Rosen, Oded Zehavi, Taiseer Elias, Bella Brover-Lubovsky, Uri Smilansky, Eitan Steinberg, Orí Harmelin, Simon MacHale, Pieter Dirksen, Andrew Woolley, Dan Tidhar, Gideon Brettler, David Lewis, Sarig Sela, Zur Shalev, and An de Ridder (from Holland Festival). Idit Shemer, Gilat Rotkop, and Nadav (Nedev) Cohen allowed me to analyze their recordings for the spectral analysis in Chapter 6. The anonymous readers for the press contributed greatly to the focus of the book and made valuable suggestions in an enlightening and effective review process.

Some of the ideas expressed in this book evolved during years of work with performers for whom I composed and arranged works. David Shemer and the Jerusalem Baroque Orchestra, as well as Myrna Herzog and Phoenix Ensemble, never missed an opportunity to involve me in their projects. For some years I was a member in the Owlos recorder quartet, which proved an invaluable laboratory for experimentation in arrangement and in programming concerts.

During my high school years I studied both the viola and the recorder, and it always seemed strange that others' expectations of me, when playing each instrument, differed significantly. As a viola player I was expected to demonstrate good musical insight, play a lot of chamber music, and develop impeccable technique (the last of which I failed gloriously). As a recorder player I was expected not only to do all that, but also to play from facsimiles, transpose on sight, change instruments, take up the crumhorn (really quickly), adopt different techniques for my 440 and my 415 instruments, master extended techniques for works from the 1960s and 1970s, search for materials in the library, look up obscure terms in encyclopedias, consult treatises, extract parts, arrange, and improvise. Thus, the strongest influence on the ideas in this book remains that of my three recorder teachers—Drora Bruck, Naomi Rogel, and Michael Melzer.

I received kind help from the library staff in the University of Haifa, as well as of the National Library of Scotland, Basel University Library, The British Library, The Bodleian, and the Pepys Library (Magdalene College, Cambridge).

The cover image is used from www.hermitagemuseum.org, courtesy of The State Hermitage Museum, St. Petersburg, Russia.

Four editors worked on various parts of this book in various stages along the past four years, and courageously faced the countless Hebraisms and idiosyncrasies that plagued the first draft (and the second, and the third . . .). I therefore thank Avshalom Guissin, David Rees, David McCarthy, and Nikole Natali Buchnik for making my ideas readable. Mistakes in this book, even when perfectly readable, are entirely my own.

The book was published with the support of the Israel Science Foundation.

My friends Ifat Mizrachi Harari, Amnon Seelig, and Avshalom Guissin were always happy to share my excitement along the process. The greatest encouragement I received from my parents, Rivka and Miki Schab, and from my siblings and their families.

The work with the editors at Oxford University Press has been encouraging and inspiring. Suzanne Ryan (who first welcomed the project), Norm Hirschy, and finally Michelle Chen and Sean Decker were ever helpful and conducted the process with virtuosity. With them, everyone at OUP made the work on this book a fascinating and enjoyable process. I am grateful to the anonymous readers for their wise advice and countless good ideas—with their positive and optimistic attitude they helped me to avoid the negative sentiment that somehow crept into the first drafts of the manuscript.

This book is dedicated to my wife Sivan, who has been enduring my HIP revolutionary zeal for fifteen years and turning a blind eye to my sneaking Tallis and Sweelinck into the musical diet of our three boys—Yotam, Yair, and Dori. It is always a pleasure to share ideas about musical performance and creativity with a wife who is Musicianship itself, at its purest and most crystallized.

Alon Schab
Herzliya, July 2021

Introduction
Early Music on the Page

How old is the "early music revival?" Should one start counting from Mendelssohn's performance of Bach's St. Matthew Passion in 1829, or from the foundation of the Schola Cantorum de Paris in 1897? Or perhaps from the foundation of its counterpart in Basel in 1933? Should one start counting from the formation of the first ensembles that recorded extensively—the Pro Musica Antiqua of Brussels or the New York Pro Musica—or from the 1960s, when the countercultural features of the revival made it both fashionable and commercially sustainable?

Whether the revival, in general, is a century old or almost two centuries, scholars may have, by now, sufficient perspective to study the rise of the historically informed approach to performance in the second half of the twentieth century. In the third decade of the twenty-first century, it is possible to critically examine not only the ideology that has been driving the early music revival, but also the performance practices that it has created, and that set it apart from other types of music making. The early music revival did not take place without resistance in some quarters, mainly by those who felt that the fashionable case for historical accuracy (whether such accuracy is achievable at all) came at the expense of musical expression and expertise, and conflicted with the pillars of their musical world: the consensus around the classical-romantic canon, and the trust in a received tradition.

From the historically informed point of view, adherence to tradition was the main weakness of mainstream performers focused on music of the eighteenth and nineteenth centuries. Initially, the objection to tradition unified the historically informed, or "authentic," musical movement, as it came to be known during the 1960s and 1970s (just as it unified other countercultural forces of the time). By the early 1980s, however, criticism was being leveled at the philosophical underpinnings of the historically informed movement, even from within the ranks of the revivalists themselves. In the long run, this criticism seems to have helped the movement to mature and to clarify its aims with less naïveté but no less vigor.

By the late 1980s, the movement reached a steady state: its festivals were attracting audiences, and it had its own "superstars" and recording labels. In

A Performer's Guide to Transcribing, Editing, and Arranging Early Music. Alon Schab, Oxford University Press.
© Oxford University Press 2022. DOI: 10.1093/oso/9780197600658.003.0001

fact, the progress that had been made by 1988, when Harry Haskell published an optimistic epilogue to his history of the revival (Haskell 1988: 189–97), has continued to grow exponentially. Moreover, additional advancements have been made: scanned manuscripts, prints, and treatises are available for all to download and use; organists install high-quality samples of original baroque instruments at home and play them on digital consoles; studio computers emulate the acoustic environment of specific historical rooms; harpsichordists can easily experiment with historical temperaments with the aid of free tuning applications installed on their mobile phones; and cutting-edge activities at festivals are broadcast live over the Internet to audiences worldwide. It has never been easier to be historically informed.

For a long time, the movement benefited from the teaching, recording, and performing presence of its founding fathers and mothers. The chronological boundaries of authenticity were pushed further—first to include Haydn, then Mozart, Beethoven, Berlioz, Brahms, Bruckner, Mahler, and even early Stravinsky (who himself witnessed the early years of the revival, and whose views on performance may have influenced some of the early exponents of the revival). At a certain point, critics could no longer act surprised when a "new" decade was annexed into the historically informed territory. The pioneers' students and their students' students enjoyed a warm familiarity and, to some extent, also a sense of inherited authority and the aura of *enfants terribles*. Slowly but surely, however, the revolutionaries' sense of legacy and routine started looking suspiciously "traditional."

With the recent deaths of some of the most celebrated exponents of the movement from its revolutionary heyday in the 1960s and 1970s, it becomes possible to examine several practical aspects of that generation's legacy. These figures essentially set the rules for early music concert life, training, and recording. Within a few years, the early music scene lost Bruce Haynes (1942–2011), Montserrat Figueras (1942–2011), Gustav Leonhardt (1928–2012), Frans Brüggen (1934–2014), Christopher Hogwood (1941–2014), Nikolaus Harnoncourt (1929–2016), and Anner Bylsma (1934–2019). Since many of these pioneers were active until their very last days, the implications of their loss were direct and immediate—orchestras hired new artistic directors, festival programs changed, and, on a more profound level, those who had been seeking the guidance of the Olympians now had to make do with their recordings, writings, and the secondhand testimony of their students and collaborators. The recent passing of these pioneers not only marked a symbolic "end of an era" but rather was a concrete crisis. It is thus time for a re-evaluation of the practices they represented.

The need for retrospection was clearly observable even before Brüggen, Hogwood, and Harnoncourt took their final bows. For the fortieth anniversary issue of *Early Music*, published in early 2013 (Hogwood was still able to contribute an article on editing Mendelssohn's symphonies), several leading scholars were invited to address, in a series of short observations, key concepts and practices of the early music community. Stephen Rose contributed a piece, titled "Towards the Digital Future," in which he pointed out that digitization programs of leading libraries, as well as websites that link to digitized sources (Rose specifically mentioned the International Music Score Library Project, or IMSLP), allow "anyone with a web browser [to] view thousands of primary sources, at minimal cost and with no gatekeepers to circumvent" (Rose 2013).[1] The primary sources played a central role in the pioneers' claim to authenticity. The young Brüggen was a prolific editor of early music before he became famous as a virtuoso. Many of Figueras's recordings are centered on a specific manuscript or print (Llibre Vermell de Montserrat, El Cancionero de Palacio, Mudarra's *Libro Tercero* of 1546). Hogwood collected an impressive library of manuscripts that informed his work as a performer. Nowadays, with so many sources available to early music performers everywhere, the mere use of source material is no longer a reliable indicator of historical erudition and discernment. The performer's claim to historical authenticity can and should be judged not by whether, but by how, he or she uses source material.

For reasons that will be discussed in detail, study of the way in which performance material was and is used allows one both to understand many core issues in the treatment of early music and to inform one's own use of performance material. The present book makes observations about recent practice and highlights possible paths forward. It is aimed primarily at those who deal with the performance of music from the late renaissance to the classical periods. By extension, the principles of sensitivity to historical context and written sources offered here are applicable to music from any period.

Transcribing, Editing, and Arranging

The six chapters of the book offer an introduction and a guide to three of the principal tasks with which performers of early music engage throughout their professional lives, whether during their studies, when on tour, in the studio, or as teachers in conservatories and in universities: (1) how to transcribe music from manuscripts and early prints; (2) how to use such historical sources when editing one's own performance material; and (3) how to reconcile one's own needs as a performer with historically informed principles, and the high artistic standards of today's early music scene when arranging a work from one medium to another.

Early music performers face various challenges in connection with source material, challenges from which performers of later repertoires are usually exempt: much of the music they explore is available only in manuscripts and early prints; the notational systems for elements such as ornaments, rhythmic alteration, and use of accidentals vary from period to period and place to place;

instrumentation is rarely specified; and textual issues such as text underlay and pronunciation are obscure. The ideology of historically informed performance, to which the early music scene inclines, means that performers are expected to engage with such challenges through comprehensive study of the historical evidence for any given period. The reputation of a historically informed performer is thus, at least in part, shaped by his or her ability to deal with the three tasks that are addressed in my book.

How important are these tasks? Let us consider a situation typical of innumerable early music festivals: a baroque ensemble has been invited to play Bach's "Art of Fugue." In order to prepare, the ensemble members may search for an existing performance edition that suits the ensemble's forces or, alternatively, prepare their own edition. The more committed the performers are to the historically informed ideal, the more likely they will choose the latter option, in which case the ensemble would probably strive to do the following:

- obtain scans of the two primary sources of the work (both available for free download on the Internet),[2]
- *transcribe* the excerpts that are to be performed,
- *edit* the transcription in order to correct mistakes and to choose among the many competing variants offered by the two sources, and then
- *arrange* the work to fit the instruments of the ensemble.

Having arranged the piece, the ensemble would then have to make additional decisions regarding the production of performance materials. Should the performers use parts or a score? Which elements of the original sources should be modernized, and which retained? Should ornaments and other such elements be decided upon and written down in advance, or should they be improvised in performance?

"The Art of Fugue" is perhaps the most iconic case of a piece whose surviving sources demand extensive decision-making on the performers' behalf. But there are many others. Polyphonic chansons from the early sixteenth century (for example, the vast repertoire published by Petrucci in Venice or by Attaingnant in Paris), dance music (from the late medieval repertoire in British Library manuscript Add. MS 29,987, through the books of Arbeau and Praetorius, to the melodies in Playford's *The Dancing Master*), instrumental diminutions of mid-century madrigals and motets, English consort music of the entire seventeenth century—these and other repertoires all require similar processes.

Preparing a performance score from the sources, especially from scratch, is time-consuming, and can easily exceed the daily scheduling constraints of active performers. Early music performers will often state that, ideally, they would always work with the sources and, if needed, make their own arrangements based on historical arrangement models—if only they had the time to delve into the material. Performers have any reason to want to choose their own favorite madrigals and motets rather than limiting themselves to those pieces selected by Rognoni or Bassano four centuries earlier, and to embellish them based on their own historical knowledge rather than performing the few written-out embellishments that sixteenth-century theorists Ortiz and Dalla Casa saw fit to include in their treatises on diminutions. Thus, musicians preparing a performance of a concerto grosso based on a trio sonata by Corelli might prefer to arrange it themselves, according to Francesco Geminiani's method (adding the parts of the ripieno without touching Corelli's original parts). Indeed, why should a performer limit herself to the six trio sonatas Geminiani arranged and published? Why shouldn't she choose from the full breadth and depth of Corelli's forty-eight surviving trio sonatas and make her own arrangements? The tailoring of new arrangements to fit the needs and constraints of a given performance, at a specific time and place, has come to be perceived as an inseparable part of the unique artistic message of many an ensemble.

For musicologists, there exists ample literature on critical music editing; for performers, helpful literature is harder to find. The most extensive monographs dedicated to editing and intended (at least in part) for performers are John Caldwell's *Editing Early Music* and Denis Stevens's *Musicology: A Practical Guide*, both published almost forty years ago (Stevens 1980: Caldwell 1985). While the editorial discipline advanced by Caldwell and Stevens remains valid, their monographs were written for an early music scene that was fundamentally different from the world of today's performers. In the years since Caldwell and Stevens's books appeared, the Internet emerged, performers developed new views of "authenticity," and the recording and publishing industries underwent a sea change, with near monopolies giving way to a plethora of new channels. Nowadays, early music performers are likely to typeset unperformed music from freely available digitized manuscripts, record it in their living rooms, and market the recording from their laptops. The practice of editing early music deserves a fresh look.

Such is the rationale behind this present book. In the following pages, I suggest that despite the effort and time it requires, performers should participate in the preparation of their performance material, and that the process of preparing performance material is as much a platform for creativity as is performance itself. Just as renaissance and baroque musicians did not canonize the scores and parts they were reading from, but often arranged, abridged, expanded, and paraphrased the music they played, so, too, should those who subscribe to a historically informed approach embrace similar creative measures, measures that inevitably make one's performance more informed, more creative, more one's own.

This book is intended to serve both early music performers and academics (especially in the field of performance-practice research). Performers will find in it an introduction to some scholarly skills that are often studied only in musicology departments. Musicologists will find in it a discussion of editorial-philological technique relevant to late-seventeenth and to early-eighteenth century music,[3] as well as an exploration of the intricate relationship between critical editing and performance practice. This book also aims to fill a gap in the existing literature on editing by discussing the creative stages of arrangement—stages that are indeed hard to theorize but are nonetheless essential for those who wish to hear their editorial projects brought to life on the concert stage.

Throughout the book, I will discuss some of the challenges involved in the preparation of a musical text for performance, especially in light of the growing accessibility of material and the increasing democratization of production. I cover those common scenarios where performers might want to assume editorial responsibilities and create their own ad hoc performance material. I am not suggesting that performers should produce scholarly editions collating all surviving sources of a piece. Those who want to perform, say, Purcell's fantazias for viols from the composer's autograph (freely accessible online) will find here much food for thought, as well as useful guidance for transcribing these works from that manuscript. The intricate technique of collating the several secondary sources of the fantazias, however, will not alter the performance significantly, and is therefore beyond the scope of the present book.

Performers and Performance Material

As described earlier, the adherence to tradition, so strongly rejected by the first generation of revivalist performers, slowly spread to those quarters of the musical world which initially defined themselves as historically informed. In fact, some of the pioneering early music conductors "showed signs of the very maestro authoritarianism the revolution had sworn to resist" (Lebrecht 2014), and some of the crises that have befallen the "Grand Tradition" in recent decades started to endanger the historically informed as well. After all the great forgotten masterworks were given their debut recording on LP in the 1960s and 1970s, and were recorded again on CD (with flawless rendition made possible by the digital recording and editing studio) in the 1980s and 1990s, the same question that record labels had asked with regard to Schubert and Schumann suddenly pertained to Sweelinck and Schütz, too: What could justify yet another new recording of an old piece?

For the individual performer who wishes to be noticed, the easiest solution in any musical genre is to cultivate a "celebrity" persona. Performers can choose to develop images as pop stars, philosophers, or activists (political, social, or environmental). Another approach is to promote oneself as an expert of a more circumscribed range of repertoire, for example as an expert for a specific composer (it is easy to find expert Mozart, Chopin, or Schoenberg performers) or a nationality (often the performer's own). The record companies that fueled the early music movement often had an interest in cultivating their own celebrity pop stars, activists, and experts of, say, Monteverdi, or French baroque music. Famous performers belonging to each of these categories will be familiar to almost any classical music fan.

There were, however, several other methods by which performers could promote themselves as original and unique—methods that persist even today. First among these was to assume the profile of the "explorer"—a performer whose reputation lies in his ability to discover unknown works, versions of works, or even unknown composers. Even if the pieces or composers discovered by the explorer were already known to the scholarly community, some credit was always reserved for the performer who brought them to the notice of a wider public. Record companies were always happy to add a "world premiere" label to the sleeve of an LP or a CD. This is not to say that the explorers themselves took a cynically utilitarian approach to musicological research. Indeed, some ensembles are motivated by genuine scholarly curiosity no less than by commercial considerations.[4]

Another way for performers to showcase their originality in early music is to turn to the field of performance practice. With only a short tradition of historically informed performance behind them, and with many gaps in today's knowledge of older performance practices, performers are free to experiment with pitch, tempo, rhythmic alteration, and ornamentation. In many cases, these experiments are taken to an extreme. Similar to jazz musicians, early music performers who extemporize diminutions on madrigals or motets shift the focus from their prowess as performers to their originality as "composers" (the anachronism of the distinction between performers and composers notwithstanding).[5]

Also common are historical reconstructions attained by the use of the historical text and the historical context. For example, situating a cycle of polyphonic mass ordinary movements on a particular date in the ecclesiastical year by adding the chants of the proper to it,[6] or reconstructing a monarch's funeral service,[7] offer the listeners the illusion of time travel. As Joshua Rifkin demonstrated, such reconstructions, though appealing, often have fundamental flaws in their historical underpinning (Rifkin 2014). The scoring of the music and even the layout of the notation may be used to reconstruct the spatial deployment of the performers: splitting an ensemble into multiple choruses in antiphonal music; arranging a small vocal ensemble around a large music stand with a single, full-size, reproduction of a chant book; playing around an open book set in table-book format—these all offer the audience the feeling that the ensemble is leaving the comfort zone of traditional stage arrangement, in order to uncover historical data that is somehow encoded in the source of the music. A historical source sometimes offers the performer a justification for programming works together. Acquaintance with, for example, the Fitzwilliam Virginal Book, may inspire the grouping together of works by Byrd, Bull, and Philips, and the result may seem to have more historical "validity" than a single-composer program.

Sometimes, ensembles make their transcriptions and editions accessible to the public on the Internet. In such cases, the performance material serves as both an archive commemorating past performances and as a proof of the performers' independence from commercial editions (and possibly of their originality, where the variant of a work justifies it).[8] While the observations and analyses presented henceforth will be as critical and unbiased as possible, it should be admitted that the present book is motivated by a proactive agenda: to encourage musicians to engage with the scholarly and creative work required from the preparation of performance material.

The Internet brought about a radical change in the landscape for musicians: it offers many new channels to those who wish to create, retrieve, and disseminate music. Assessment of an ongoing technological revolution such as the Internet must be done cautiously: referring to technology, software, or websites too specifically might cause a study not only to miss the general picture, but simply to become outdated and feel irrelevant quickly. For example, the radical changes in the copyright ethics of Internet users in response to Napster in the period 1999–2001 are still highly relevant for any study of contemporary music consumption, although the specifics of how Napster operated become less and less relevant as file-sharing technologies evolve.[9] In all probability, at the time when the present book is published, most undergraduate students will be those who were born around 2000 and will never have had the chance to run the relevant version of Napster themselves.

For early music performers, two defining factors of contemporary, Internet-influenced, musical culture are an increase in accessibility, and democratization. Audio and visual materials are largely obtainable by any performer (accessibility), and they in turn may extend the materials' accessibility further on various platforms (democratization). The essence of these processes and the principles of handling them are not new, however. Even the course of writing the present book demonstrated for me the force of the aforementioned processes: many of the preliminary analyses I made were based on hard-copy facsimiles I had in my home library, but as research progressed and I tried to locate additional sources, I found myself working more and more with online archives and libraries. And time and again I found that, even in the rare cases when I could not find a decent reproduction of a manuscript, the Internet enhanced the traditional networks of academics—I could quickly contact acquaintances (and strangers) from overseas who were happy to share the contents of their own libraries, be they physical or virtual. The longest I had to wait for a manuscript scan was no more than a day or two.

Some of the most influential studies of the present-day early music scene, for example, John Butt's *Playing with History* (2002) and Bruce Haynes's *The End of Early Music* (2007), were written shortly before it became impossible to ignore the Internet's influence. This reflects, for example, in Haynes's treatment of period composing. Period composing is usually encouraged as a part of the study program in conservatory (where it is usually called "style composition") but meets fierce objection in the "real world" of public music making. Haynes (2007: 209–13) commends the Vox saeculorum guild—an Internet community that specializes in period composing. Such communities would be met with very little encouragement among concert organizers, and even among audiences, but are independent and unlimited under the democracy of the Internet. Haynes does not mention the fact that, to a large extent, it is the very platform of the Internet that facilitates the potential growth of such phenomena. Occasional references to online resources appear in periodicals and give a clear picture of the changing attitude toward discussion groups, databases, and social media groups.[10] For example, review sections in periodicals, which have traditionally dealt with books and scores, nowadays often discuss online catalogues and databases. Periodicals themselves, especially those published by specialist societies for the advancement of specific instruments (lute, viol, recorder), reach out to ever expanding audiences by adopting an "open access" policy, exposing amateur and professional performers to cutting-edge scholarship.

Historically informed performance of early music is one of the musical genres most influenced by the Internet. The performance of early music is dependent on the conflation of many kinds of information—musical and textual sources, recordings, treatises and paintings—and all of these have become increasingly accessible in recent decades. And while the change in access to historical evidence is seemingly only a matter of quantity, there are qualitative changes as well.

One such qualitative change occurred in the field of intellectual property rights. Of course, commercial recordings may be bought and downloaded in seconds, but illegal downloads, of both recordings and scores, are also available, at least until they are discovered by the copyright owners and a "cease and desist" letter is issued. When Rose mentioned that IMSLP provided links to digitized sources, he must have been aware that IMSLP had been doing much more than that. IMSLP's official policy regarding copyright was not yet strict when the site started operating in 2006. The strict policy was in reaction to legal threats the site faced in 2007, and even after adopting that policy, the complexity of the copyright issue (stemming mainly from conflicting copyright laws in various countries) kept jeopardizing the IMSLP initiative. While many editions' prefaces and critical commentaries are clearly under copyright and are more rarely made accessible, the copyright on the main musical text of many up-to-date critical editions is much harder to protect and, as a result, performers can often find these online.[11] Other websites react differently to legal action, and may change name, domain, and file-sharing method. In other words, material that is under copyright still circulates freely over the Internet, and its availability blurs the practical difference between legal and illegal, especially in countries where copyright laws are not enforced consistently.

There has also been a radical change in the training process of young musicians over the past few decades. Until the middle of the twentieth century, students' acquaintance with repertoire was largely dependent on their score-reading ability and their access to proper music libraries. Opportunities to hear music performed live were not to be missed. While recordings of common-practice repertoire became more accessible during the 1950s and 1960s, it was not until the early 1980s that entire corpora of earlier composers' works were recorded—the complete works of Monteverdi, Dowland, Purcell, Corelli, F. Couperin, and, of course, J. S. Bach. In the field of early music, however, an available recorded "canon" is not enough to satisfy young students' wish to explore further repertoires.

Many students of early music now acquire substantial knowledge of performance style from recordings—many enroll to earn early music degrees when they are already able to imitate the performing styles of French and Italian baroque as reflected in commercial recordings. Although early music performers have been learning with the aid of recordings for several decades now (since the creation of a preliminary corpus of recordings made in the 1950s and 1960s), the increase in accessibility makes the learning process even easier and faster. In her recent study of improvisation in the performance of medieval music, Angela Mariani makes a useful distinction between "living" and "imagined" models: a "living" model is a performer whose performance one may imitate from hearing (and thus a recorded performer may be dead and still considered a "living" model) while an "imagined" model is an idealized reconstruction of a performance based on historical evidence (Mariani 2017: 15–27). When taken from the realm of medieval music into later repertoires, the two terms might prove misleading. Although the term "imagined" hints at something less tangible than "living," the baroque "imagined" model (reconstructed according to treatises and primary sources) can be supported much more strongly than its medieval counterpart.

The decline of physical media for storing music radically changed the dimensions of the artistic platform and offered new media, such as the short video—initially a promotional tool, and now an independent art form. Soloists and ensembles today are likely to benefit more from a "viral" three-minute video than from a flattering review of their recent CD in the written press.

Contemporary home recording techniques allow far more than simply recording. Beyond the use of artificial acoustic surroundings that flatter the ensemble or imitate a historical venue, multitracking, fading in or out, and other effects that go beyond the imitation or idealization of a live performance, are available. Although effects were experimented with in projects such as Philip Pickett's *The Alchemist* (1988), and sophisticated digital reverb machines like the "Lexicon" were in use at that time, experimentation with such effects cost a lot of money. Now, similar effects may be installed on one's laptop without cost. In some cases, advanced recording technique is joined with advanced video-production technique: Sting's video of himself singing in consort with three other "Stings," to the sound of his multitrack rendition of Dowland's "Can she excuse my wrongs," was released in 2006, more or less when the creation of such cinematic effects became feasible even in home production.

The Internet has accelerated, if not triggered, a sea change in audiences' expectations from artists' creativity. For those interested in early music, platforms like YouTube reintroduced renaissance principles such as cantus firmus and participatory modes of creativity. For example, toward the end of the first decade of the twenty-first century, a new genre of musically conceived satire boomed: filmed speeches (mainly by politicians) were made ridiculous by the addition of an instrumental track, doubling the prosody at the unison and with musical accompaniment, mostly using jazz idioms. As the speakers' prosody is natural and unmeasured, reinterpreting it as improvised outbursts of free jazz improvisation, adding instrumental "commentaries" to pauses, and forcing musical meter on unmeasured speech served to make the speeches chaotic and laughable.[12] Other techniques include "bad lip reading"—substituting the speech track of a video for a new, false, and ridiculous speech track, or the addition of intentionally wrong subtitles to movie scenes in languages other than English, could be attempted by users with very little technical skill, and did not require any special equipment. In some cases, the same speech was paraphrased by more than one artist, and the evident rivalry between some of them seems remarkably similar to the tradition of *emulatio*, evident in some paraphrases on Escobar's "Clamabat autem mulier," in *L'homme armé* masses, and in settings of the In Nomine.[13]

Performers and Musicologists

Earlier in this introduction I mentioned the celebrity "explorer," and described musicological research as a site for performers to exhibit distinctive qualities. That the early music revival owes much to the collegia musica that bloomed in American universities after the Second World War is well known. The fact that the leaders of the revival during the 1960s and 1970s combined, to some extent, characteristics of both performers and academics was one of the easiest targets for attack from traditional performers. Even from within the scene itself, the combination of emotion and logic was not always seen as possible or desired. Nonetheless, early music conductors such as Harnoncourt, Leonhardt, and Hogwood kept stressing the importance of collaboration between performers and scholars well into the twenty-first century. Since the present study is dedicated to the task of critical manuscript preparation, a task that was considered musicological but gradually became a part of early music performers' daily bread, it is important to make several remarks on these two groups.

The professionalization of early music performers during the early 1980s influenced their relationship with academia in two opposing directions: on the one hand, performers strove for independence and justification in a competitive recording scene saturated by excellent performers, both historically informed and non-informed. On the other hand, their busy schedule did not allow them to spend too much time on comparing editions against the original sources or other such scholarly ventures. For scholars, the relationship became much more rewarding and, at the same time, they witnessed how much of their academic caution was being sacrificed on the altar of showmanship and pizzazz.

The challenge for the historically informed cause from the early 1980s onward was that it became more profitable, and performers became motivated to jump on the bandwagon of authenticity for reasons other than aesthetics or ideology. During the 1960s and 1970s, the Oxbridge scene (mainly in faculties other than music) was a hotbed of well-read, curious, and intellectually independent musicians. Later, the foundation of specialized early music departments in conservatories proved a double-edged sword: it facilitated the formation of many full-size baroque orchestras and choirs specializing in early music, but it also shifted some of the weight from study of sources and texts to acquiring knowledge from the experienced teachers. In recent years, this tendency has gained further force as players of modern instruments take up period instruments for purely financial reasons. For the talented, it is even possible to "fake" the mannerisms of historically informed performance.

A growing demand for authentic-sounding performances and the crystallization of authentic-sounding performance styles (both potentially unrelated to the ethos of historically informed performance itself) create several problematic byproducts. Mannerisms of historically informed performance are being unthinkingly adopted by many: lists of all the instruments used in a recording, or of the editions used; musicological explanations (sometimes far-fetched) for performers' choices; choice of specific historical temperaments without historical justification; and many more. Any comprehensive discussion of the phenomenon and the ignorance (and sometime deceit) that it reflects might all too quickly turn into an indictment. This is contrary to the purpose of the book—which is to assist performers. It is, however, important to say that working on this book involved the study of many dozens of recordings from the past few years, and brought about many moments of disappointment at the sight of what seems to be a prevalent simplistic approach to issues of historical performance.

For those who, like myself, maintain that musicological research is not only relevant but also crucial for the historically informed, there are two possible ways to deal with a situation in which performers seem to ignore important scholarly aspects of performance: one is to lock oneself up in the ivory tower and complain bitterly about any manifestation of ignorance; another is to raise awareness of the importance of research, the possible consequences of scholarly oversight, and the merits of immediate contact with historical evidence. Similarly, lamenting the prevalent non-critical approach to online information, without taking active measures to educate people, risks the fundamentals of democracy. This book is therefore an optimistic reaction to the complicated state of historically informed performance.

Interference and Non-Interference

Transcribing, editing, and arranging—while these three tasks are grouped together in the title of this book, they represent different points along the continuum between a non-interventionalist approach to the musical text (neatly captured in teachers' common request to "play what is written on the page") and an interventionalist approach to the text (which, taken to the extreme, might entail changing or re-writing the musical text, only to modify that text again during performance). These two opposite approaches are to be found even among just those who subscribe to a historically informed agenda. For some, being historically informed means that they should play solely from historical sources, and even without amending textual errors, because that would lead to a result close to what was heard in the distant past (which, naturally, requires that they use exactly the same instruments that are required to perform the music as the sources transmit it).[14] For others, being historically informed means to assume all those freedoms that performers in the distant past would have assumed—for example, a harpsichordist who would play a harpsichord suite by Handel might choose an edition that gives what she perceives as the authoritative one, add an overture she arranged from one of Handel's operas, change the order of the movements or omit a movement, replace a movement with a movement by Pepusch, write her own double for a saraband, improvise two or three added variations to the chaconne, or perhaps even add her own original chaconne. Handel would hardly have been shocked to see his works treated in this way. It is certainly more historical to see Handel's own constant adaptation of his own or others' works as an accepted early eighteenth-century practice than to dub it as theft or plunder. Most historically informed performers, however, take different approaches with regard to different aspects in their performances, and make all the necessary fine-tuning for every project that they work on.

The present book consistently negotiates these two tendencies. On the one hand, the majority of music examples in this book were edited directly from renaissance and baroque sources, and the practices described here all draw on direct work with the sources. In many of the cases I encourage performers to do the same (for example, in Chapters 1, 3, and 4). On the other hand, I find the interventionalist approach almost inevitable in performers' attempts to keep themselves and their audiences interested. Therefore, much attention will be given to issues of improvisation and arrangement (in Chapters 2, 5, and 6).

Criticism leveled against practices of "period composition" (or "style composition") is often centered on implicit presuppositions borrowed from a late-romantic view of music and of musical creativity in particular: an old musical style is someone else's language; composers nowadays should find "their own voice"; music in an old style is good for the classroom and for the classroom only; music written in earlier style is all too similar to art forgery. My choice not to dedicate a chapter to period composition does not in any way reflect my adherence to such view of music creativity, but rather my belief that any serious discussion of the subject would require another book. Any arguments for and against period composition—arguments that would certainly have a place in such a book—are, to me, on an entirely different plane than the aforementioned arguments. As to my personal opinion on the issue, suffice it to note that I slipped in my own example of an Ortiz-style solo recercada into my discussion of improvisation in Chapter 2 and that several of the examples in Chapter 5 (like those relating to Campion, Van Eyck, and Sweelinck) explore the far interventionalist end of the spectrum.

The Structure of the Book

The following book consists of six chapters. Chapter 1 explores the advantages and disadvantages of various types of editions and some of the common issues that arise when working from historical sources. Three historical sources are examined: the printed sources for a fantasia by Jacob Van Eyck (from the 1640s), the printed sources for a ricercar by Andrea Gabrieli in keyboard intabulation, and the manuscript partbooks containing a gigue by James Paisible. The chapter shows how, for a person engaged in creating tailor-made transcriptions of sources, a thorough understanding of the historical sources allows some flexibility when deciding which notational features to modernize and which to retain.

Chapter 2 analyzes the various paths that performers may take when performing from a musical source that aims to instruct rather than to document finalized texts. Many of the readers of my book will be familiar with Diego Ortiz's *Tratado de Glossas* (1553), one of the most important treatises on performance and improvisation—and if not with the more technical "catalogue" of ornaments that opens the book, then at least with some of the recercadas from it. The chapter shows discrepancies between Ortiz's theoretical teachings and his exemplary works. It also elucidates various ways a performer can approach such treatises: the performer can treat the exemplary works as closed texts, but may alternatively add counterpoint to them, or improvise newly composed glossas.

Chapter 3 focuses on the issue of multiple versions. In the field of early music, performers are particularly sensitive to the fact that many works survive in more than one authoritative version, and they tend to inform their audience about the specific versions they perform. While it is, of course, the responsibility of the specialist musicologist-editor to give full critical consideration to the issue of multiple versions and its implications, there are some challenges that fall squarely in the performer's domain. Which elements from one version can and should one intermix with those from another, and how? At what point should one rethink or redefine a variant source as an independent composition? How can one use the multiplicity of versions to enrich one's artistic message? In this chapter, I survey the corresponding problem-solving skills necessary for engaging with multiple versions—skills I consider essential for the early music performer's toolkit.

Chapter 4 examines one of most valuable assets of the performer—musical intuition—and evaluates the advantages and the disadvantages of using intuition to resolve textual problems in a musical source. The chapter focuses on the common problems of missing accidentals and redundant accidentals, and encourages performers to distinguish between cases where intuition offers a useful guide to solving textual problems, and cases where the use of intuition goes against the very essence of a historically informed approach.

Chapter 5 goes on to consider the creative task of arrangement. In it, I seek to alert readers to those levels of the composition that the performer must re-examine and arrange. In particular, I outline the way in which generic and instrumental idioms affect the musical source text. I analyze seventeenth- and eighteenth-century arrangements and examine the apparent priorities of and the techniques used by arrangers from that period. I walk the reader step by step through the process of arranging extensive excerpts from works by Sweelinck, Van Eyck, Bach, and Huwet. In addition to the How, I also highlight the Why, giving detailed descriptions of the dilemmas that an arranger might encounter and, as a case study, demonstrating the solutions I chose in my arrangements of those same excerpts.

As postscript, Chapter 6 extends the chronological boundaries of the book and deals with various problems that arise from the process of arranging early twentieth-century music. After discussing the spectral features of various early instruments, I add two more examples to complement those from Chapter 5, this time the works of Frank Bridge and Anton Webern.

At the beginning of my introduction, I stated that "it has never been easier to be historically informed," but here at the end, I offer a path that is far from the easiest. Reading this book; playing over the examples; digesting the principles that come up from the analyses; experimenting with improvisation; starting to read more meticulously the apparatus of editions we have been using for years; sketching new arrangements modeled after the historical examples surveyed here—these are all time-consuming tasks, and quite the opposite of the "never been easier" state of mind. Yet I offer this contribution to performers and early music lovers nonetheless, knowing that while our generation need not apologize for having manuscript scans at our fingertips and the convenience of high-quality recording devices at home, reading a book like this is but an invitation to experience something of the excitement of early music scholarship that was the daily bread of the movement's pioneers. We will never know what renaissance and baroque music sounded like in real time, but that is hardly a reason not to try and understand that music better.

Historical Sources on the Concert Stage

Performance Material and the Early Music Movement

Notation is central to the Western music tradition. It is so central that, collo-quially, it is often synonymous with music itself (as when people "play from the music" or "put the music on the stand"). The broader term "performance mate-rial" usually refers to the various kinds of music, either printed or handwritten—such as scores, instrumental parts, charts, and lead sheets—which musicians use in their daily work in rehearsal rooms, studios, or on stage. Performance material may sometimes be purely textual or graphic—for example, an outline of an arrangement, or a "set list" with the order of the pieces in the concert (which is sometimes no more than a copy of the same program given to the au-dience at the door), but more often it will be encoded in some form of notation.

Another important property of performance material is that it bears the markings of its users, the performers. Performance material "matures," undergoing a process of personalization and customization, gradually accumulating penciled-in information such as breath marks, bowings, fingerings, and registration, as well as other markings (often in shorthand) and highlighting, not to mention dog ears making for easier page turns, and further personalizations, such as scribbled notes and pictures and coffee stains. One of the first markings performers tend to add is their name, not only a sensible pre-caution to prevent loss or theft, but also a symbolic act establishing ownership in a deeper sense. Markings give performance material great professional and personal value for performers, as well as scholarly value for future generations. While most markings bear witness to a performer's personal study of a piece,

A Performer's Guide to Transcribing, Editing, and Arranging Early Music. Alon Schab, Oxford University Press.
© Oxford University Press 2022. DOI: 10.1093/oso/9780197600658.003.0002

for some performers the markings constitute the very core of their study, not unlike a theologian's glosses on Scripture.

The way in which musicians use performance material depends in no small part on the style of music they perform. While historically informed, early music performers will employ the same technical markings (breath marks, fingerings, etc.) and interpretative markings (usually dynamics, articulation, and phrasing) as do their colleagues occupied with later repertoires, they are usually alone in adding a third type of markings, namely those related to style-dependent interpretation.

While markings from this third category may appear similar to technical and interpretative markings, their function is a different one. Unlike the average seventeenth-century musician, performers nowadays regularly program works from different periods and places, which means that the same musical symbols must be interpreted in myriad different ways, depending on the time and place in which the music originated. Performers therefore use special markings to decode the musical text according to its historical context. In a piece by Purcell, for example (such as the suite discussed in Chapter 4), historically informed keyboard players would be sure to decode the ornamentation sign ⌁ according to contemporary English sources, namely, as a "beat"—a trill from the note below, whereas, in a piece by Couperin (such as "Les Rozeaux," discussed in Chapter 5), they would decode the same sign according to contemporary French sources, that is, as a "cadence"—a trill from the note above. A trill, in other words, is not a trill is not a trill. Similarly, if the performer is not entirely comfortable with the conventions of the French late baroque, for example, he or she may write down explicitly which melodic passages are to be played *inégal* and which *égal*. The constant mental acrobatics demanded of the performer by the historical multivalence of symbols makes markings of this third category essential for the performer.

Naturally, traditional and historically informed performers also differ in the kind of sheet music they use, just as the publishing history and performance history of their respective repertoires vary. The music libraries of early music performers are usually heterogeneous, containing a blend of facsimiles, modern editions, excerpts of *Denkmäler* volumes, and independently engraved scores prepared either by themselves or by private individuals who had made them accessible on the Internet. In many cases, a large part of the collection is photocopied rather than original. It is harder to guess the makeup of a lutenist's personal music library than that of a clarinettist's. In other words, an early music performer's music library says a lot about their artistic persona, and the performance material they go on stage with represents an individual artistic statement.

Sources and Facsimiles

How important are the sources for early music performers? Why do facsimiles of the sources occupy so much space in their libraries (and on their hard drives)? The function of notation in early music performance is hard to define and varies from one repertoire to another. In some medieval and early renaissance music, none, or almost none, of the music survives in notation: ensembles base entire programs on poetry, and the music is largely improvised. Benjamin Bagby, a founding member of the medieval-music ensemble Sequentia, described re-creating medieval epics as "a long process of trial and error [that] cannot be worked out on paper before-hand. . . . There is no "score" and no master plan which everyone receives on the first day of rehearsal. The work is done with the human beings who inhabit that space at that time. It is an organic process" (Bagby 2011). In later repertoires, however, relevant musical notation does exist, even if it requires some transcription or adaptation. Sometimes the ensemble may work from a "narrow" transcription of just the main melodic material, and then memorize the basic outlines of the arrangement. Jordi Savall describes how his ensemble Hespèrion XX used such a process while working on one of their early recordings: The ensemble members "copied the melodies from the manuscript with the rhythmic values and pitches found in the source . . . together with the text, and no one had a single extra note in front of them" (Savall 1992: 650). Other ensembles arrange monophonic repertoires (such as the *Carmina Burana* or the *Cantigas de Santa Maria*) down to the finest details, so that the structure, harmonization, and orchestration extend beyond what could be improvised with just the "raw" musical material.[1] Since the format of an hour-long song-recital (common in the performance of nineteenth-century Lieder) does not always work for early music (imagine an hour-long concert of fourteenth-century motets!), anyone compiling an early music program has to figure out how to keep the audience alert and interested.[2]

In later repertoires, pitch and rhythm are notated more accurately and performance stems more directly from the notes. For that reason, many of the prominent figures of the early music revival agree that early music performers should not make do with a modern edition but, at the very least, consult the historical sources themselves (or their facsimiles). Barthold Kuijken, looking back at more than four decades as a pioneer of the baroque flute, wrote in 2013 that "a responsible performer, especially, but not only of Early Music, should study the scientific editions and their critical comments, but also see the sources for himself" (Kuijken 2013: 94). Kuijken's expectations are moderate in comparison to what Trevor Pinnock wrote in the same year, for the fortieth anniversary volume of the journal *Early Music*:

> Ensembles and orchestras with an established nucleus who lay any claim to authenticity should work from totally unmarked parts. They should also seek out original source material. It is too easy to accept the convenient tyranny of "Urtext" editions that are readily available without recognizing that these are not of a uniformly high standard. I mention this topic with some feeling as I myself made wrong decisions by failing to go back to source material. (Pinnock T. 2013: 21)

As obliging as Kuijken and Pinnock may read, they merely echo the prevailing authoritative view among early music performers during the 1970s and 1980s, namely that performers should ideally perform from the historical source itself. Again, *Early Music* served as an important platform for that view, both explicitly in articles and implicitly in the variety of affordable facsimile editions advertised among its pages. In one of the journal's first issues, Joscelyn Godwin argued that he "would not hesitate to say that a mere pianist who can play from the original score of *Parthenia Inviolata*, for example, has penetrated further into the Jacobean musical world than someone who plays from a transcription on a Ruckers-type virginal, with the proper bass viol accompaniment" (Godwin 1974).

To this day, performing from facsimile is considered standard among early music students and professionals with regard to seventeenth- and eighteenth-century printed instrumental music (with the exception of keyboard music), lutenists play almost exclusively from facsimiles. Keyboardists, singers, and performers of later repertoires also are usually acquainted with the sources, but not always perform from them on stage.

The way the music is laid out on the paper in the source encodes much information about the way an ensemble was "staged" when the music was performed, and it therefore complements other primary sources like paintings, literature, and formal records (which are crucial for determining the size of historical ensembles). The decision to read from a single "choir book" placed on a high music stand, or from a folio in tablebook layout with the musicians seated around it, or from copies of the original parts,[3] may influence the attention of the performers, the communication between them, the way in which they look at the performer who leads the performance (if there is one), and the intensity of the performance.

The historical sources, whether they are used on stage as performance material or offstage as the basis for transcription, affect the very way in which early music ensembles work. Whereas much of the classical and romantic repertoires are available as performance material in the public domain, many modern performance editions of early music are still under copyright, which motivates ensembles to produce ad hoc editions based either on scholarly editions (that are old enough to be in the public domain) or on the sources themselves (Pinnock A. 1995). Preparing such ad hoc materials, and assuring their textual integrity, often involves collaboration with professional musicologists. An ensemble such as a college-based choir may be able to recruit the in-house services of musicology grad students or faculty members for no charge; if not, it may have to hire the services of a freelance musicologist, thus inflating production costs.[4]

From Facsimile to "Semi-Facsimile"

Producing a new edition of a musical piece is a process that requires some planning in order to make the product useful to its intended users. The edition must be notated in a way that is comprehensible for the performers on the receiving end, who are concerned, not least of all, with practical questions: Is the musical text clear and unambiguous, informative, and free of errors? Is the layout easy to use, without any awkward page turns in the middle of phrases? Is the type large enough to be legible, but small enough to keep the number of pages—and page turns—to a minimum? To meet these requirements consistently, the editor needs a style sheet, or editorial policy.

Thurston Dart (1921–1971), an eminent pioneer of the early music revival, offered such a policy. In his landmark book *The Interpretation of Music* (1954), Dart supplied a concise set of "hints to editors"—hints that reflect the policy of many editors of early music editions to this day. Dart's policy had two main concerns. The first was to make the music accessible to performers. Apparently, Dart did not expect his readership to be acquainted with early notation, for he asked editors to modernize time units, key signatures, and clefs, and to give the original symbols and units in prefatory staves only. He also called for the addition of reference marks, such as measure numbers. Dart's second concern was scholarly transparency. He asked editors to make their contribution to the edition distinguishable from the composer's, to give indications of ligatures and coloration marked in the source, to identify sources by library code and shelf mark, to warn the reader of any substantial changes made in the original musical text, and to provide a short scholarly preface (Dart 1967: 21–28).

One instruction that Dart gave in considerable detail shows that he considered the decoding of the old notational signs and the elimination of any ambiguity a high priority. Indeed, his emphasis on the modernization of notation conventions suggests that he tried to cater to the requirements of "the average music-lover" of his time (Dart 1967: 23). Retaining too much of the original notation would, he feared, result in what he termed a semi-facsimile:

[The] composer's accidentals should be in front of the notes to which they refer; any missing ones supplied by [the editor] should be in smaller type above (or in front of) the notes, and they should hold good to the end of the bar. Eliminate redundant accidentals, and use today's notational conventions wherever you can; a semi-facsimile of the original is of no use to the scholar and it is a nuisance to the performer. (Dart 1967: 21)

Dart's negation of the semi-facsimile was apt perhaps during the 1950s, when there were fewer performers who were capable of reading unedited facsimiles. But is it nowadays still a nuisance to the performer? As we will see, the original sources often pose serious obstacles when used as performance material, and making a semi-facsimile of a source is a process whereby performers might learn to evaluate and criticize the text.

In order to understand the idea of a semi-facsimile, let us take Kuijken's and Pinnock's advice and consult the source. A short "Fantasia & Echo" for recorder by Jacob van Eyck (1589/90–1657) is well suited to illustrate the problems a performer would encounter in playing from a facsimile because its earliest source, printed in the first edition of van Eyck's *Der Fluyten Lust-Hof* (1644), was designed for use by performers, and because, being written for a single melodic instrument, its typesetting is relatively straightforward (compared, say, to a piece for keyboard). Another advantage of this piece is that its earliest source originated from within the composer's own circle, which means it is likely authoritative. In the following, I shall refer to the version of the piece that appears in the second edition of *Der Fluyten Lust-Hof* (1649) (Figure 1.1), which corrects mistakes in the first edition and provides additional dynamics. Thus, this edition is free from most of the blunt problems posed by historical sources.

So how might a performer—let us call her Jane—fare in the attempt to perform the "Fantasia & Echo" from a facsimile of the original print? Jane would encounter several obstacles. For one thing, Jane would discover that the short notes are not beamed, as a result of which she would have a hard time distinguishing long and short note values. Although Jane has a head for numbers and a reputation for her ability to sight-read even the most complicated rhythms, she is baffled by the visual jumble of unbarred eighths and sixteenths she encounters here. The reason for this jumble, of course, is that *Der Fluyten Lust-Hof* was printed with movable type, which had the advantage of being cheap, even if visually unimpressive, and was therefore the most common method of printing music for almost two centuries. To be sure, the printer of our example, the Amsterdam printer Paulus Matthysz, seems to have made an effort toward readability by grouping the notes by beats. Unfortunately for Jane, however, the groupings are frequently upset by other technical requirements, such as the addition of accidentals (for example, in m. 13, one sharp sign helps to group the notes of the fourth beat together, but upsets the grouping of the second beat).[5] In fact, in Matthysz's types, the flags of the notes sometimes resemble noteheads, especially in cases where the inner flags of sixteenth notes received even slightly less ink than usual. It thus takes Jane some time to make sure that she is not mistaking some of the sixteenths for half notes. In particular when the

FIGURE 1.1 J. van Eyck, "Fantasia & Echo," *Der Fluyten Lust-Hof*, 2nd ed. (1649), pp. [18v]–19[r]. The images are reproduced by kind permission of the National Library of Scotland. This work is licensed under the Creative Commons Attribution 4.0 International License. To view a copy of this license, visit http://creativecommons.org/licenses/by/4.0/ or send a letter to Creative Commons, PO Box 1866, Mountain View, CA 94042, USA.

FIGURE 1.1 Continued

melody moves unexpectedly from one octave to another, her eye, seeking the next notehead, will stumble upon flags that look very much like noteheads (for example, in mm. 15 and 28).

After mastering the visual subtleties of Matthysz's type, Jane realizes that Matthysz's way of notating music differs somewhat from what she is used to. She is unsure whether accidentals apply only to the notes to which they are attached (as seems to be the case in mm. 25 and 44–45) or remain valid for the remainder of the measure (as seems to be the case in mm. 12–13 and 41). Upon reaching the concluding section with the triplets (mm. 41–48), she rightly wonders why Matthysz chose to complicate the last note in every measure by writing it as a dotted-quarter-made-of-three-triplet-eighth-notes, instead of simply putting in a quarter note.

For most modern performers, the absence of beams in van Eyck's book is the most visible deviation from modern notational conventions. Indeed, it is a deviation that they would encounter almost in every measure, one that distorts the visual grouping of notes into discrete beats. While van Eyck's music is based on the principle of *breecken* ("breaking"; essentially diminution),[6] which means that the performer can usually expect rhythmic repetitivity, the "Fantasia & Echo" contains several rhythmic "traps" that are likely to startle the performer, especially when sight-reading the piece. The work does not seem complicated at first. The opening 39 measures are based on a very limited variety of rhythmic formulae, which makes sight-reading it rather simple. In measures 1–39, 75 percent of the quarter-length beats are played either as simple quarters; divided into two equal eighths; divided into four equal sixteenths; or tied to another quarter, thus forming a half note. The remaining 25 percent always fall into one of three simple sixteenth-derived formulae (2:1:1; 1:1:2; and 3:1). Arriving at measure 40, the performer who is sight-reading the work would be surprised to see, for the first time in the fantasia, three new elements: thirty-second notes, a quarter rest, and triplets. Without warning, most performers would probably interpret the thirty-seconds as sixteenths, and then find that the measure is "too long." When arriving at measure 41, understanding that the triplets' indication "3" should be applied to eighths, although a triplet-eighth does not appear on the first beat, is also very counterintuitive, at least for modern players like Jane. Moreover, the triplet indication "3" is not consistently placed halfway through the range of notes to which it applies. Modern performers may therefore be excused if they wish to avoid performing these works in concert from facsimile.

Does dealing with the lack of beams in van Eyck's print inform the performer historically in a way that playing from modern notation does not? Isn't the lack of beams merely a technical limitation imposed by using movable type, a method often chosen by seventeenth-century publishers for its low production costs? Can it be that after some period of studying the piece, when one already knows it by heart (and many recorder players do!), the lack of beams stops being an obstacle? Let us think about the original buyers of van Eyck's *Der Fluyten*

Lust-Hof in the 1640s: how many times would they have played the piece? How did their memory and their processes of memorization operate? Did they attempt to learn the music by heart at all (as the piece must have been perceived by its composer, who was a blind carillonneur)? Was this music performed in situations in any way comparable to the modern concert situation?

If one prefers not to play from a facsimile of van Eyck's book, one obvious alternative would be to use a modern edition, as many editors nowadays try to supply performers with a text that is both authoritative and easy to use. Editors have reacted to the rise of historically informed performance to the point where the borders between scholarly and performance editions have become blurred. In their work on scholarly editions, on the one hand, editors have taken several steps toward the performer, adjusting their editorial policies to address more practical aims (in terms of format, editorial method, and production of parts). In performance editions, on the other hand, they have adapted to a new generation of scholar-performers who demand higher critical standards by following some of the guidelines advanced by Dart, that is, they add an introduction, list their sources, and mark editorial interventions (Grier 1996: 12).

Yet modern performance editions of the "Fantasia & Echo" do not offer solutions to all the problems posed by the original source—for the simple reason that every editor perceives different notes to be ambiguous (a principle that will be discussed in greater detail in Chapter 4). The issue of editorial accidentals, necessary for the elimination of ambiguous pitches, triggers many of the editorial interventions in available editions. Although most of these interventions seem to follow principles similar to Dart's, differences between the edited texts demonstrate that the elimination of ambiguity depends entirely on how an editor defines what is missing and what is redundant.

In order to resolve some of these disagreements, or at least arrive at their own opinions on some of the ambiguities, performers might need to turn to the source. In the case of a printed source, familiarity with the printer's house style might help to solve textual problems. First, both editor and performer should observe features of the printer's house style, as these naturally must be taken into account when interpreting the text. In the "Fantasia & Echo," for example:

- The printer consistently omits bar lines at the ends of systems.
- The lack of beaming reveals that the typesetter always directed the stem of the note b′ (on the middle line of the staff) upwards.
- As noted earlier, the method of applying accidentals is inconsistent.
- As was customary in many places in the seventeenth century, the original score does not use the natural sign, and so the note b♯′ (on mm. 26 and 28) probably denotes the pitch b♮′, even if there is no preceding accidental (such as a b♭′), that requires canceling.
- The dynamic indications used are "forte" and "pian.," with the exception of a single instance where "for." replaces "forte" (m. 42). The abbreviation

probably stems from space limitations: all the dynamics are vertically placed at the same height as the first ledger line below the staff (that is, where the note c′ would be). The abbreviated indication implies that the setter tried to save space, and the collision with the note c′ is a likely reason. Thus, the position of the indication "for.," below the note e′, is likely to be musically inaccurate and should be corrected.

Even a thorough understanding of the printer's house style does not eliminate possible ambiguities with regard to pitch. Measure 26 offers a case in point: printers of movable type could easily apply accidentals to wrong notes.[7] While we observed two instances of the note b♯′ in the piece (in mm. 26 and 28), only the second one is contextually justified (the ♯$\hat{6}$ of the scale). The note b♮′ is relatively rare in the piece. After the b♭′ of measure 7, the supposed pitch b♮′ appears, in passim, only in measure 14 and then again in measures 23–24. However, there seems to be little reason to cancel the b♭′ only as late as measure 26 and not earlier. Moreover, there is no contextual reason to indicate a redundant natural sign, as in the cadential figure of measure 28. Is it therefore possible that the ♯ sign applied to the note b♯′ in measure 26 is wrong, and should have been applied to a different note? The ♯ sign is on the third line of the staff (hence, the setter did not intend to apply it to the preceding a′ or the following c″), but that does not rule out an error in the printer's copy (from which the setter worked), or that the setter misinterpreted the printer's copy. If there really was a ♯ sign in the printer's copy, it makes more musical sense that it be applied to the c″ after all, corresponding with the c♯″ of measures 27–28.

If the c″ in measure 26 is indeed a c♯″, then any modern edition that, following Dart's instructions, makes it its policy to eliminate redundant accidentals risks ironing out a significant hint to a textual error that the performer might want to identify and correct. Thus, creating a quasi-facsimile, or at the very least making a careful study of each and every note in a source, is an important stage in the creation of scholarly editions, performance editions, or performance material for one's own use. Knowing the sources is crucial, since their technical specifications (in this case, the use of movable type) may at times hold the key to questions regarding the text.

Ironically, the more one studies the sources, and the more aware one becomes of the challenges that make the editorial process more interesting (multiple sources, variant readings, and blunt errors), the less one is inclined to take those sources, in form of facsimile editions, on stage. On the other hand, performers who work from a modern edition run the risk of overlooking textual problems of the kind observed in measure 26, or "simpler" ambiguities regarding the application of accidentals (see Table 1.1, mm. 14, 30, 40, and 49). When these ambiguities are resolved by the editor, performers are discouraged from thinking for themselves. As we see in Table 1.1, editors often arrive at conclusions that are still debatable (Kuijken 2013: 74). Thus, neither facsimiles nor modern editions are ideal for historically informed performance.

Table 1.1 Editorial interventions in three modern editions of Van Eyck's "Fantasia & Echo"

Measure	Item	Category of modification	Details	Michel (Amadeus, 1984)	Vellekoop (Ixijzet, 1957)	Linde (Schott, 1965)
14	11	Editorial accidental	Sharp sign, probable on stylistic grounds, added and marked as editorial			✓
25	5, 7, 8	Editorial deletion of "redundant" accidental		✓	✓	✓
26	2	Editorial deletion of "redundant" accidental		✓	✓	✓
26	6, 7	Editorial accidental	Sharp signs, probable on stylistic grounds, added and marked as editorial			✓
26	9, 10	Editorial accidental	Natural signs, added and marked as editorial in order to cancel previous editorial sharps			✓
28	3, 4	Editorial deletion of "redundant" accidental		✓	✓	✓
28	6	"Certain" cautionary (not marked as editorial)	Assuming that lack of sharp sign indicates natural (in contrast to item 4 on the same bar)	✓		
30	9	Editorial accidental	Natural sign, probable on stylistic grounds, added and marked as editorial		✓	✓
36	8	"Certain" cautionary (not marked as editorial)	Added due to a flat sign in previous bar			✓
40	7	Editorial accidental	Flat sign, probable on stylistic grounds, added and marked as editorial	✓		✓
40	9	Editorial accidental	Flat sign, probable on stylistic grounds, added and marked as editorial	✓		
44	9, 11	Editorial deletion of "redundant" accidental		✓	✓	✓
45	9, 11	Editorial deletion of "redundant" accidental		✓	✓	✓
43–47		Modernization of rhythmic notation	Dot of augmentation omitted from the fourth beat of every measure, according to modern conventions of triplet notation.		✓	✓
49	3, 11	Editorial accidental	Sharp signs, probable on stylistic grounds, added and marked as editorial			✓

In terms of textual integrity, using a facsimile naturally helps to bypass several centuries of possible transmission errors. There is no guarantee, however, that the facsimile itself is free of errors.

Reservations regarding the use of facsimile editions on stage say nothing about the value of using them for educational purposes during the training of students. They will learn the kind of information conveyed by the notation of each period, and of possible ambiguities in the text, and they will develop flexibility in reading various styles of notation. It has become more and more common for students to encounter a work first in recorded format, rather than as notated music; but the merit of handling early notation and confronting the potential textual problems it entails has been at the heart of the early music revival for a good reason. Even the sheer excitement of handling a centuries-old document (or a copy thereof) may inspire the performer and make him alert to notational subtleties. After all, not only autographs but also facsimiles are displayed behind glass windows in museums, and seeing them makes the general public feel somehow closer to a long-dead composer, and not less effectively than seeing Schubert's glasses or Beethoven's chamber pot.

There are, to be sure, more alternatives than just the facsimile of an original source and a performance edition. Scholarly editions, the result of many hours of research, put the performer in a good position to read the text critically and learn about the various sources and, provided that no new primary sources surface, they remain usable for several decades. It must be acknowledged, however, that in order fully to understand the scholarship embedded in such editions, one must spend a considerable amount of time reading the preface, the source descriptions (which often fail to convey the character of the sources, such as their size and the impression they create), the editorial policy, and the critical commentary.

Working with a scholarly edition brings with it a cluster of fundamental paradoxes of editing: The less a source is represented in the edited text, the more it is represented in the critical commentary; the more it is represented in the critical commentary, the harder it becomes for the reader to picture it. The more concise the critical commentary, the more it conceals the reasons for the variants documented by the sources; but the more detailed the critical commentary, the harder it is to justify excluding the variants it relegates to the commentary. For example, a glance at an original source can easily reveal, say, a copyist's tendency to err on the first note of a new system, but the same tendency will be nearly impossible to detect in the variant list of a modern edition (unless the editor has chosen to preserve the system changes or has already identified the recurring error and explicitly describes it in the source description).

Another paradox of critical editions is no less "dangerous": the more exhaustive an editorial project (in terms of the number of sources collated and the number of errors corrected), the more distant from any given primary source it tends to be. By extension, one may argue that monumental editions that aim to present a homogeneous series of collected works, and volumes that eliminate any trace of textual unclarity, create a distorted image of the composer's creative life. For example, Purcell's "Three Parts upon a Ground" Z.731 survives in a version in D major for violins, in a manuscript copied by John Reading,[8] and in an autograph version in F major for recorders. While the latter version certainly has the stamp of the composer's authority, its only surviving source is as fragmentary as a source can be: a few measures from one of the recorders' parts (Ring 1996). But in the Purcell Society Edition, the piece appears in its F major version, reconstructed by transposing the violin parts in accordance with the fragment of the recorder part.[9] Though it is probable that the recorder version is indeed "the original" (if the concept is applicable at all to a seventeenth-century worldview), it is still remarkable that most of the text in the collected edition is not extant in any physical source. The spirit of *Gesamtausgabe*, which motivates many of the monumental editions to this day, sometimes prefers phantoms over empirically verified texts. On an even larger scale, monumental editions that collect works attributed to individual composers, but with varying degrees of authority, may construct an image of those composers quite different from the historical figures they aim to construct. The two markedly different images of "Josquin" (that is, the markedly different corpora of musical works) projected by the two complete Josquin editions, prepared in the early twentieth century and early twenty-first century respectively, may serve as a case in point (Elders 2013: 11–12, 57–64).

Let us now examine the "semi-facsimile of the original," which Dart found useless for the scholar and a nuisance to the performer (Dart 1967: 21). For the purpose of this study, "semi-facsimile" will refer to a diplomatic copy with minimal editorial intervention. In the case of van Eyck this means, for example, retaining the separation of notes even in modern, digital typesetting (as in Example 1.1). This may help to retain something of the seventeenth-century reading experience, an aspect that would be entirely altered if one applied consistent beaming according to beat division. The "semi-facsimile" does still eliminate other aspects of the original, such as the quality of the paper and the printing, and color contrasts. Most important, it substantially alters the performer's feeling of reading an original or a facsimile. The question of whether reading from an original that "feels" old actually distances modern performers from their forebears (for whom the same music "felt" new) remains open.

I believe that most scholars and performers would find insisting on retaining the separation of notes unjustified. However, dismissing the use of separated notes by arguing that all other aspects of the music-reading experience (the type of paper, the music stand, the setting, the musical knowledge that van Eyck assumed from his readership) are essentially modern is an approach tinged with nihilism. There is another reason that the separation of notes should

EXAMPLE 1.1   Van Eyck, "Fantasia & Echo," "semi-facsimile," measure numbers added and "direct" signs at the end of each staff omitted.

32

EXAMPLE 1.1 Continued

not be insisted upon: because it is secondary to the proper interpretation of the musical text. Reading from the original, because it gives one the illusion of being closer to the text, puts too much effort in the wrong place. If one puts the effort to understand the fine details of the printing in *Der Fluyten Lust-Hof*, then one would probably be in a position to make sure the text is accurate and, in such a case, one would also probably be in a position to overcome the notational challenge relatively easily.

It is also important that those aspects of the text that are ambiguous should be decided upon in advance. This is *not* to say that spontaneity should be banned—on the contrary! It is just that issues like accidentals should not be considered as subject to whim. (As I argue in Chapter 4, it is too often the case that editors and performers leave such decisions to intuition). It serves no purpose for the performer to waste attention on decision-making regarding aspects that could be decided in advance and marked in the performance material.

From "Semi-Facsimile" to Tailor-Made Transcription

The production of a "semi-facsimile" copy is a process by which the performer gives, even if temporarily, the most serious consideration to a given source, whether it is a "good" source or a "bad" one. Similarly, if the music survives in parts, then assembling a full score is the surest way to spot textual errors. In many cases editors do not have the time, budget, or will to take each source, copy it, and then scrutinize it. Copying, however, is the simplest way to study a piece (or a source), and the efficiency of this method has been recognized for centuries (Purcell 1694: 144). Moreover, close acquaintance with the historical source allows the performer a glimpse of the immediate contact that people in the distant past had with the performed piece: were there notes that were unclear? Were there implied accidentals that past users felt obliged to explicate? Is there any important information entailed in the details of the bass figuring (which is often standardized in modern editions)? All these and more can inform performers' decisions.

A similar conclusion is reached by Kuijken in his aforementioned overview of the issue of editions:

We should use Urtext editions more as the beginning of our investigations into a piece than as the version that we strictly have to adhere to. If we play them as the truth and nothing but the truth, we are certain to miss a great deal. I do think that a responsible performer, especially, but not only of Early Music, should study the scientific editions and their critical comments, but also see the sources for himself. He can then formulate his own conclusions or preferences, discuss them with colleagues and test them in rehearsals and concerts, in order to come to "valid" but necessarily always temporary solutions. (Kuijken 2013: 74)

Obviously, some discretion must be used in the choice of sources. Sources that are clearly corrupt should be avoided, and sources known to have unrivaled authority should be preferred. The performer does not have the privilege of footnoting possible readings outside those performed (Grier 1996: 2), but the performer also does not have the duty to exhaust all available sources—only to prepare the performance material sensibly.

Reading Van Eyck's "Fantasia & Echo" from a semi-facsimile of the kind suggested in Example 1.1 is as cumbersome as it is illuminating. Moreover, at no point during the transcription did I take into consideration the performer's needs—only the proper study of the source. Producing such semi-facsimile, however, puts the performer in an excellent position to create yet another version, this time a personalized version that reflects one's acquaintance with the text. Using a typesetting program, it is but a few minutes' work to modify a previously typed semi-facsimile into the kind of transcription that I suggest in Example 1.2. It is not only possible, but even recommended, to make the transcription easy to use: beaming may be applied, knowing that whether they reflect divisions to half notes or to quarter notes is insignificant; layout may reflect the formal division of the piece; page turning may be taken into consideration; breath marks may be included.

Keyboard Tablatures and Other Curiosities

Modern recorder players who encounter Van Eyck's print (it is available online) are likely to try and perform the music from that source. According to the previous section's analysis, they have a good chance of succeeding, at least until they encounter rhythmic surprises starting in measure 40. But other sources from roughly the same time stretched the boundaries of contemporary printing technology even further, and some used a different notational approach altogether. Such prints are challenging for the performer, and the decision to use them as performance material cannot be made offhand. One such type of source is the Italian keyboard tablature. We will take an example from the *Terzo Libro de Ricercari* by Andrea Gabrieli (c. 1532–1585), a volume published posthumously by Gardano in 1596, in order to examine some of the challenges when performing from tablature.

Like many sixteenth- and seventeenth-century ricercari, Andrea Gabrieli's are set in four-part polyphony. In the composer's time, however, there was no agreement as to the preferred way of notating such polyphony, especially in print. Two approaches developed. One was idealistic, presenting the polyphony in "open" score (*partitura*), usually with four staves per system.[10] In open-score layout, the player needed to read several staves simultaneously, often with four different clefs, but gained an excellent bird's-eye view of the contrapuntal workings of the piece: how many parts sound at any given time, when each part enters or exits, or how the contrapuntal manipulation operated

EXAMPLE 1.2 Van Eyck, "Fantasia & Echo," personalized transcription, containing beaming and reflecting formal division of the piece.

EXAMPLE 1.2 Continued

on each part (it is relatively easy to observe diminutions, augmentations, and inversions when reading from a score). The other, arguably more practical, approach involved tablature notation. Italian keyboard tablature (*intavolatura*) is a notation system that tells the keyboard player when each note is to be played, and with which hand, hence shortening the time required to establish the fingering for the piece. Of course, the *intavolatura* does not offer the same contrapuntal overview that is offered by the *partitura*. In both approaches, the printing technique employed was usually movable type, so the repertoire poses problems similar to those we encountered in Van Eyck's fantasia: the absence of beams, the position of one type being affected by the position of another, and the risk of assigning an accidental to a wrong note (Silbiger 1991).

The standard way of notating keyboard polyphony from the eighteenth century onward can thus be seen as a compromise between the *partitura* and the *intavolatura*. From the latter it takes the use of only two staves and only two clefs at a time; and from the former it takes the clear differentiation between the parts—each staff usually transmits two parts with opposite stem directions. In modern editions, diagonal lines sometimes indicate when a part crosses the lines from one staff to another.[11]

Let us now consider Gabrieli's Ricercar del Primo Tono (Figure 1.2). Most keyboard players nowadays, who are unfamiliar with sixteenth-century keyboard notation, must at first get used to the C2 clef in the right-hand staff and to the six-line staff and its two clefs in the left hand. In addition, the use of rhythm dots over the measure line (bottom staff, mm. 4–5) and the inconsistent use thereof (cf. top staff, mm. 3–4) was very common in general.

A potential performer playing a keyboard ricercar of Gabrieli's time may expect an intricate four-part fugue or a succession of intricate four-part fugues related to one another. Even before mastering the unusual staves and clefs, our potential performer's eyes might perceive the similarity of contour in the melody, first played in the left hand and then in right. Indeed, these are the first two subject entries of the fugue. However, those who are experienced in reading modern editions of Bach fugues might expect to distinguish the parts of the fugue by the stem directions. This is not necessarily the case in Gabrieli. Which of the four parts participate in measures 1–6? This is hard, even impossible, to say. This feature of the source offers a valuable insight: The original performers of this repertoire were not always informed by the score as to which of the four parts were playing at any given moment.

Is it, then, fair to conclude that the notion of immutable parts of the fugue (Voice 1, Voice 2, etc.) does not apply to this period? Not necessarily. While the graphical layout of the sources makes it nearly impossible to identify parts while playing the piece in "real time," it is sometimes possible to identify parts through careful score study. The contrapuntal work of Gabrieli and his contemporaries often exhibits strict four-part texture, and may even

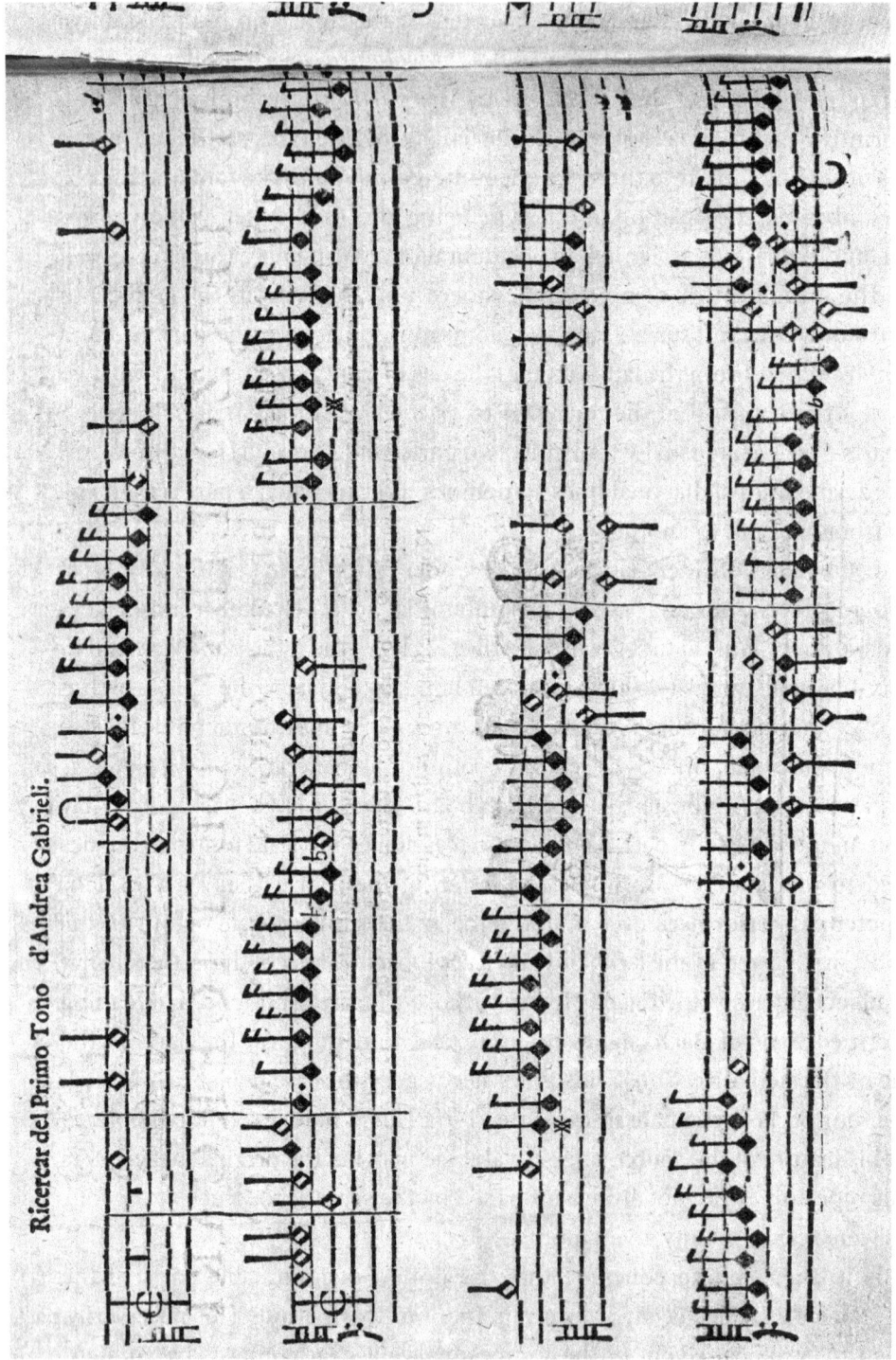

FIGURE 1.2 Andrea Gabrieli, *Terzo Libro*, Ricercar del Primo Tono. Basel University Library, kk IV 28:5.

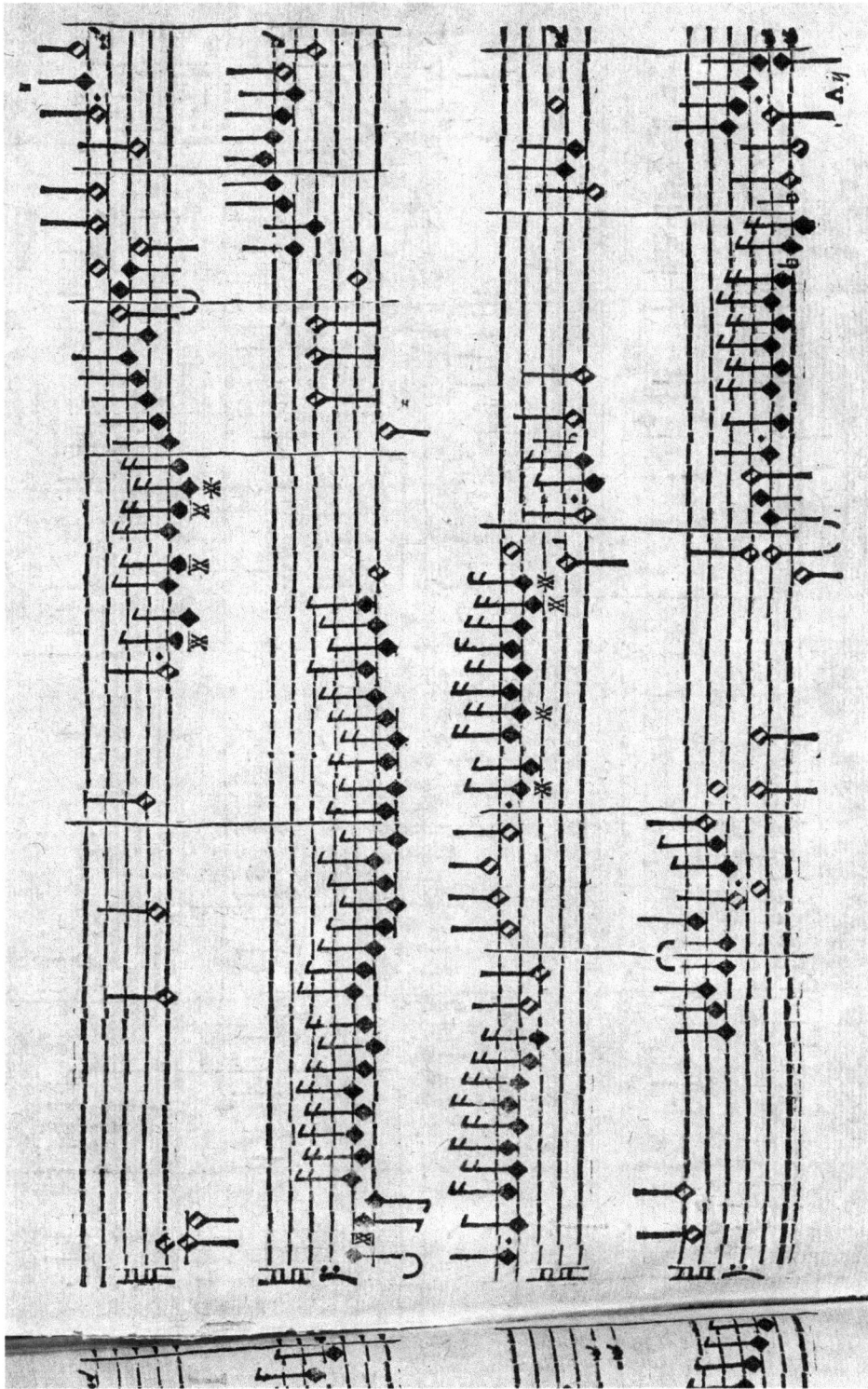

FIGURE 1.2 Continued

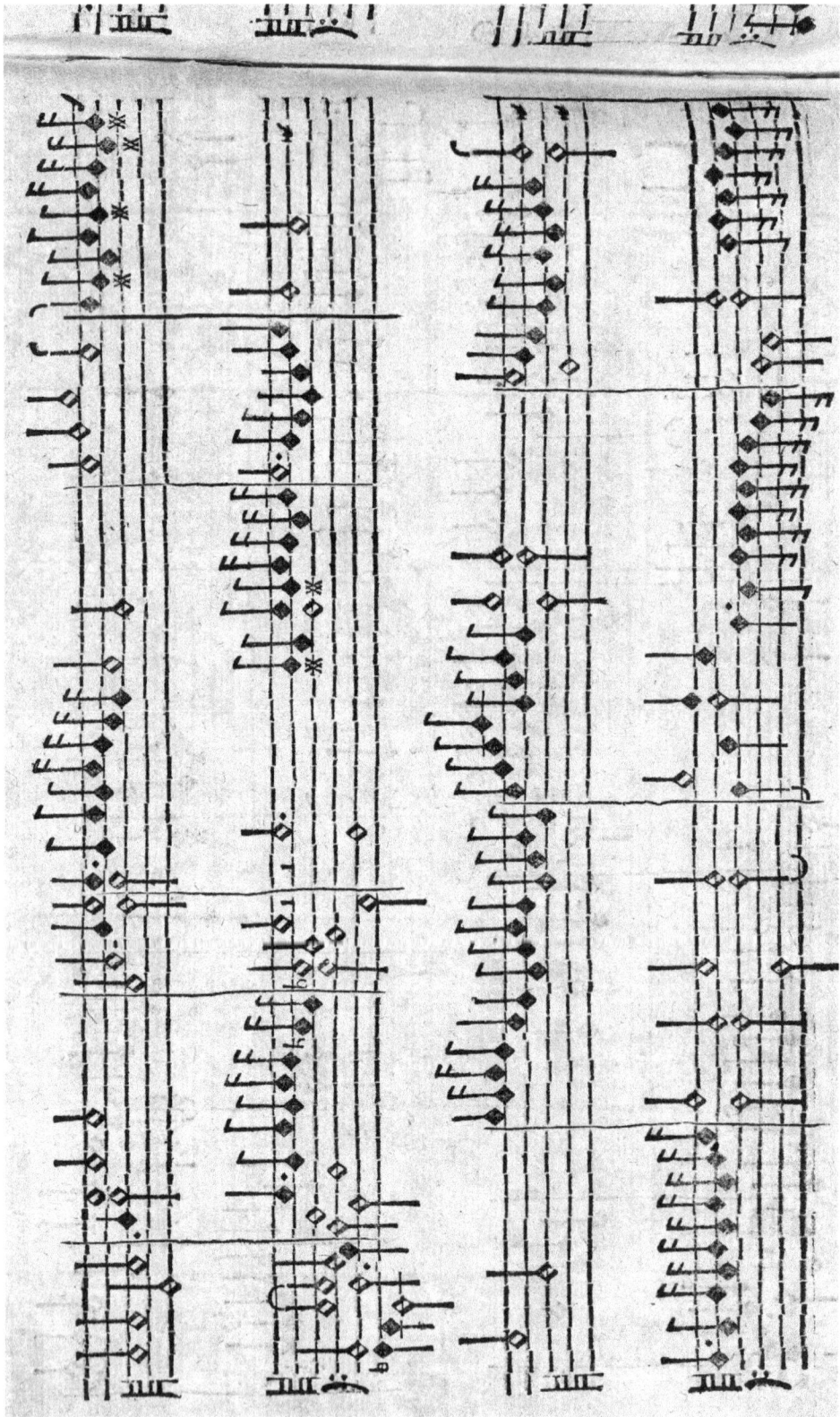

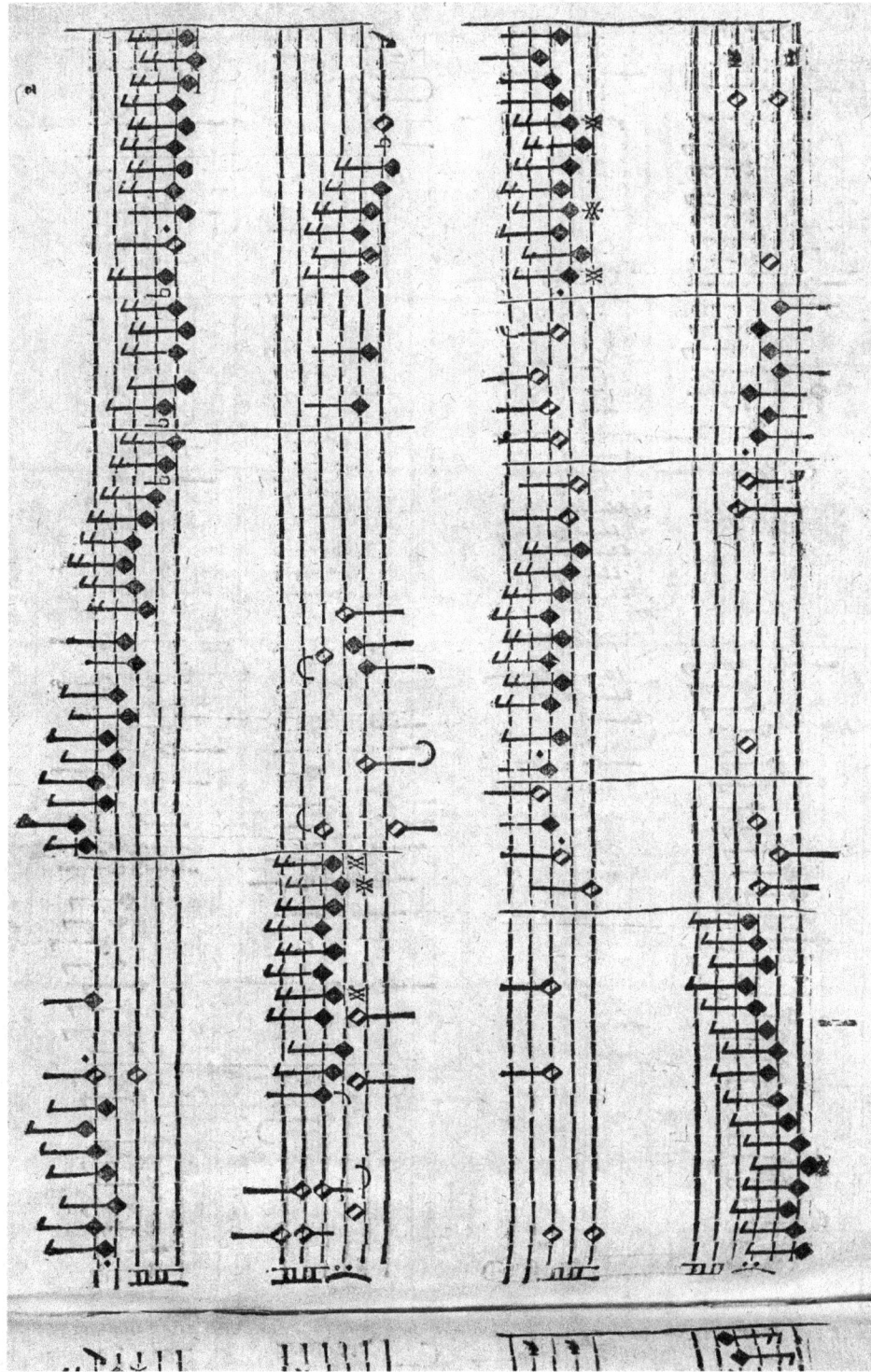

FIGURE 1.2 Continued

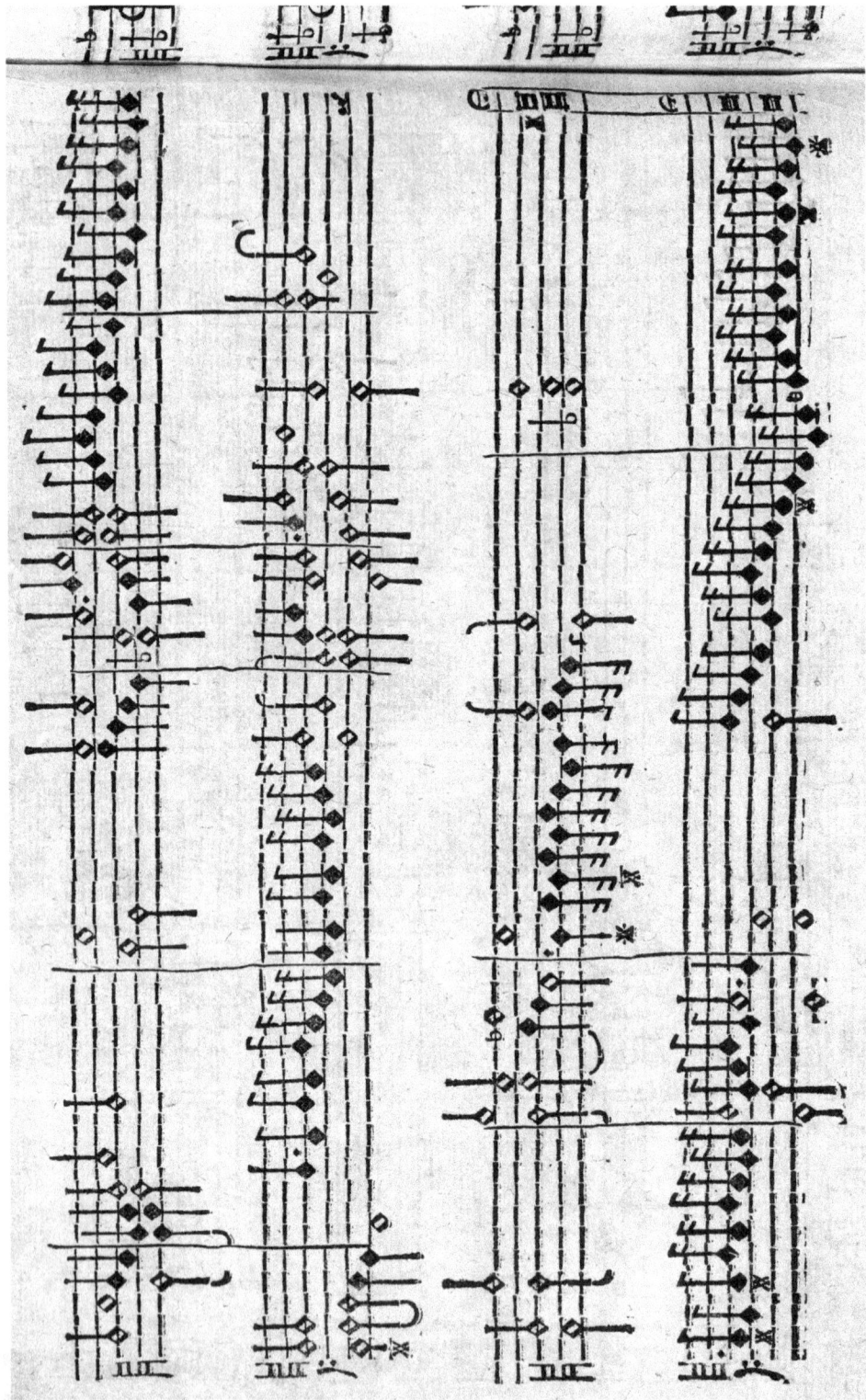

FIGURE 1.2 Continued

be transcribed for melodic instruments if one examines the piece as a whole. Sometimes the identity of a part becomes clear only in hindsight, and contrary to one's initial assumptions. Those acquainted with later notational standards, say, from the classic Riemenschneider edition of Bach chorales, might assume that the part played by the left hand in the beginning is the tenor. The part in question is set relatively high in the left-hand staff, and the stems of its notes (at least in mm. 1–3) go upward, just like the tenor part in those old Bach chorales. What seems to be a bass entrance in measure 7 might at first reaffirm our suspicion that it was indeed the tenor that opened the piece, but in measure 8 a third part enters in between the two parts that had already entered and clarifies that the left hand was actually playing the alto at the beginning.

As demonstrated by the entrance of tenor in measure 8, where the first note of the entrance falls on the bottom staff, with the second and third notes continuing on the top staff, the division between the staves reflects the division between the hands and has little to do with the clarity of melodic continuity. Counter to modern convention, three notes of the same pitch (a) are printed on different staves. This allows performers to "improvise" workable fingering in real time, but at the same time blurs subject entries—both characteristic of tablature systems in general.

Identifying contrapuntal imitation in Italian keyboard tablature, as challenging as it may be, is still immeasurably easier than in tablatures for plucked instruments, where notational symbols and their meanings changed radically from one place to another, and over time. A Spanish mid-sixteenth century vihuela printed tablature (like Mudarra's 1546 *Tres Libros de Musica*) and a turn-of-the-century English lute manuscript (like the c. 1600 Margaret Board Lutebook) share many fundamental principles and yet these principles are realized as almost-perfect opposites. The former type of tablature employs numbers, the latter, letters; the former's top string is notated at the bottom of the tablature, the latter's, at its top; the former usually indicates when to stop a string from vibrating, the latter, when to let it vibrate.[12] Other systems, like the Italian *alfabeto*, are founded on different principles altogether. Whereas the various lute tablatures offer valuable, sometimes unique, information about the musical text (for example, they eliminate *ficta* ambiguities that plague sources in staff notation), an *alfabeto* guitar book would hardly allow one to reconstruct a simple song melody.[13]

Let us compare the situation in Gabrieli's ricercar with a few measures from Adrian le Roy's Prelude from his *Tiers Livre de Tabulature de Guiterre* (1552). Le Roy's book is set in French guitar tablature and the passage we want to examine contains stretto imitation on a stock subject with all-quarter-note motion. Even in what is an unusually simple example of tablature (with notes of only one type of rhythmic value, for an instrument of four strings only), it is difficult to observe the stretto entrances just from looking at the tablature

(Example 1.3a)—much more difficult than to hear them. Even in simple transcription to staff notation (Example 1.3b) it would take a few seconds to observe the imitation, which only becomes evident and clear when we apply different stem directions (Example 1.3c).

Unsurprisingly, Gabrieli's four-part polyphony occasions more textual errors than Van Eyck's solo fantasia. In measure 10 (the last measure of the first page of Figure 1.2), for example, the tenor (the upper part in the bottom staff) has a redundant eighth note (see the tenor part isolated in Example 1.4a). There are quite a few possible corrections that one may offer. If one assumes that the first eighth note was inserted by mistake, then it is possible to omit it (Example 1.4b). If one assumes that the setter used a quarter-note type instead of an eighth-note type on the third beat of the measure, the mistake can be rectified simply by changing the quarter back to an eighth (Example 1.4c). One may also conclude that, writing a strict fugue, Gabrieli wanted the tenor entrance to resemble the

EXAMPLE 1.3   a. A. Le Roy, Prelude. Guitar tablature based on the *Tiers Livre* (1552), p. 2r; b. transcribed into staff notation without part separation; c. transcribed into staff notation with part separation.

EXAMPLE 1.4 a. A. Gabrieli, *Terzo Libro*, Ricercar del Primo Tono, m. 10, tenor part, copied with a redundant quaver, as it appears in the source; b.–f. possible corrections.

other entrances (Example 1.4d), or perhaps that some more complex typesetting error occurred, allowing additional corrections (Example 1.4e and 1.4f).

Any choice one makes with regard to measure 10 might have further implications on the interpretation of the source. The choice of the correction in Example 1.4e, for example, might commit an editor to the assumption that if Gabrieli used a subject in a certain way here, he would have used it in the same way elsewhere. In this case, how should one read the bass part in measure 11 (first measure on the second page of Figure 1.2)? Should one assume that the sharp sign on the first C in was actually intended for the second C (as already heard in m. 5)? Or perhaps a sharp sign should be added in measure 5, in keeping with the sharp sign in measure 11? Or perhaps one should add sharp signs to all the Cs, following the example of measure 18? Such puzzles, of transferring readings from one passage to another, are essentially similar to a problem of a higher scale—that of borrowing readings from other versions of a piece—a problem that will be discussed in detail in Chapter 3.

We have seen that the "forte" indication in measure 42 of Van Eyck's fantasia was truncated into 'for.' to avoid a collision with a note positioned below the staff. Similar typesetting considerations seriously affect the alignment of notes in Gabrieli's ricercar. Measures 22–24 provide two such examples, and would have been very difficult to sight-read. Example 1.5 offers both a diplomatic copy of these measures as they appear in Gabrieli's book (marked "a") (see also third page of Figure 1.2), and a "corrected" version, where all the parts are aligned with the soprano part (marked "b"). In measure 22, the entrance of the soprano part is graphically shifted from the first to the second beat, probably to avoid collision with the stem of the alto. In measure 24, all the parts are out of alignment. The placing of sharps on the staff, rather than above it, may explain some of the disorder in that measure, but on the whole it is very difficult to read.

EXAMPLE 1.5 a. A. Gabrieli, *Terzo Libro*, mm. 22–24, layout of notes follows the source; b. notes aligned according to beat.

Problems of alignment notwithstanding, performers' attention might be drawn to the real textual problem of the passage: three notes (f′, g′, and a′) in the top part of measure 22 that do not conflict with any of the other parts but may have been the result of the common copying error of writing a note or a group of notes a third too high or a third too low. If, again, we assume that Gabrieli would have wished to leave the imitative subject intact, then it would make sense to transpose the three notes a third higher (resulting in a′, b′, and c″ respectively). The contrapuntal validity of the wrong reading, added to the fact that the *intavolatura* format deprioritizes the clarity of the counterpoint, may explain how the error survived proofreading, assuming such a process took place.

The preceding analysis suggests that intabulations often constitute poor performance material. A reservation should be made, however, for it is mostly by today's standards regarding previous acquaintance with the musical text, with its form, and with its contrapuntal workings, that intabulations prove challenging. That is exactly why attempting to play from these sources provides an invaluable firsthand experience with the process of studying the musical text in the context of its own time. Performing from the source also shows, for example, how much weight Gabrieli (or his posthumous printer) placed on the running sixteenth-notes passages notated note by note! While it would have been possible to simplify the notation by replacing ornamental figures with shorthand symbols, such as *tr* or +, the printer, working after the composer's death, found the ornamentation essential to justify precious space on the page (doubting, perhaps, potential buyers' ability to ornament properly). As matters stand, the ricercar takes up the first five pages in the *Terzo Libro*; reduction of the ornaments would have saved at least one page.

Performers who wish to study Gabrieli's ricercars will do well to begin the process by studying the *intavolatura*. Indeed, this may require, as already mentioned, that performers familiarize themselves with various C clefs, six-line staves, and over-the-bar-line dots, even before they play the first note. By reading the pieces from their original *intavolatura*, however, they will acquire a sense of historical fingering, and something of the physical sensation of historical performance practice. Performers who wish to study Gabrieli's ricercars will also do well to retranscribe the works in open score. Indeed, this labor involves time-consuming scrutiny and writing. Yet those who make the effort will acquire precious knowledge about Gabrieli's contrapuntal mastery, knowledge that is simply inaccessible to those who limit themselves to playing from the original source. During the process, one may decide to reduce some of the ornamental figures, thereby simplifying the counterpoint. This knowledge about Gabrieli's contrapuntal technique may not necessarily have been the same knowledge acquired by those who performed Gabrieli's music around 1600, but it may certainly clarify to modern performers why Gabrieli's music is "worth the trouble" of such close study.

If the original intabulation constitutes poor performance material, and if an open score gives an excellent theoretical acquaintance but is justly considered challenging for performance, what kind of edition should be used in performance? Of course, if one took the pains to transcribe the piece as a score using notation software, producing a modern two-staff edition based on that score should be a matter of a few minutes. But even careful study of the tablature, without the added effort of transcription, should put the performer in a position to criticize and correct an existing performance edition. As we saw with the Van Eyck example, the process of studying the sources shows the performer that even excellent editions overlook significant details. Not only do modern editions contain textual errors (the aforementioned error in m. 23, where three notes were apparently set a third too low, is sometimes accepted as a valid reading by modern editors), but they also rarely convey a sense of the original division between the hands. Again, performers may decide that making a tailor-made hybrid transcription, taking the best from each format, most completely suits their needs. One possible hybrid solution (Example 1.6) would be to retain the original clefs, staves, and division between hands from the intabulation while modernizing the beaming and the placement of accidentals, reducing the ornaments, and using diagonal lines to indicate the crossing of parts from one staff to the other—as in modern keyboard scores. Similarly, one could also decide, for example, to modernize the clefs but to retain the ornamental sixteenth notes, or to use an open score with modernized clefs.

EXAMPLE 1.6 A. Gabrieli, *Terzo Libro*, mm. 1–9. Beginning of a possible performance edition.

Transcribing a Score from Original Parts

We have seen that the production of a "semi-facsimile" helped us to identify textual errors that might otherwise have been overlooked, either because they resembled redundant accidentals, or simply because they happened to fit in with the harmony. In some cases, the textual errors are more acute, and their solution requires some creativity. Indeed, errors in historical sources sometimes require serious intervention, correction, and marking. This is not easily done on facsimile, and material must be tried out in rehearsal. In cases where errors abound, the preparation of a transcription is no longer a privilege but a necessity.

Let us take, by way of example, a short gigue from the repertoire of Queen Anne's band, a repertoire comprising a few hundred short pieces and preserved in a set of four partbooks in the British Library.[14] Most of the short pieces in the manuscript are grouped into suites. Many of the pieces in the manuscript are by James Paisible. (It is hard to say exactly how many are by Paisible because explicit attribution usually appears only at the beginning of a suite and, in other manuscripts of this kind, suites often mix movements by various composers.) Historical inquiry may lead us to the conclusion that the partbooks were intended for a woodwind ensemble consisting of two oboes, a taille (tenor oboe), and a bassoon. Nonetheless, the titles of the various parts (treble I and II, tenor, and bass) allow some flexibility (for example, the repertoire can easily be performed by a four-part string ensemble). Let us assume that a group attempts to read through the vast repertoire contained in these partbooks in order to collect material for their next program. If they are reading from a facsimile or "semi-facsimile" of the parts, when they arrive at the gigue, probably by Paisible, on folio 2r,[15] the rehearsal will have probably reached a dead end. Halfway through the second section of the piece, the tenor and the bass will probably have noticed that they are playing in parallel ninths, and that the second treble has already finished. All attempts to repeat the section with more attention given to counting, or to the notes and rhythms, will inevitably have the same result. The reason is that the original parts are simply wrong.

If an editor attempts a scholarly edition, he would have to know that the gigue in question appears in another contemporary source, the Magdalene Partbooks; to consult the other source; to weigh the variants against each other; and to arrive at a satisfactory text.[16] But a performer might (justly) want to avoid searching for concordances, fetching microfilms or scans, and correcting the errors according to the best reading. Such apparent abstention should not be seen as laziness if the partbooks from which one plays are the same partbooks used by a band in the late seventeenth century (or copies thereof) since it makes sense that the original users tried to solve the problem as well, and that they could not refer to catalogues or scans.

Again, a faithful transcription of the source, errors included, is the best way to begin (Example 1.7). Especially if we retain the original clefs, it is evident that the "parallel ninths" were merely the result of the notes of the bass in measures 15–21 having been copied into the wrong staff (the tenor). When a notehead placed on a staff with an F4-clef is copied to the same location on a staff with a C2-clef, it will indicate a note that is a ninth higher. The philological implication of this error—that the copyist of the partbooks (or of the exemplar from which they were copied) extracted the part from a score—is in itself an implication of considerable scholarly value, and an editor should certainly make note of it. For the performer, however, the direct implication is simpler: we are missing the "real" tenor part for measures 15–21, and for our purpose, the question of whether the real part survives in a manuscript to which we have no access, or whether it has been lost, is irrelevant. The treble II part also seems

EXAMPLE 1.7 J. Paisible (?), Gigue, mm. 9–24. GB-L*bl* Add. MS 30,839; 39,565–567 f. 2r. A score reproducing all reading from the partbooks, including suspected errors.

EXAMPLE 1.7 Continued

to be shorter than the rest—but which measures are missing? The final measure, a half-measure, does indeed work with the harmony of the half-measure 24. The previous measure works well with measure 23, as does the measure before with measure 21. Since measure 19 still worked well with its treble I and bass, we may conclude that the missing measures are measures 20–21. At this point, a transcription with blank measures indicating those measures that we know that are missing (Example 1.8) may at first look like an assignment in harmony class. Indeed, the completion of those measures is not essentially different from what is expected in harmony class (Example 1.9). At this point, after we have already learned something from the original notation of the tenor part with its C2 clef, there is no reason not to modernize the clefs to the standard G2, G2, C3, and F4 clefs.

Since the treble II and the tenor go with the bass rhythmically, the completion of measures 15–19 is relatively simple. As in harmony class, it is even possible to write down the Roman numerals for the various chords, write down all the possible notes that may be completed (see below the tenor and treble II staves), and then complete the missing notes. In some cases, it is even possible to weave a relevant motif into the fabric (see mm. 20–21). This is a valid completion that makes it possible to perform the gigue. Assuming that the performers in Queen Anne's band did not have access to the Magdalene Partbooks, the completion process we have traced would have been a logical solution. Some manuscripts even preserve drafts of that kind.[17]

Now, after we have a valid completion in hand, let us enjoy the unfair advantage that we have over the players in Queen Anne's band—the advantage of comparing our results with concordances. As mentioned, the Magdalene Partbooks provide a complete text of the gigue (Example 1.10). The tenor part is very much similar in spirit to our completion, although we can see that we

EXAMPLE 1.8 J. Paisible (?), Gigue, mm. 14–24. Blank measures replace suspected wrong readings.

insisted on completing the chords even where Paisible was comfortable using incomplete sonorities. (Whereas we added the thirds of the chords in m. 17, third quarter note, and in m. 19, sixth quarter note, Paisible omitted them.) If we compare our reconstructed second treble part with the Magdalene version, we find a surprise. It appears that, although we identified the three final

EXAMPLE 1.9 J. Paisible (?), Gigue, mm. 14–24. Missing measures with suggested completion.

measures of the incomplete part measures 22–23 (and the half-measure 24), and although they work perfectly with the harmony in those measures, they appear in Magdalene as measures 20–21! Indeed, the variant in Magdalene is far from perfect. It may even be more corrupt than the incomplete variant in the British Library set of partbooks. It may well be that an incomplete text was

EXAMPLE 1.10 J. Paisible (?), Gigue, mm. 14–24. Magdalene Partbooks. Set 34/ 10.

in circulation, and that one of the copies offers a possible correction or completion. Thus, in the case of Paisible's gigue, a careful new completion might be as historically informed as the accurate execution of an "authentic" completion that contains wrong notes.

A performing ensemble can, of course, bypass the textual problems of the gigue by skipping the gigue altogether. And yet, if we assume that the original partbooks were used in performances, then we should probably ask ourselves how the original performers handled textual problems of that kind.

The examples discussed in this chapter—a fantasia by Van Eyck, a ricercar by Andrea Gabrieli, and a gigue by Paisible—demonstrate the problems embodied in using original sources as performance material. Whether printed or handwritten, original sources require study, acquaintance with notational standards that are foreign to our own, and in many cases, correction and completion. It surely is reassuring to imagine that if we take up an original instrument (or a replica thereof) and play from original performing material (or a copy thereof) we are getting as close as possible to what musicians in the past really did. Considering that most early music performers and scholars nowadays accept that the early music movement is better off having withdrawn its claim to authenticity, however, we should consider it worth some effort to ensure that historically informed performance is underpinned by at least a hint of historical curiosity. Adopting the intensity with which past musicians were involved in producing their own performance material is almost as valuable an asset for the historically informed as is the use of original instruments. Being historically informed entails considerable time and effort. Yet rather than copying music "authentically" by hand, we might use our time more effectively by first studying the sources and then typesetting a historically informed hybrid edition that best suits our performance needs.

Chapter 2

The Musical Text as a Point of Departure

The existential situation of many early music performers is one of a constant hunt for "new" material. On the surface, such a hunt may seem utilitarian: like their colleagues who specialize in contemporary music, early music performers must expand their repertoire in order to devise new programs, sustain audience, and stir the interest of new listeners. That, however, is only part of a bigger picture. Undoubtedly, there had never been so many sources and editions available for one to retrieve in a matter of seconds as there are now, but musicians keep looking beyond what is readily available to them—a tendency that must be ingrained somehow in the early music revival from its earliest generations. Many early music performers frequent archives, antiquarian shops, and flea markets in the hope to rediscover a manuscript of musical worth, and some even keep track of auction catalogues. They spend long moments in museums in front of paintings with depicted musical fragments: more than wanting to identify the fragment (which would itself be a scholarly feat indeed), they hope to be able to reconstruct an unidentified piece.

In earlier generations of the revival, performers showed no less originality in excavating material to perform. Noah Greenberg (1919–1966), the director of New York Pro Musica, spent many hours in the New York Public Library and in the Columbia University Library, accompanied by his "captive musicologist" Joel Newman, in search of material for his ensemble's programs. Since, regarding access to manuscript sources, Greenberg was working on the wrong side of the Atlantic, he found his material mainly in collected editions, from which he extracted parts, and to which he often added instrumental parts in order to fit his ensemble's voices-and-instruments approach (Gollin 2001: 155, 189–191). However, alongside the majority of material found in volumes of *Musica*

A Performer's Guide to Transcribing, Editing, and Arranging Early Music. Alon Schab, Oxford University Press.
© Oxford University Press 2022. DOI: 10.1093/oso/9780197600658.003.0003

Britannica or *Tudor Church Music*, some of Greenberg's eventual choices hint that collected editions were simply not enough for him—he apparently looked for examples outside these editions: a music example from Reese's *Music in the Middle Ages* (whose author's firsthand advice Greenberg often sought and received), excerpts from Davison and Apel's *Historical Anthology of Music*,[1] music examples from unpublished dissertations,[2] or an occasional facsimile illustration from Peter Warlock's *The English Ayre*.[3]

If a music example in a dissertation, a book, or an anthology is complete and set clearly enough, it can easily be performed or used in order to prepare performance material. Nonetheless, different source types pose different methodological problems, and scholarly writing, when used as a source for music, indeed raises several questions. Should an example in a historical survey book be taken as representative of a certain time in the history of music? Can it be taken without fully understanding the scholarly argument it illustrates and its context? Does it illustrate a historical norm or the exception to that norm?

Performers nowadays might look down at Greenberg's desperate reliance on sources like Gustave Reese's surveys, books that reflect mid-twentieth century scholarship and that have been since replaced by more updated scholarship. However, at least one type of source that is used by many early music performers to this day—historical treatises—poses problems that are remarkably similar to those posed by Greenberg's examples. The use of historical treatises as a major source for repertoire nowadays, just like the use of Reese's examples in the 1950s, reflects performers' reliance on whatever available sources they can access.

The following chapter will overview the ways in which treatises and examples from treatises may be used as source material for repertoire. As one purpose of this book is to encourage performers to take creative initiative and responsibility for their artistic endeavor, I will focus on extracting principles of composition and improvisation from treatises. In this way, I will suggest that, at least with relation to some types of sources, the most intensive engagement with historical sources (often identified with a non-interventionalist approach) may yield a seemingly source-free, but nonetheless historically informed, creative mindset (identified with an interventionalist approach).

It is important to stress that, while many of the techniques here relate to improvisation technique, the following chapter is not a self-contained course in improvisation. It does, however, clarify goals and techniques that are integral to the study of stylistic composition and improvisation.

Performing a Treatise

There is no single rule as to the way a musical example in a treatise should be interpreted and used—by historian, theorist, or performer. Each treatise uses examples differently, and each theoretical text relates differently to the illustrations that accompany it. The topical and chronological range of treatises, from which interesting examples could be extracted, is mind-boggling: from twelfth-century manuals on singing organum to late seventeenth-century instruction books aimed at amateur viol players; from eccentric sixteenth-century attempts to reconstruct the Greek modes to eighteenth-century harmony books. But even within a narrower scope, for example that of printed treatises on keyboard playing, the variety does not allow the making of a rule: In Matthew Locke's *Melothesia* (1673), a short (albeit important) theoretical essay precedes a substantial collection of pieces, most of them unrelated to the text. In François Couperin's *L'art de toucher le clavecin* (1716), the theoretical essay far outweighs the short preludes that are appended to it, although they are more integral to Couperin's discussion of performance issues than Locke's works are to his theoretical text. The two volumes of C. P. E. Bach's hefty *Versuch über die wahre Art das Clavier zu spielen* (1753 and 1762) contain several finished pieces as examples. Whether Bach himself saw the Freie Fantasie in D from the second volume as a finished piece or as mere illustration, Heinrich Schenker certainly applied to it the same analytical technique that he had been applying to a Beethoven symphony or to a Brahms quartet, and performers echo that seriousness in the many recordings of the piece. Usually, the canonization of examples, even marginal ones, takes place when their composer's catalogue raisonné is compiled. But what about composers of lesser renown, mostly earlier, in whose cases the examples form the bulk of their surviving output?

How did Diego Ortiz (c. 1510–c. 1570), whose entire surviving output consists of two books—a treatise and a collection of sacred vocal works—consider the many theoretical examples in the former? We know that he titled his second book (1565) a *Musices liber primus* (a *first* book of music), so should we conclude that he himself considered his (chronologically) first book as something other than a book of music? That first book, the two-volume treatise *Tratado de Glosas sobre Clausulas y otros generos depuntos en la musica de Violones nuevamente puestos en luz* (1553), groups together various improvisational skills and genres under the umbrella term *glosas* and is considered among the earliest and richest treatises of its kind. The first volume offers a repository of ornaments and passages over cadences and basic melodic cells, most of which are just one or two measures long. The second volume, however, contains more extensive written-out examples of various kinds of improvisations: free unaccompanied fantasias, improvisations over a plainsong, diminutions over existing polyphonic works, and improvisations over repeated harmonic progressions. Each of the twenty-seven pieces in the second volume is entitled recercada, and each group of recercadas demonstrates different types of glosas. Evidently, both performers and listeners nowadays find these recercadas appealing, and they usually treat them as finished pieces for all intents and purposes. All twenty-seven recercadas have been recorded commercially and, collected, they have even stood alone as the program of an album.[4] Alongside Ortiz's treatise, early music performers draw extensively on examples from other diminution treatises, and many concerts and albums of virtuoso sixteenth- and seventeenth-century instrumental music feature works extracted from (or inspired by) the treatises by Ganassi, Bassano, Dalla Cassa, Rognoni, Bovicelli, and Virgiliano.[5]

The many recordings of Ortiz's recercadas allow an overview of performers' various approaches to early music, and particularly to "theoretical" music examples. Three general approaches emerge: treating examples as text, as cursory text, and as a model. Performers who adopt the first approach (example as text) treat the surviving notation as self-contained, not requiring any substantial addition. The Amsterdam Loeki Stardust Quartet, for example, recorded a set of three of Ortiz's recercadas in their disc *La Spagna: Music at the Spanish Court* (1996), stressing the common compositional principle to the recercadas and to "proper" works by others.[6] Two of Ortiz's recercadas on the Spagna cantus firmus closely follow Johannes Ghiselin's Spagna setting, and Ortiz's recercada on Sandrin's chanson Doulce Memoire prepares Cabezón's "Glossada sobre Susana un jour" and "Diferencias sobre Un gay bergier," which are built around similar principles.

Another aspect of Loeki Stardust's recording that reflects a literal reading of the score also treats the text as finite by reading the two-part notation of the Spagna recercadas as genuine two-part music playable on two recorders: one plays the cantus firmus, while the other plays the glosas on the cantus firmus. However, Ortiz's commentary implies that the cantus firmus is intended for the harpsichord, capable of much more than playing a single melodic line with breves (in itself, not necessarily fitting an instrument that cannot sustain long notes). It is left to ask, therefore, if Ortiz did not intend the harpsichordist to add some melodic or harmonic filling with the right hand. There are, however, arguments in favor of the example-as-text approach: First, Ortiz published his *Tratado* half a century before the emergence of the single-staff basso continuo notation. Second, in his recercadas on "tenores" (short harmonic progressions), Ortiz wrote out the full four-part harmony on a four-staff system.

Performers who adopt the second approach (example as cursory text) assume that the examples in treatises convey only the information that serves the author's methodological aims, and that the music, when it was performed originally, may have contained more parts, more notes, perhaps even more sections. In the case of Ortiz's Spagna recercadas, this would mean that Ortiz notated only the essential framework for the violist to understand how to improvise above the cantus firmus, and little beyond that. In other words, musicians who hold this approach do not rule out the possibility that the harpsichordist should improvise with the right hand, but assume that Ortiz did not find this essential for understanding the improvisation of the viol part, and therefore did not offer a written-out right-hand part. Jordi Savall's album *Diego Ortiz: Recercadas del Tratado de Glosas* (1990) demonstrates this approach most clearly. Savall turned these six two-part pieces into three-part pieces: the lute (in the Recercada Primera) and the organ (in all the others) play elaborate counterpoint against the viol part, from which they borrow material. The resulting three-part texture is substantially richer than what is notated in Ortiz's book, yet it should be noted that if Ortiz sought to write down exemplary versions for what, ideally, should be improvised, then Savall's rendition of the Spagna recercadas takes these works one step *away* from the improvised ideal. Savall's added parts were not improvised but had been carefully worked out at least two decades before the aforementioned recording (they are almost identical to those heard in Savall's first recording of the *Tratado* from 1970).

The third approach (text as model) is arguably the hardest to implement and sees the text as a mere tentative surface result of the creative process, which is what the author really meant to address. Thus, if Ortiz in his Spagna recercadas gives an exemplary written-down improvisation, then those who adopt the text-as-model approach will seek to operate similar improvisatory creative process themselves and generate their own results, rather than to perform Ortiz's tentative result. Put simply, they will improvise their own recercadas, based on Ortiz's model. This approach has gained currency in recent years, as for example in Vicente Parrilla and More Hispano's CD *Glosas* where Ortiz's recercadas over Sandrin's Doulce Memoire serve as the model for Parrilla's own recercada on the chanson. Parrilla's glosas, either improvised or written out, are on other sixteenth-century "hits" like Rore's "Anchor che col partira."

In the same way that Savall's counterpoint to Ortiz, in strict sixteenth-century style, may evoke the debate around period composition, so may those who adopt the third approach evoke the debate around period improvisation. There is little question that our musical culture, steeped as it is in romantic concepts of authenticity in composition and in jazz-inspired concepts of authenticity in improvisation, is somewhat suspicious toward composition and improvisation in past musical styles. Without digressing to the core of the aesthetic debate around the adoption of a "foreign" style, it is important to stress that many early music specialists have not only been promoting period improvisation, but regarding it as an integral part of being historically informed. In the words of Barbara Thornton, cofounder of the Sequentia ensemble:

I feel it is very unauthentic to perform with the point of view which says, "I am now going to perform someone else's music from long, long ago, not my music." As an audience member I would want to say something like, "Well go home and find out what your music is and then come back." . . . The building blocks of medieval tradition are known and available. They are stable principles which won't go away. If you want to train yourself in them, you can create medieval music. (Rosenwald 2000: 288)

The three approaches can be implemented on other repertories described in treatises: Christopher Simpson's *The Division Violist*, for example, contains many fine examples that merit performance, and that could be further elaborated and arranged, but his professed aim was to instruct his readers so that they could write or improvise their own divisions on whatever ground they chose. C. P. E Bach's previously mentioned Freie Fantasie may be read as a finished piece, but its author gives concrete advice for those who wish to improvise such fantasies themselves, using but "thorough understanding of harmony and acquaintance with a few rules of construction" (Bach 1974: 430).

In the context of the present study, not much can be said about the first approach—if a certain example requires transcription, then the technique of producing one is essentially similar to that employed in "ordinary" repertory, as was discussed in Chapter 1. Moreover, as treatises often attempt to provide instructions, taking the first approach essentially ignores the context in which the example appears. The second and third approaches, however, fall neatly into the modern categories of arrangement and of composition (or improvisation) respectively, and are therefore pertinent to the core of the present discussion. One of the main problems in learning about these techniques from Ortiz's treatise is that, like in many diminution treatises, the detailed instruction provided on one page does not always lead to a relevant example on the other, and the example that *is* provided on the page does not necessarily illustrate the description that precedes it. In Ortiz's case, the first volume teaches one technique, while most of the second demonstrates others.

Embellishment

At the outset of the first volume of the *Tratado*, Ortiz explains the fundamentals of improvisation over a written melody. Put simply, he demonstrates how one may take common cadential formulae and simple melodic cells of 2–5 notes in long rhythmic values, and embellish them using shorter rhythmic values (Example 2.1).[7]

Let us return to Jane, who in Chapter 1 attempted to play Van Eyck's "Fantasia & Echo." Jane ventures to dedicate a week-long holiday (or two-week lockdown) to polish her improvisation skills by studying the *Tratado*. As she plays the various cadences and the passages in the first volume, she cannot escape the feeling that, although she had never read Ortiz's book before, she somehow knows many of his ornaments already. Had she been asked to ornament an ascending fifth, an ascending fourth, or a descending fourth *without* reading Ortiz, her fingers might have come up with figurations that are not at all different from Ortiz's. For example, with Van Eyck's fantasia still fresh in her

EXAMPLE 2.1 a. D. Ortiz, *Tratado*, Vol. 1: an example of a cadence in "D la sol" and three embellishments based on it. b. an example of a downward third in half notes and six embellishments based on it.

(a) [cadential formula]

1

2

3

(b) [melodic cell]   1   2   3

4   5   6

head, she might even instinctively ornament those intervals using fragments that "her fingers remember" from practicing Van Eyck (even though the latter's book was published almost a century after Ortiz's). Eventually, if Jane does put the effort in memorizing some of Ortiz's exact formulae for these intervals, she might find herself with melodic fragments that are very similar to those she already knew (Example 2.2a). Even the entire opening phrase in Van Eyck could serve Jane as an ornamented ascending fifth, remarkably similar to one of Ortiz's formulae (Example 2.2b).

Ortiz's book gives the illusion that studying its first volume somehow prepares the reader to produce pieces like those that appear in the second. This, however, is not the case. The embellishment of cadences and passages, as catalogued in the first volume, does appear relevant to only eight recercadas in the second volume—those based on vocal polyphonic models. Ortiz offers four

EXAMPLE 2.2 Basic ornamental figures: a. ascending fifth, ascending fourth, descending fourth, based on van Eyck's "Fantasia & Echo" and on Ortiz, *Tratado* Vol. 1, pp. 23r–24v. b. ascending fifth, based on Ortiz, *Tratado* Vol. 1, p. 24r.

(a)
[melodic cell]   [from Van Eyck]   [from Ortiz p. 24v]

[melodic cell]   [from Van Eyck]   [from Ortiz p. 23r]

[melodic cell] [from Van Eyck]   [from Ortiz p. 23r]

(b)   [from Van Eyck]

[Ortiz: melodic cell]   [Ortiz: ornamented cell p. 24r]

recercadas on Arcadelt's madrigal "O felici occhi miei" and four on Sandrin's chanson "Doulce memoire." In his first recercada on "O felici," Ortiz embellishes the bassus part. Looking at Arcadelt's original, it is easy to isolate some of the basic melodic cells treated in the first volume. In fact, it is possible to apply some of Ortiz's suggested embellishments and arrive at an embellished version almost identical to his perfected recercada (Example 2.3). Most important, if one wished to adopt the text-as-model approach, one could embellish the basic melodic cells with formulae different from those that Ortiz eventually chose and create a "new" recercada on Arcadelt's madrigal (Example 2.4).

Improvising a Solo Recercada

The second volume of the *Tratado* explores various improvisation techniques intended for bass viol with harpsichord accompaniment, each demonstrated with several recercadas. While the eight recercadas on polyphonic models seem to demonstrate the diminution technique explained in the first volume, the other recercadas relate to that technique more loosely. The fundamentals of free improvisation, of improvisation over a cantus firmus, and of improvisation over a harmonic progression are beautifully demonstrated in the recercadas but sadly

EXAMPLE 2.3   J. Arcadelt, bassus part from the madrigal "O felici occhi miei" (mm. 4–11). Staff 1 gives the original vocal part, staff 2 suggests embellishments from Ortiz's *Tratado*, vol. 1 that correlate to basic selected melodic cells from staff 1. Staff 3 gives written diminutions from Ortiz's *Tratado*, vol. 2.

EXAMPLE 2.4 J. Arcadelt, bassus part from the madrigal "O felici occhi miei" (mm. 4–11) in its original form (top staff), and with new embellishments taken from Vol. 1 of *Tratado*.

left without any commentary. One additional type, that of free accompanied fantasia, is mentioned but not represented at all. The great appeal that these recercadas have to performers requires that we try and extract guidelines for composing or improvising recercadas along the same lines.

Despite Ortiz's focus on accompanied music, the first four recercadas he presents in his book are written for solo viol. Ortiz explicitly aims these works to be warm-up pieces but, being situated immediately after a short discussion of tuning (Ortiz explains that the viol's G string should be tuned according to the harpsichord's Gamut) (Hoffmann 2004: 38–39), it is possible that they serve a function in the tuning process: all are set in G, all end on the low G string (Ortiz recommends that the tuning process should commence with that string), and perhaps even try to supply ample opportunity to test the tuning of the open strings (musically convincing context for the tuning of the strings D, G, c, a, and d' can easily be contrived, but Ortiz manages to introduce e on a strong beat as well). The recercadas also explore the whole effective range of the viol (going up to g' and a'), a fact that provides further evidence to their purpose as warm-up pieces.

Those who attempt to improvise a solo recercada in the style of Ortiz, one must keep in mind that, whatever instrument they play, their recercada should explore the instrument's range, be an effective warm-up piece, and perhaps also help in establishing proper tuning.

Ortiz's commentary on the solo recercadas tells us very little about the construction of the four pieces. However, their respective modal and motivic unfolding is consistent, and, with some analysis, one may generalize rules of thumb for composing one's own solo recercadas. In fact, very little in these four pieces requires prior planning and with some practice, they can indeed be extemporized.

The notes of the recercada tercera (Example 2.5) show how the piece evolves by way of a chain of short melodic cells, divided in the example by broken bar lines. Each cell either repeats its former in transposition, or otherwise offers a new, often subtle, modification of its former or of the simple opening subject. These modifications are usually either inversion, elision, rhythmic alteration, or combination with a cadential formula. Note that throughout the discussion, the term "cadential formula" denotes a melodic progression that is characteristic to a cadence (usually the so-called cantizans, ascending to the final from its leading note), but it is not a complete polyphonic cadence. Indeed, writing for solo instruments has its own peculiarities: none of the four solo recercadas end with a "cantizans" progression. While many occurrences of the "cantizans" cadential formulae in them do supply some measure of articulation to a phrase, not all of them function as substitute for full cadences.

While Ortiz notates the piece in common time, the example shows that the cells are of various lengths—two, three, or four half notes each—this creates metric variety, but not necessarily metric sophistication. Every cell either presents a new idea, or derives a variant of the cell that preceded it.

Unlike in later musical forms, where one may clearly observe composers to avoid a conclusive cadence on the tonic until the very end of the piece, here the tonal scheme is loose. Occasional cadential formulae occur here without logical order—on D, G, C, G, D, G, B♭, D, G, C and G—a direct result of employing them in cells that undergo constant transposition. Indeed, this recercada, with its haphazard tonal scheme, *could* have ended on any of the cadences on G that appeared along the way. However, the frequent cadences help to divide the flux of transposed cells into syntactical musical phrases.

The performer's challenge in improvising such recercada may be summarized thus: Play a basic melodic cell, repeat it in various transpositions 3–6 times, and then modify the cell. Repeat the procedure as much as you please, but make sure that some of the modifications contain cadential formulae.

Ortiz recercadas for solo viol are often performed on other instruments as well. As mentioned earlier, Ortiz's possibly intentional focus on the open strings of the viol becomes meaningless when played on the cornetto or the violin. Those who attempt to improvise their own recercadas should take into consideration the effective range of their own instruments, their accordatura (or scordatura), and what they find fit to transpose around while most of their attention is two steps ahead—in the next cadence, or the next modification to the cell. An

EXAMPLE 2.5 D. Ortiz, Recercada tercera, development of melodic cells indicated.

EXAMPLE 2.5 Continued

example for a new recercada for violin appears in Example 2.6. Note that the piece closely follows the summary outlined earlier, while assuming an effective range of g–b′♭ (safe within the violin's first position, as befits a warm-up piece) and the open strings of the violin. It is, however, important to note that Aurelio

EXAMPLE 2.6 Recercada for solo violin, based on principles from Ortiz's *Tratado*.

Virgiliano's ricercatas "per Flauto" (apparently an alto recorder in G) explore the high register of the instrument far more than one would expect in a warm-up.

With the concrete example of Ortiz's recercada tercera in mind, several questions arise: What did Ortiz really sound like when he improvised?

Are the four recercadas a real transcription of his extemporized playing and, by extension, can viol players nowadays achieve the same coherence and finesse when improvising according to the instructions I have set out? These questions are, naturally, relevant to other "documented" improvisations, and scholars have been grappling with these questions beyond the realm of performance practice as well. Rob Wegman, when discussing Ippolito Chamaterò di Negri's transcribed polyphonic introits of 1574 (Wegman 2014: 48–50, 60–62), offers an illuminating comparison: in the same way that those who transcribe spoken English would not hesitate to correct obvious errors, and thus write down what was *supposed* to be said, so did Chamaterò transcribe "not just what was being sung, but also how a proper listener would have heard it" (Wegman 2014: 62). The same could be said of Ortiz: slips and wrong notes had surely crept into his improvisations, and he had no reason to document them in his *Tratado*. Similarly, if Jane attempts to use the instruction offered in this section and tries to train herself in improvising solo recercadas, such slips are bound to occur during her practice (but hopefully less so as she gains confidence). Indeed, learning how to improvise is first and foremost a continuous personal process that cannot be learned with a book. But Ortiz never imagined that anyone would "study improvisation" from his book—he simply offered a model to be learned and to serve as a goal in others' learning process. So does the present chapter—it merely tries to help in reading and learning from Ortiz's model.

Improvising Recercadas upon a Plainsong

Like the four recercadas for solo viol, the six recercadas on the "La Spagna" plainsong (referred to henceforth as **I–VI**) cannot be convincingly interpreted as elaborations of vocal-like melodies. Even if the previously proposed instructions—constant transposition and occasional cadence or modification of a cell—really resemble what Ortiz expected improvisers to do when playing a solo recercada, they do not necessarily hold for other types of recercada. In fact, it *cannot* have been the process that Ortiz imagined would yield a recercada upon a plainsong. When playing upon a plainsong, the plainsong itself limits most of the improvisers' freedom: when playing a cell against any plainsong note, they must make sure that the result is contrapuntally valid. Whenever they transpose the cell, they must again make sure that the result is contrapuntally valid. If the cell is longer than the duration of a single plainsong note, then it must work against a *sequence* of notes in the plainsong, which is even harder to ascertain. In other words, improvisers must take the plainsong into account in each and every moment, so they should either know it by heart, or have the notes of that plainsong before them. Assuming that performers have the plainsong written in front of them and that the plainsong is performed by another instrument, can we offer them concise instruction (as we did earlier with relation to the solo recercada) as to how to improvise over that plainsong?

An intuitive way for many conservatory graduates nowadays is to try to compose a first-species counterpoint to the plainsong—placing a single consonance (a unison, a third, a fifth, or a sixth) against each plainsong note. Those who improvise first-species counterpoint do not have the composers' privilege of placing the climactic high point of their melody in advance, as is often recommended in counterpoint textbooks, and it is therefore possible that the melodic contour will turn out dull. The fact that it is possible to improvise first-species counterpoint says nothing about improvising other species. In fact, first-species is the only species that really allows one to find a consonance for each measure without having to look ahead to the next plainsong note (with the exception of avoiding consecutive fifths and octaves).

The near impossibility of improvising species counterpoint in any other but the first species is evident if we try to estimate how fast one must think when improvising. Let us assume a moderate tempo of $\downarrow$ =92 (very close to Savall's tempo in five out of the six "Spagna" recercadas). This means that every note of the plainsong takes about 2.6 seconds, and this is the time one has to decide what note to play when against the next note of the plainsong. In second species, one may opt to play two consonances against a note and still enjoy 2.6 seconds to decide what two notes to play against the next note of the plainsong. However, in order to use a dissonant passing note, one must figure out what note to play at the beginning of the next measure *and* figure out if the note that is being played and the note planned for the next measure allow the use of a passing note between them, and this must be done in the first half of the measure, leaving the improviser only 1.3 seconds to make a decision that is more complicated than in first species. If one wants to improvise third-species counterpoint and wants to use dissonant passing notes or a *cambiata* figure, one is left with 0.65 seconds to figure out what to do.

What trick could possibly allow the improviser to bypass the rigid time frame? This is where, again, analysis might reveal something of the inner workings of Ortiz's improvisations. Let us observe an important feature of the construction of the beginning of **I** (Example 2.7): measures 3–4 and 6–7, as well as 9–10 and 12–13, show that similar segments in the viol part are written over similar two-note patterns in the plainsong (in this case an ascending third). This is already in stark contrast to the idea of basing the improvisation on species counterpoint—an idea proven earlier as limited. In other words, it is possible that Ortiz, as the improviser-composer of these works, paid attention to the recurrence of *patterns*, rather than to single notes, within the plainsong. Perhaps Ortiz even had an improvisatory procedure that "generated" certain musical gestures above certain segments of plainsong notes, without forcing the improviser-composer to continuously invent new material.

EXAMPLE 2.7 D. Ortiz, Ricercada primera on "La Spagna," mm. 1–14. Similarity between mm. 3–4, 6–7, 9–10, and 12–13 highlighted.

Motivic economy is apparent in all six *recercadas*. **IV** begins with a triadic subject that repeats itself, in transposition, with an awkward leap that disrupts the melodic continuity (Example 2.8a). The disjunct repetition creates the impression that, since any measure can be fitted with the same subject (one

EXAMPLE 2.8 a. D. Ortiz, **IV**, Triadic subject in m. 1 (over D in the plainsong), transposable to fit the plainsong note in m. 2. b. D. Ortiz, **IV**, Triadic subject in m. 1 (over D in the plainsong), transposable to fit the plainsong notes in mm. 2–7. c. D. Ortiz, **IV**, mm. 1–5.

needs only to take the plainsong note as the root of the subject's triad), an entire *recercada* may be based on it (Example 2.8b). The result is not only unimaginative and mechanical, but also contrapuntally erroneous: the subject starts and ends on the fifth above the plainsong note, so repeating it results in repeated

EXAMPLE 2.9 Anonymous, "Green Sleeves, to a Ground with Division," mm. 25–32, from *The Division-Violin* (London: John Playford, 1685).

consecutive fifths. However, for other authors, similar mechanical repetition was deemed acceptable—both theoretically and aesthetically. John Playford's *The Division Violin* (London, 1685) contains a set of divisions entitled "Green Sleeves, to a Ground," where some of the variations seem contrapuntally careless and coarse (Example 2.9).

"Green Sleeves, to a Ground" and Ortiz's **IV**, while both being diminutions upon a plainsong played in the bass (a ground, as is the case in "Green Sleeves," may be seen as a short, repetitive, plainsong), focus on quite different skills, as is evident in the first four measures of **IV**. Measure 2 modifies the tail of the subject into a cantizans cadential formula over the descending step in the plainsong, now interpreted as a tenorizans formula. Immediately after that, in measures 3–4, Ortiz pushes the subject forward by a single quarter note, and consequently the last note of the subject now falls on the following measure, and on the next note of the plainsong (Example 2.8c). That is, of course, the crux of the skill displayed in the six *recercadas*: when improvising, successfully starting a cantizans figure over a plainsong note requires that one knows what the next plainsong note is. Similarly, using a subject that extends over more than one plainsong note requires that it works with both.

Ortiz's six plainsong *recercadas* draw consistently on subjects that cover two (occasionally three) plainsong notes. This is often camouflaged at the beginning: the subjects are not pulled *forward* by a quarter note, as just described. On the contrary, the "real" subjects (i.e., the form in which they appear most frequently later in the piece) exceed a single measure and are pushed *back* by a quarter or half note at their first appearance, thereby creating a sense of development when they are finally revealed (see beginnings of **I**, **III**, and **VI** in Example 2.10, as well as the beginning of **IV** in Example 2.8c).

EXAMPLE 2.10 D. Ortiz, Beginnings of **I**, **III**, and **VI**. The opening subject always appears on the first quarter note or half note before its "normal" beginning, on the second quarter note or half note, is revealed.

EXAMPLE 2.11 D. Ortiz, **IV**, mm. 1–5, opening subject modified to hypothesized original form.

1. descending fourth   2. descending step

3. ascending third   [2. descending step]

The subject that opens **IV** is one that may fit above several possible pairs of plainsong notes. In fact, if one reverts the subject's variants back to a hypothesized original form (as appears in mm. 3–4), one may postulate that Ortiz set out to demonstrate that his subject may be superimposed on three possible melodic intervals: a descending fourth or ascending fifth (mm. 1–2), a descending step (mm. 2–3, 4–5), and an ascending third (mm. 3–4) (Example 2.11). This is added to two possibilities already hinted at, with modified appearances of the subject (see Example 2.8c). First, in measures 1–2 of the finished work, the subject is pulled one quarter note forward, so that both its first note and its last note (being the same) would fit the plainsong if it repeats notes. Measures 2–3 show that this can be modified into a cadential formula over a cadential descending step. Another possibility, not used by Ortiz, is placing the subject over a descending third.

Let us try to reframe the contrapuntal knowledge embedded in measures 1–5 in a format similar to the one Ortiz proposes with relation to his recercadas on Arcadelt and Sandrin. In the first volume of the *Tratado*, Ortiz lists basic melodic cells, and for each cell he proposes several realizations (see Example 2.1). In the written recercada, one may look at a subject, of the kind observed in measures 1–5, as a "cell," and at the melodic intervals upon which the subject may fit consonantly as the possible realizations of that cell. Analyzing **I–VI** as a group, one may easily compile a repository of subjects, equivalent to the repository of cells in the first volume of the *Tratado*. It is left to ask if memorization of such a repository is an efficient, or even possible, tactic for improvisation.

The performer who wishes to use the subject that opens **IV** as a basis for improvisation needs to memorize the five possible melodic intervals over which

EXAMPLE 2.12 Summary of possible combinations of the opening subject of **IV** (first variant) and melodic plainsong intervals below it: 1) descending fourth or ascending fifth; 2) ascending third; 3) unison; 4) descending step; 5) descending step (cadential variant); 6) Descending third. Missing intervals: Ascending fourth and descending fifth; descending step.

it will work, and be able to retrieve that knowledge while reading the plainsong. The melodic intervals common in plainsong range from the ascending fifth to the descending fifth—nine intervals in total (including the repeated note). Excluding the descending fifth and the ascending fifth, which are equivalent to the ascending and the descending fourths respectively, we arrive at seven melodic intervals against which the subject must be checked.[8] This subject cannot appear above two important melodic intervals—the ascending fourth (and its complement—the descending fifth) and the ascending step (Example 2.12). Apparently aware of this, Ortiz presents a second variant of the subject in measures 7–9. The second variant may also appear over five melodic steps, including the two that do not work with the first one (Example 2.13). The two variants combined are sufficient for an improvisation over any common plainsong. There are additional combinations of the subject variants with melodic plainsong intervals—these will be clarified in the following text—but these two groups are sufficient for a basic improvisation upon any plainsong.

If one remembers which melodic intervals fit each variant, then the process of performing the variants fluently becomes almost automatic, and is very close to the common meaning of the term *cantare super librum*—one reads a plainsong and improvises a counterpoint to it. Let us take, for example, the beginning of the Kyrie *cum jubilo* and mark each interval with either the first or second variant ("A" and "B" respectively),[9] and apply modifications at cadences (Example 2.14a). With a little concentration and practice, this can be done mentally. Unlike a previous example which used a single subject over single plainsong notes (see Example 2.8b), here, the use of two variants of the same subject over various pairs of notes results in greater variety of sonorities (Example 2.14b). The relative license with which Ortiz treats consecutive fifths

EXAMPLE 2.13 Summary of possible combinations of the opening subject of **IV** (second variant) and melodic plainsong intervals below it: 1) descending fourth or ascending fifth; 2) descending fifth and ascending fourth; 3) ascending step; 4) descending step; 5) descending third. Missing intervals: ascending third; unison.

and octaves perhaps indicates the practical, performance-oriented nature of his advice, and that the same restrictions on compositional technique were applied to improvisations only loosely.

Voice-Leading Combinatorics

To this point, I have suggested that those who practiced Ortiz's implicit method were basing their use of subject variants on prior knowledge of the melodic intervals of the plainsong upon which they improvised. The question of how to arrive at such prior knowledge, Ortiz leaves to his reader to answer. It is possible, however, to suggest one possible way of extracting that knowledge from Ortiz's artful examples.

Let us reduce the problem into simple note-against-note counterpoint in two parts. Instead of an elaborate subject, let us assume a sequence of two notes played by the viol, for example, e′ and g′. What are the possible two-note sequences in the "La Spagna" plainsong that the sequence would fit? In order to simplify the calculation, I will consider only consonances within the octave—unison, third, fifth, and sixth—without their compounds, for the first interval. Since there are also four possible consonances under the viol's second note g′ (unison, third, fifth, sixth, and their compounds), there are 4×4 options (16 in total) (Example 2.15a). Since we are only examining pitch "classes," the actual melodic steps contain also those fourths and fifths that complement the fifths and the fourths among the 16 intervals in question (Example 2.15b), and two contrapuntally invalid melodic steps—those resulting in consecutive octaves and fifths (see options marked with [x] in Example 2.15a). Ortiz's part-writing takes some freedoms that are uncharacteristic for stile antico vocal polyphony (Example 2.16), and it may therefore be redundant to invoke the strict rules of vocal counterpoint here.

EXAMPLE 2.14 a. Kyrie *cum jubilo* (*Liber Usualis*, p. 40), transposed down a fifth, with markings for a potential improvisation of a viol part. Possible placement of two subjects taken from Ortiz's **IV** are marked "A" and "B." Potential modification of subject "A" into a cadence marked with an exclamation mark. b. Realization of Example a.

(a)

(b)

EXAMPLE 2.15 a. Sixteen possible plainsong notes under e′–g′. Combinations that are contrapuntally invalid are marked with x. b. Additional possibilities of plainsong notes under e′–g′.

(a)

1   1   1   3   1   5   1   6   3   1   3   3   3   5   3   6

5   3   5   5   5   6   5   8   6   5   6   6   6   8   6   10

(b)

1   6   3   8   5   10   6   12   8   8   8   10   8   12   8   13 *etc.*

EXAMPLE 2.16 D. Ortiz, **V**, mm. 1–10. This short passage features the use of consecutive octaves (albeit in contrary motion), part-crossing, and a loose use of consecutive fifths.

EXAMPLE 2.17 Sixteen possible ways of imposing an ascending third on possible plainsong melodic intervals.

EXAMPLE 2.18 Kyrie *cum jubilo* with a counterpoint entirely based on ascending thirds.

Having derived a list of valid melodic intervals under the notes e′-g′, we can now reverse our vantage point, and recast it as a list where the fixed elements are the plainsong intervals upon which an ascending third (whether major or minor) may appear, and of all the vertical intervals from the plainsong on which the thirds can begin (Example 2.17).

If we try to use this exhaustive list in order to write actual counterpoint, the result is likely to be dull or awkward, and with occasional moments where notes must be held in order to avoid contrapuntal errors (Example 2.18). Moreover, if an improviser must memorize similar lists for all melodic intervals, then the improviser would, for every couple of notes in the plainsong, have to decide between 16 possible pairs of notes that can appear above them, hence mastering no fewer than 112 possible scenarios of matching pairs of notes in the plainsong to pairs of notes in the improvised part. This seems impractical.

However, Ortiz did not use skeletal note-against-note formulas, but ornamented figures, often beginning after the first beat of one measure and ending on the first beat of the next, leaving room for several notes in the first measure that, because of their metric position in the measure, must all be consonant with the plainsong note against which they are played. If there are four possible consonances for each structural note of the subject (cases 1 and 2 in Example 2.19), then the possible consonances for a subject with *two* structural notes will consist of all the possible consonances *common* to both notes. If the first measure of the subject contains two such notes a third apart (case 3 in Example 2.19, combining together cases 1 and 2), there are only *three* possible consonances that could fit under that measure. Now, together with the four possible consonances under the single note that ends the subject (beginning the next measure), there are not 16 possible scenarios but only 12 in total (3×4). If the two notes are a fourth or a fifth apart, it could fit above

EXAMPLE 2.19 Possible plainsong consonances under subjects with: 1 and 2) one structural note in their first measure; 3) two structural notes a third apart; 4) fourth apart; 5) second apart.

only two notes (case 4 in Example 2.19), together with four possibilities for the next measure, yielding 8 options in total (2×4). If the structural notes are a second apart (case 5 in Example 2.19), then it could fit above just one note, yielding 4 options (1×4). Thus, the improviser has much less to memorize and calculate.

The Incompleteness of Ortiz's *Tratado*

The underlying principle of Ortiz's method is thus that the more harmonic implications a subject has, the fewer contexts in which it can appear and hence the fewer cases one needs to memorize. Let us explore Ortiz's subjects from the least flexible to the most. Example 2.20 consists of two lists that, between them, contain all the main subjects that Ortiz used in **I–VI**—those designed to work against two and three plainsong notes respectively. Rhythmic values of subjects from **I**, **V**, and **VI** (where the plainsong is in whole notes) are doubled in order to allow comparison with subjects from **II**, **III**, and **IV**. I will henceforth refer to subjects by [list]/[number]—the two variants from **IV** I have discussed are thus A/4 and A/5.

Example 2.20a gives, for each subject, the possible plainsong notes above which it may appear, and the interval, relative to the plainsong note, on which the subjects may begin. A/1 and A/2 serve as a good starting point for practicing Ortiz's technique. Each of these two closely related subjects (indeed, they may be considered two variants of a single subject) from **IV** contains no fewer than four different notes that, metrically, should be consonant with the plainsong note upon which they appear. Therefore, these subjects must begin on the octave above the plainsong note. The two subjects differ in their endings, and while both may appear above an ascending fifth (or a descending fourth), A/1 may appear above three intervals that cannot accommodate A/2—an ascending

EXAMPLE 2.20 Lists of possible contrapuntal combinations between subjects in Ortiz's *Tratado* and potential plainsong fragments. List A gives subjects fitted with two-note plainsong fragments. List B gives subjects fitted with three- and four-note plainsong fragments.

A/1

A/2

EXAMPLE 2.20 Continued

A/3

A/4

A/5

A/6

86

EXAMPLE 2.20 Continued

A/7

A/8

or

or

A/9

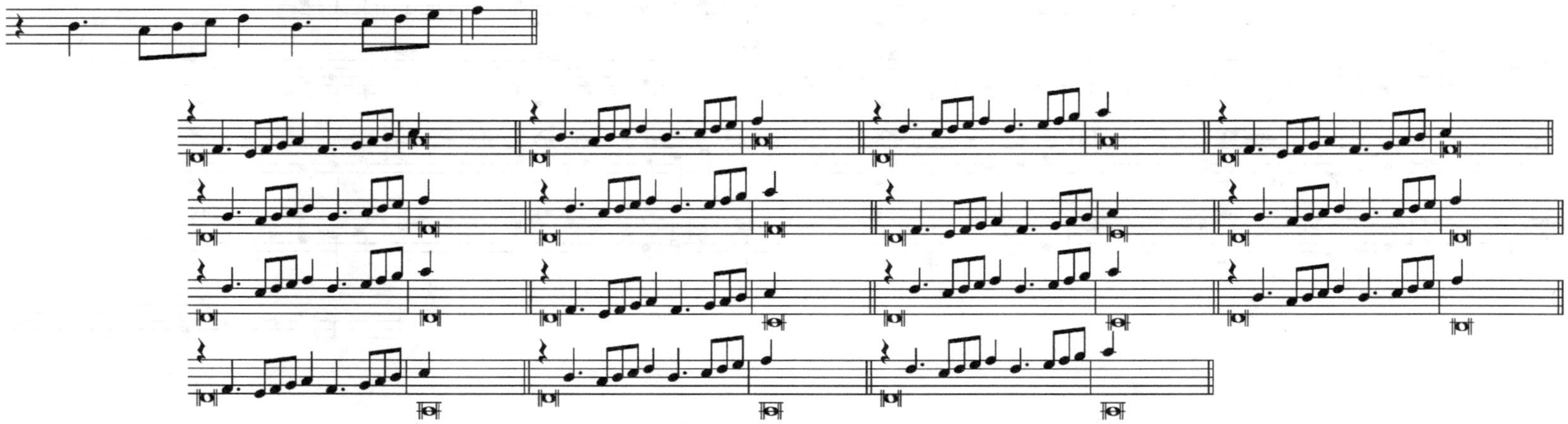

A/10

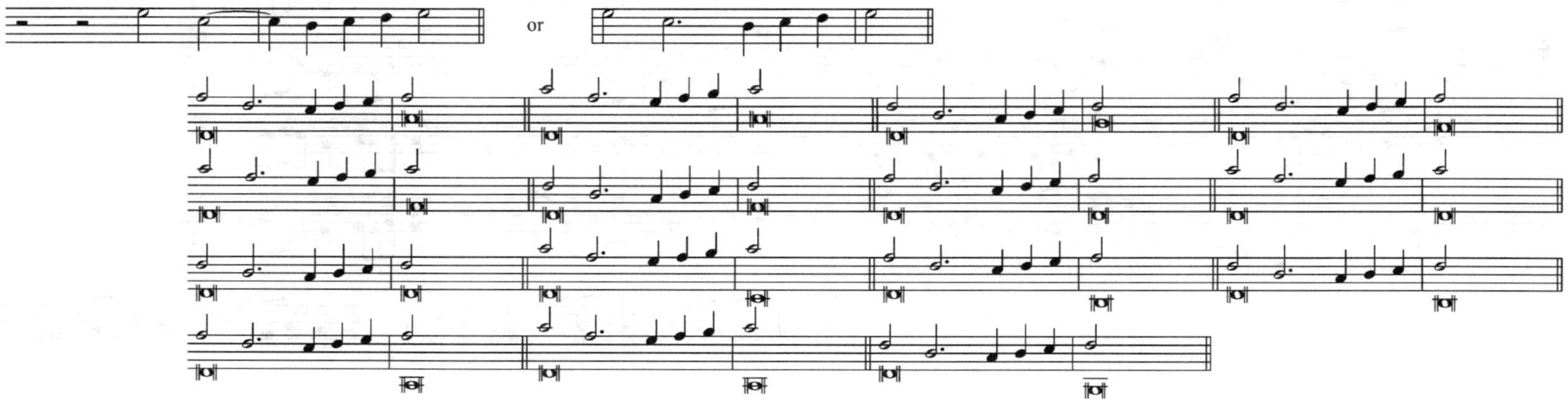

88

EXAMPLE 2.20 Continued

A/11

or

A/12

A/13

EXAMPLE 2.20 Continued

B/1

B/2

B/3

B/4

B/5

B/6

B/7

or

B/8

third, a unison, and a descending third—and A/2 may appear above three intervals that cannot accommodate A/1—an ascending fourth (or descending fifth), an ascending second, and a descending second. Improvising upon any plainsong with A/1 and A/2 allows the performer to decide between only two subjects, without having to decide on which interval to begin either of them—it must be an octave.

Compared to A/1 and A/2, subjects A/4 and A/5 (discussed earlier) are more flexible. Each opens with an arpeggiated triad, whose three notes may either be the unison, the third, and the fifth, or the sixth, the unison, and the third, relative to the plainsong note. There are three plainsong intervals that may accommodate either subject (the ascending fifth or rising fourth, the descending second, and the descending third), and only two that are exclusive to either subject. On the other hand, unlike with A/1 and A/2, there are choices as to which note to start on. For example, A/4, when it appears above a descending second, must begin on the fifth above the plainsong; but when it appears above a descending third, must begin on the third. This relative freedom is slightly harder to handle than what appeared earlier, where only melodic plainsong intervals were discussed. One may take the same beginning of Kyrie *cum jubilo* as in Example 2.14 and, using exactly the same two subjects, construct an entirely different melody (Example 2.21).

Example 2.20b requires a different approach to organizing contrapuntal possibilities. In Example 2.20a, each subject is checked against seven possible melodic intervals in the plainsong.[10] If one tries to treat subjects played against three plainsong notes similarly, then one must check each subject against $(7 \times 7 =)$ 49 possible two-interval sequences. The number of possible counterpoints for each two-interval sequence is $(4 \times 4 \times 4 =)$ 64. Example 2.20b gives a loose survey of the subjects played against three notes, and of the three plainsong notes against which they are played, as they are found in Ortiz's recercadas, without additional possibilities. The reader can see that Ortiz sought subjects that work upon more than one two-interval sequence or, in some cases, identified recurring two-interval sequences within the plainsong that could accommodate recurring subjects.

Even if, at the beginning of this chapter I implied that Ortiz did not properly explain the technique underlying **I–VI**, it should be said that he was very methodological in his examples—each of the various recercadas seems to address a different aspect of technique. **III** and **IV** use smaller rhythmic divisions, and their subjects are designed to work against two plainsong notes; **II** and **V** have subjects that work with three plainsong notes; **I** and **VI** use subjects over both two and three plainsong notes; **IV** uses the most restrictive (hence also the easiest to memorize) triadic subjects; while **VI** uses very flexible subjects that are harder to master. In fact, among the 17 two-note subjects, 10 use unique combinations of structural notes. For example, A/3 is the only subject outlining a triad and descending a fourth from the triad's top note to the last note of the

EXAMPLE 2.21 Potential improvisation of a viol part upon Kyrie *cum jubilo*, exploring different use of subjects A/4 and A/5 compared to those in Example 2.14b.

subject; A/4 and A/5 outline similar triads, but remain on the top note and descend a step respectively. In other words, Ortiz seems to have used **I–VI** to give as many different examples as possible, without wasting space on multiple subjects that function similarly.

Conclusion

This chapter opened with the image of the hunter-performer who gazes at a painting in an attempt to identify a musical fragment. Those who would visit the Musée des Beaux Arts in Brussels might encounter a beautiful still life (Inv. 3893) by the early seventeenth-century painter Evaristo Baschenis. At the center of the composition, Baschenis depicts an open music book, framed by string instruments in a jumble on a table (with fruit). The open music book is clearly an imitation of a page from Diego Ortiz's *Tratado*. While a bass viol dominates the painting, there are also a violin and no fewer than four other plucked instruments of various kinds on the table.

Having dedicated the chapter to dealing with treatises as a special type of source, we may rightly ask how we should deal with the painting of Ortiz's book. With all precautions taken, Baschenis's still life may indeed raise interesting questions that might affect musicians' treatment of the *Tratado*. The painting might inspire the performance of Ortiz's recercadas with plucked instruments accompanying the viol. It might hint that Ortiz's works were indeed performed as "works" and were even perceived as an ideal graphic representation of Music itself. It might lead us to conclusions about the author's enduring fame into the early seventeenth century, or at least about the circulation of Ortiz's music more than fifty years after the *Tratado* had been published, around Baschenis's area of activity (mainly Bergamo).

However, while all this insight from Ortiz's cameo appearance in the painting could have direct influence on performers—it may inspire to "orchestrate" the recercadas in a certain way, or to program the works with later music, or to suggest other works from Bergamo—a painting of this kind does not substitute an in-depth analysis of the *Tratado* and an attempt to understand, with regard to each type of example it contains, how the music itself should be approached. As was demonstrated by Noah Greenberg, we should look for good music to perform wherever we can—in paintings, treatises, newspapers, books, stone tablets—but in order to really exhaust the potential of the source, we must try and understand if, and in what ways, it differs from an "ordinary" music manuscript or print, why it contains music at all, and whether the music should be understood as text, or perhaps as a cursory text or even a model.

Chapter 3

Different Works, Different Versions, Neither or Both?

The first chapter of this book examined procedures required by the work with historical sources: interpreting early notation systems, working with manuscripts and early prints, correcting mistakes, and preparing tailor-made performance material. The second chapter focused on one specific type of source—treatises—and the challenges one might face if one chooses to use treatises as a basis for musical performance. One conclusion that may be drawn from these two chapters is that the historically informed approach to these sources may sometimes, perhaps paradoxically, take one step *further* away from the source, either by modifying and simplifying details of notation, or by adapting historical material as a model for one's own text. The present chapter deals with situations that are somewhat opposite—situations in which the performer attempts to get *closer* to the text as it is transmitted by a source. This chapter, along with the next one, thus takes us to the realm of critical editing.

The following chapter highlights some of the ways in which scholarship affects performance. As often discussed with relation to early music, scholarship affects performance practice in general: research informs choices of instruments, dynamics, articulation, tempo, ornamentation, and pronunciation. All the aforementioned aspects are applied to a given text, even when that text remains fixed within a manuscript or a treatise. The present discussion, however, is more circumscribed and focuses on the way in which scholarship shapes the text itself: which sources we look at. How do scholars define the boundaries of a certain work—does it have a single authoritative text or perhaps

A Performer's Guide to Transcribing, Editing, and Arranging Early Music. Alon Schab, Oxford University Press.
© Oxford University Press 2022. DOI: 10.1093/oso/9780197600658.003.0004

several versions? I will argue that, especially when they work directly from the sources, performers should not only be aware of recent scholarship, but also be able to examine that scholarship critically, and perhaps look at the sources afresh. Most important, I will try to offer ways in which the study of the available sources of a piece can enrich one's artistic concept.

On the surface, one's decision to trust a critical edition, prepared by a scholar who had examined the surviving sources and their historical background, might help to bypass most of the contemplation about sources. Indeed, some of the ideas expressed in what follows are often perceived as belonging within the domain of the editor rather than of the performer.

However, the tenor of this book, being that historically informed performers may want to take responsibility over the preparation of material and to study the sources themselves, justifies a brief discussion of the decision-making that is involved in dealing with works, their versions, and their sources. To offer a selection of such case studies that performers can take ideas from is more feasible and more modest in scope than to offer a comprehensive account of approaches to multiple-source and multiple-version scenarios for the editor. The latter is an impossible, perhaps even futile, task.

Most of the cases discussed in the chapter involve pieces that have survived in at least two versions, or that are transmitted in at least two sources. Hitherto, the only case examined in this book, in which performers had two competing texts to work with, was James Paisible's gigue (see Chapter 1), where we observed a textual problem in our two principal sources, intentionally focused on one source, *refrained* from seeking a solution in another, and instead opted for a third solution—completing a few missing measures ourselves. In fact, the absence of alternative sources was probably the common point of departure for the late seventeenth-century musicians who used these sources originally, and yet one must not equate a historically informed mindset with the self-imposition of "authentic" limitations.

Sources and Works

First, we must clarify some aspects of the terms "source" and "work," so common in the early music lingo. A historical source, being a physical object that transmits musical text, is relatively easy to define. Every source is unique in its combination of several attributes: its physical medium, its production method, the motivation for its production, the identity of the copyist or the printer, the identity of its owners, its provenance, and the text it transmits.

The sources, either directly or through the mediation of an edition, play a significant role in the context of music performance, and especially of historically informed performance. Not only do performers sing and play from the source, but programming concerts and recordings of early music is also affected by it. In many cases, constructing a concert or a recording around a specific source provides the performers with a skeleton of a program, even with a "concept" or a "story."[1] In such cases, performers deliberately avoid any claim for Urtext and, instead, choose to breathe life into a historical document and into the environment that produced that document and its repertoire—a dark medieval monastery, a lavish renaissance court, a seventeenth-century London tavern—at the risk of performing idiosyncratic variants and even errors that are besides "the composer's intention" (however unverifiable those intentions are bound to remain).

Compared to the easily defined source, a work is an elusive term. First, the way in which we classify and list composers' works is not necessarily similar to the way the composers listed their works. For example, ask any Bach fan about Bach's major works, and they will give a relatively well-organized list, grouping sets of works together according to genre and despite their origin in different times (like four orchestral suites), using anachronistic titles (like "Toccata and Fugue"), and adding common nicknames that would have surprised the composer (the "Great" Mass, the "French" and "English" suites, the "Goldberg" variations, the "Forty-Eight" or the "Air on G String").

Second, performers today tend to accept (even if tacitly) nineteenth-century assumptions about the musical work as a fixed and autonomous text. The issue of the Work Concept has preoccupied many authors over the last decades, and while many accept Lydia Goehr's identification of the Work Concept as an essentially Romantic phenomenon, John Butt points out several work-oriented tendencies from as early as the mid-fifteenth century (Butt 2005). In fact, arguing about the relevance of the Work Concept in the context of baroque and renaissance thinking is but a part of the whole picture: twenty-first-century patterns of consumption simply force early music into later framework, anachronistic by definition. One can argue for the fluidity of works in the sixteenth century, and yet nothing is fluid in the recordings of these works, which are the form in which many people nowadays, at least among the audience, know these works by. In other words, the centrality of recorded media creates a situation whereby many among the audience of early music accept a Work Concept that is close to that of pop music.

Let us examine an extreme example by looking at medieval music. Many performers of medieval music, as well as their fans, know the few late-medieval dances preserved in manuscripts F-P*n* Fr. 844 (the Chansonnier du Roi) and GB-L*bl* Add. MS 29,987. These fans are most likely to know them by their titles—like the "first" to the "eighth and last" estampie royal, Saltarello, or Lamento di Tristano. It is by those names that many music listeners, not only of early music but also of early music–inspired folk and pop acts (like John Renbourn, the Albion Band, or Dead Can Dance), know the tunes. For many listeners, these titles evoke the memory of their favorite recording of the piece, or those details that are common to several recordings that they know. Few performers know these dances purely from reading the manuscripts and ignore the half-century-long tradition of recording that popularized them. The way these short works are treated is essentially like that of Tin Pan Alley songs—songs that had been initially published in print, then recorded countless times, and are by now transmitted solely through performance and recording, while their "original" published sheet music is obsolete.[2] In other words, while historical sensitivity requires that we treat many early pieces of music as fluid texts and subject to significant intervention, the way in which these works are retrieved and consumed by audiences today forces them into nineteenth- and twentieth-century Work Concept molds. Streaming services, for example, would probably add a title and a composer name even when these are unknown, standardize spelling, and match their catalogue numbers with other tracks with similar attributes,[3] and listeners may equate the work with a single recording that they know.

Works and Versions

A harpsichordist rehearses for a concert—a recital dedicated to works from an English virginal book. However, she finds some of the cadences and the ornaments in that book somewhat awkward. She assumes that these are the copyist's idiosyncrasies and, although she could check these details against other sources (perhaps even more reliable ones), she is fascinated with the way the *copyist* understood the music, and sticks to the variants as they appear in that manuscript. Our harpsichordist's colleague attends the recital and, excited, he decides to play his own recital based on the same manuscript. However, he decides to take a different approach by avoiding the idiosyncratic cadences and ornaments by consulting other sources that sound to him more convincing. To their disappointment, a common friend that attended both recitals claims that she did not notice any difference. An occasional difference in a cadential formula or an ornament, so they realize, does not necessarily justify the identification of two distinct versions.

For the present discussion, let us define "versions" as two or more musical texts of the same piece that, unlike the versions in the two friends' recitals, are different enough to be perceived as distinct, even without close scrutiny. This is, in some cases, a matter of quantity rather than of quality: two people might disagree as to when there are enough added or omitted measures, significant differences in the melody and harmony, or significant changes to the scoring, to justify the identification of a version. The fact that we resort to questions of quantity when deciding if two texts are in fact the same piece, two distinct versions of the same piece, or two distinct pieces altogether means that even a fundamental reference like a composer's catalogue of works may not be as "factual" as it is often perceived.

Situations whereby various versions of a work exist are common in music of the renaissance and baroque eras. Awareness of that does not always require profound knowledge of the sources—it suffices that a performer knows the music in several recordings to be aware that some of them sound different from others. Thus, for example, Tallis's anthem "Remember not, O Lord, our old Iniquities" exists in one version in the Lumley Partbooks, and in another version in the Mulliner Book, where it is untexted but allows the reconstruction of a second vocal version with more elaborate polyphonic texture. In Frescobaldi's canzonas the situation is even more confusing: his Canzona detta l'Ambitiosa was published in his first book of canzonas (1628) and then again, radically modified, in his second book (1634). The opening phrases of the two respective versions share but vague family resemblance; from the first cadence on, their second section sounds almost similar, up to the cadence that concludes it, and then the two versions split again. Both in Tallis and Frescobaldi, those who know one version and listen to the other for the first time might feel that familiar moments alternate with moments that are entirely new. The composer's motivation (or someone else's) to create a second version is different from one case to another: in the aforementioned cases, Tallis's revision probably had to do with the swinging religious pendulum in England during the 1550s; Frescobaldi's has more to do with the composer's tendency to improve on his older material, or simply to justify reselling his canzonas in a second book, only a few years after selling the first. It would therefore exceed the scope of this book to overview those most common motivations.

Historically informed performers are often aware if a piece they perform survives in more than one version. This is not always easy to do, especially when one is acquainted with a piece in recorded medium: "the text," when performed, is often added ornamentation and accidentals, its rhythm altered according to performance conventions, and its continuo part (where such a part exists) realized. A safer way to learn of the existence of versions is by working with a critical catalogue, but this method, as we shall see, states facts that might limit, rather than free, the performer.

Versions and Catalogues

The existence of multiple sources does not, in itself, pose a problem. If each source transmits a plausible text that performers and hearers find meaningful, then even sources conflicting with one another do not pose a serious problem but, at worst, result in the identification of multiple versions of a given piece. A hypothetical early eighteenth-century performer in Dresden playing a Vivaldi concerto (reading from a hypothetical source [x]) and another performer in Venice playing the same concerto (but reading from another source [y]) could call the works they were playing by a similar name [*title*] (although not yet with the similar future catalogue number [n]); and not care that the sources x

and *y* differ substantially from one another (for example, if the second movement in [*x*] is entirely different from the one in [*y*]), as they probably did not know of one another. The approach of both our hypothetical Dresdner and Venetian could be described as directed "from the sources up." At the very most they may have been concerned with how to call the piece that was copied on the paper.

Problems begin to occur only when musicians are aware of multiple versions and of multiple sources. This situation, which is essentially a modern one, results in attempts to classify, catalogue, and identify sources with "versions," and to identify those as versions of "works." For the musicologist who holds two facsimiles of the Vivaldi concerto (reproductions of both [*x*] and [*y*]) on their desk, the conflicts between the two sources pose an ontological problem. The musicologist's approach is directed "from an abstract catalogue entry down": having multiple sources at hand, seeking to explain what the essence of [*title*] is, and usually supplying that explanation in the form of a single critically-edited score.

Identifying a source with a catalogue entry (that was formulated centuries after the copying) has far-reaching consequences, stemming from the way in which traditional musicology perceives the relationship between work and source. This is reflected in the common structure of a catalogue: as mentioned earlier, the basic building block of analytical catalogues is the work or, sometimes, a movement within the work. Each work or movement refers to the sources that transmit it. But the relationship of work and source is asymmetrical: while each title may be transmitted by multiple sources, each source usually refers back to a single title only.

However, there might be cases that challenge this principle of asymmetry. Let us imagine a literary scholar who compiles a catalogue of Franz Kafka's autographs. During his research he stumbles upon an unknown autograph sketch of Kafka's short parable "Before the Law." How should the sketch be catalogued? As a sketch for the parable as it was published independently in 1915? Or as a sketch for the important novel "The Trial" in which the parable was integrated? Can a source be linked both to a whole (for our purpose, a novel) and to a part of the whole (a parable)? Is the method of linking sources to multiple catalogue entities valid and fitting for every cataloging project, or is it necessary only in Kafka's case?

In music, a similar problem occurs with relation to Mozart's G minor Symphony K. 550, which is often referred to with the added clause "version without clarinets" or "version with clarinets." As the oboes are the only parts (other than the clarinets) in which the two "versions" differ, scores or sets of parts that survived in fairly good state may easily be linked with one version or the other. Thus, a manuscript containing the oboe parts may be linked with the "version without clarinets." But what about an incomplete set that contains only the viola and cello parts? In cases where two versions originate in different times, then linking a fragmentary source to one version and not to the other may have crucial implications on setting the earliest date of that version. Fortunately, Mozart's symphony is unusual in the fact that, although it survives in two versions, these are encoded within a single autograph containing the "version without clarinets" and an appendix with only the clarinet parts and the modified oboe parts—only what is necessary in order to produce a score of the "version with clarinets." It seems that the composer did not find it important to register two versions in his own-compiled "List of all my works" and he entered only the "version without clarinets" into that catalogue on July 25, 1788.[4] Can we refer to the original version as "missing" parts, when those parts are not necessarily supposed to be there?

Some sources may, at the same time, be considered complete for one work and fragmentary to another. Handel's autograph GB-L*bl* R.M.20.g.5 is the source of his 1727 Coronation Anthems. Some of the movements he later reused in his oratorios *Esther* and *Deborah*. It may be awkward to state that GB-L*bl* R.M.20.g.5 is a source for *Deborah* when all that ties it to *Deborah* is that the composer added, more than five years after the composition, an alternative text to one of the anthems, to integrate the music in the new oratorio. Handel did not even bother to copy the recycled anthem into the score of the new work.

Two Sources and Two Versions

Two versions of the same piece have, by definition, a lot in common. In the case of K. 550, when all that Mozart wanted was to modify the oboes and add the clarinets, he should be excused for not wasting paper on copying the entire symphony anew. But in cases where there is a stand-alone source for each version and where there is considerable overlap between the two sources of the two distinct versions (had Mozart copied, for example, the score again for the "version with clarinets"), an editor might want to improve the text of one version by collating readings from another. Henry Purcell's Trio Sonata Z. 809 provides a case in point. The sonata survives in two different versions, one in the composer's autograph GB-L*bl* MS Add. 30,930 and another in the posthumous print *Ten Sonata's in Four Parts* (1697). While only one of the sonata's five movements (the Largo) is entirely different, there are several passages in the rest of the work where the editor of one version may justly consult the other. For example, in the autograph version, measures 40–44 of the first violin part were copied incorrectly by the composer and were then scribbled over. Consulting the print is the easiest way to reconstruct the passage.

But in another passage in the autograph version of Purcell's sonata, consulting the print version may blur an interesting variant. In the autograph, the rhythm in measure 3 of the second violin part does not add up to a four-quarters measure (Example 3.1). The posthumous print suggests that the third eighth

102

EXAMPLE 3.1 H. Purcell, Sonata Z809, mm. 1–4. Illogical reading in the autograph (m. 3), with two solutions (from *Ten Sonata's in Four Parts* [1697] and an alternative).

note in that bar should be a quarter note (see example) and that the composer merely overshot the beam of the preceding two eighth notes in the autograph.[5] Purcell's print, as previously mentioned, is posthumous and, like others of his posthumous prints, may have involved considerable editorial intervention. If so, one should also consider solving textual errors in the autograph *without* resorting to the later print. Thus, one may also suggest alternative corrections for the wrong rhythm. For example, if one assumes that Purcell omitted a dot rather than overshot a stem, then adding such a dot to the first quarter note changes the measure into an alternative (valid) reading, and even results in an imitation with the first violin that is more convincing than the that in the print version (see example).[6]

Posthumous prints, like corrupted copies of works, have unquestioned *historical* authority, but they are often the result of processes that are *editorial* in nature. In some questions, two editorial suggestions, even when separated by three centuries, should be applied the same criticism and weighed with equal seriousness. The two passages from Purcell's sonata demonstrate that each conflict between sources must be considered independently and according to the historical background of each source—indeed, a reason musicologists cling to their monopoly on critical editing.

Like Purcell's sonata, Bach's "The Art of Fugue" exists both in autograph and in a heavily reworked posthumous print (1751). Unlike in Purcell's case, however, Bach's posthumous print enjoys the trust of scholars and performers alike. To be sure, as far as music is concerned, Bach's estate was in better hands than Purcell's. However, the authority given to the print (by virtue of its later date, the apparent revisions it contains, the fugues that were added to it, and the coherent and logical ordering of the works contained therein) overshadows the significance of the composer's own autograph of the work (D-B Mus. Ms. Bach P 200) (Schulenberg 1992: 344–355). The autograph version is rarely recorded and is considered secondary to the print. Those who know the Purcell precedent might ask whether Bach's print really reflects the composer's intentions faithfully. If, inspired by the Purcell case, one chose to doubt the authority of the posthumous print and prefer the autograph, one could also question some of the later readings in the print.

When comparing the autograph and the printed versions of Contrapunctus 1, it is apparent that the work was heavily revised and added a more modern touch—measures were halved, a coda was added, and some smaller details were changed throughout. But even if we assume that Bach wished his last work to accord with more modern taste (which is not self-explanatory! Why set it in open score in the first place?), some of the figurations that were added are simply not convincing. Let us compare measures 8–13 in the autograph with their equivalent measures 15–25 in the print (Example 3.2) While the eighth notes added to the bass part in measure 16 (in the print) help to retain the ongoing eighth-note motion without changing the overall contour of that part, the eighth notes added to the treble in measure 23 (in the print) break the melodic contour, disturb the imitation with the bass, and further blur the already-hidden subject entrance in the alto. In the case of "The Art of Fugue," there is no reason to ignore the autograph since, at least in some cases, it provides a better text.

Variants in Performance

Both of the cases discussed here—Purcell's sonata and Bach's "The Art of Fugue"—confront the composer's autograph with a posthumous print of a different version of the same piece (within the same entry in the composers' respective catalogues). Let us now consider the validity of mutual consultation in another scenario, this time confronting two autographs of two versions of a piece by Bach that are different enough from one another to actually be considered not as versions but as separate works, and are allocated different catalogue numbers—the fourth Brandenburg Concerto in G major BWV 1049 (D-B Am.B 78) set for violin, two recorders, and orchestra, and its later adaptation for harpsichord, two recorders, and orchestra in F major BWV 1057 (D-B Mus. ms. Bach P 234).[7]

In many respects, the two concertos are more similar than different. The main differences between the two versions are the change of one solo

EXAMPLE 3.2 J. S. Bach, "The Art of Fugue," Contrapunctus 1, mm. 7–12 (in following the autograph measure numbering) compared with mm. 15–25 (following the 1751 print measure numbering).

EXAMPLE 3.2 Continued

EXAMPLE 3.2 Continued

instrument from an idiomatic violin part to an idiomatic harpsichord part and the transposition of the entire work a major second down. Also, the dialogue-like second movement is changed from the two recorders and violin against the orchestra (in BWV 1049) to the harpsichord against the orchestra (BWV 1057). But a more surprising change appears in measure 59 of that movement (Example 3.3): the g″♮ in BWV 1049 (in the violino principale, flauto I, and violino I ripieno).

The change in measure 59 extends beyond the realm of orchestration and instrumental idiom into the realm of stylistic syntax, with an uncharacteristic melodic ascent containing an augmented second (e″♭–f″♯–g″ in flauto I and cembalo). Several paleographic questions arise from the autograph of the concerto BWV 1057: two of the three sharp signs in question, in measure 59, are located above the noteheads and not to their left; the ink color of the sharp signs is slightly lighter than the color of the notes to which they apply. Could they be a later addition? Are they autograph? But two fundamental questions go beyond paleography—are the two opposed readings interchangeable? And if one wants to see them as interchangeable, can this be done with two works that are different in chronology, key, orchestration, and catalogue number? From these two fundamental questions one may go further and ask if any question regarding the validity of the reading from BWV 1057 would have risen without the comparison with BWV 1049. A survey of the recordings of BWV 1057 shows that, as far as performers today are concerned, the two readings are interchangeable indeed.

A remarkably similar problem occurs in Handel's Trio Sonata Op. 5, no. 6 HWV 401 and in his Organ Concerto HWV 295. The trio sonata was one of two new sonatas that Handel composed toward the publication of his Op. 5 in early 1739. By April of that year, Handel already reused the sonata as the basis for an organ concerto. The equivalent measures—measure 14 of the trio sonata and measure 15 of the concerto—both contain aborted cadences in D minor, and the e″ in the top part has no accidental in both autographs (GB-L*bl* R.M. 20.g.14 f. 6r GB-L*bl* R.M. 20.g.12 f. 14r). In the 1740 print of the concerto, however, a flat sign is applied to the e″, a fact that changes the harmony and aborts the cadence one quarter note earlier (Example 3.4). The e″♭ given in the print was not taken lightly by the editors of the collected Handel edition, and it is given in parentheses and in small print in all critical editions of the organ concerto. As a result, practically all recordings of the concerto contain the e″♭, but those of the trio sonata contain an e″♮. The question remains: as far as the composer was concerned, were the two opposed readings interchangeable?

Frans Brüggen, in one of his recordings of Vivaldi's concertos, made an inspiring statement with regards to the dividing line between versions and works. Five of Vivaldi's *VI Concerti a Flauto Traverso [. . .] Opera Decima* (Amsterdam: Le Cène, 1728) exist in earlier versions as chamber concertos. On the original 1979 record sleeve, and in deviation from the title of the record—"6 Concerti a Flauto Traverso e B.c., op. 10"—Brüggen declared that the versions printed by Le Cène are "dull and unmusical" ("matt und unmusikalisch"), that they may have been adapted on Vivaldi's behalf but without Vivaldi's supervision, and that, as a performer, he found no wrong in reverting back to the older versions of the concertos.[8] What is implied by Brüggen's act is rather provocative: at a moment in the early music revival when many recordings were being based on a complete opus performed from

EXAMPLE 3.3 a J. S. Bach, Brandenburg Concerto No. 4 BWV 1049, Andante, mm. 57–61. b. J. S. Bach Concerto in F major BWV 1057, Andante, mm. 57–61. 3a and 3b

facsimile, Brüggen argued that the "Opus" is not necessarily the historical document, nor the sequence of the RV catalogue numbers that one may identify in the print (433, 439, 428, 435, 434, 437) but rather a sequence of "ideas" whose exact manifestation (either as the early chamber concertos or as the later concertos for transverse flute) is of secondary importance. Brüggen perhaps took his cue from Nikolaus Harnoncourt, who styled an earlier version of RV439—the chamber concerto RV104—as Op. 10, no. 2,[9] but he took the idea a few steps further, showing that even when playing an entirely different sequence of concertos, even if related (RV98, 104, 90, 435, 442, and 101), the identity of the opus remains. Brüggen undoubtedly made a bold claim based on his dislike of the Amsterdam versions of Vivaldi's concertos. As noted above, proper study of the historical circumstances may prove helpful and, indeed, Vivaldi's Opp. 10–12 were printed on Le Cène's expense, they do not contain dedications, and Vivaldi's involvement in their printing process was probably limited (Talbot 1978: 58–78).

EXAMPLE 3.3 Continued

(b)

The second concerto in the set, "La Notte," allows us to examine Brüggen's choice by analyzing several textual conflicts of the kind previously highlighted in Bach, between the Le Cène print (transmitting RV439) and Vivaldi's autograph in I-T*n* Giordano 31 (transmitting RV104).[10] The different scoring and the comprehensive re-composition of measures 22–31 in the second movement makes it futile to treat these two versions as two sources of the same piece, and yet comparison of the apparently similar passages leads once again to fascinating questions about the boundaries of Vivaldi's musical language. The clearest challenge is posed by the beginning of the first solo episode in the final Allegro. The key signature is *cantus mollis* with only B♭, and no E♭. The bass line in RV104, played by the bassoon, contains an e♭ (specifically adding a flat sign) while the high bass line in RV439, played by the viola, is not given a flat sign and therefore implies an e′♮ (Example 3.5).

EXAMPLE 3.4 G. F. Handel, Trio Sonata Op. 5, no. 6 HWV 401 (GB-L*bl* R.M. 20.g.14 f. 6r, figuring based on Walsh's edition) and in his Organ Concerto HWV 295 (GB-L*bl* R.M. 20.g.12 f. 14r, information from Walsh's edition in brackets). Cadences in D minor (in mm. 14 and 15 respectively) compared.

For those well acquainted with the available recordings of RV439, this e'♮ might not sound unusual but, if compared with RV104, it makes little sense.[11] Exactly as with BWV 1049 and BWV 1057, one should ask if the two readings are really interchangeable, or if RV439 is simply wrong.[12] The diatonic "lament bass" figure in RV104 is a common harmonic progression that Vivaldi used extensively (Brover-Lubovsky 2008: 151–168), while the modified descending tetrachord in RV439 is not. Comparison with first solo episodes in other Vivaldi concertos in the minor mode (Op. 8, no. 9, in D minor RV454, mm. 22–29; RV495, mm. 57–71) shows that the Phrygian

EXAMPLE 3.5 A. Vivaldi, Concerto "La Notte" Allegro, first solo episode, mm. 15–19. Versions RV104 and RV439 compared.

tetrachord repeated twice is a recurring opening gambit in the composer's ritornello-form movements.

Some Helpful Leads

The examples presented earlier show how hard it is to define the musical work and how, in certain cases, any scholarly attempt to help one define the work actually complicates things further. Every musical work poses different problems with regard to the choice of sources and to their handling. Thus, as it is impossible to formulate an all-embracing method for dealing with musical works and musical sources, we can at least offer a tentative set of three clusters of questions to be asked when setting out to perform a work.

1. What are the available sources of the work? Does the work exist in more than one version? Are there other, seemingly independent, works that are nonetheless related to the work?

2. Do any of the sources particularly inspire the performers, by virtue of its transmitted text, its contents, or its historical context? The choice of source may in turn trigger the choice of other works as well.

3. Does the source offer a plausible text? Are there any details that are suspected as errors and that could be checked against other sources, versions, or works? Are there any particular details that seem source-specific? Any details of that kind may either be retained or modified, depending on the extent to which performers want to make them "present" in the projected performance.

As a final example, let us now implement this set of lead questions on a musical director's hypothesized process of devising a new program for an ensemble. Our music director is a fine violinist, an old-time enthusiast of the music of Corelli and Purcell. Knowing that Purcell declared, in the preface to his set of trio sonatas, that he sought to imitate Italian composers, our musical director's initial plan was to play a program with works by his two favorite composers, and he even thought of several nice titles for the project. He quickly finds facsimiles of all of Corelli's original prints of trio sonatas (Rome, 1681, 1685, 1689, and 1694) as well as of Purcell's (London, 1683 and 1697)—all free for download and in partbook format. He selects four sonatas from each composer and, already at this point, his draft concert program looks like a textbook example of a historically informed concert:

> Arcangelo Corelli (1653–1713)
> Sonata IV in A minor from *Sonate a tre . . . Opera Prima* (1681)
> Sonata VII in C major from *Sonate a tre . . . Opera Prima* (1681)
> Henry Purcell (1659–1695)
> Sonata VII in E minor from *Sonnata's of III Parts* (1683)

Sonata VIII in G major from *Sonnata's of III Parts* (1683)
Arcangelo Corelli
Sonata XI in G minor from *Sonate a tre ... Opera Terza* (1689)
Sonata V in D minor from *Sonate a tre ... Opera Terza* (1689)
Henry Purcell
Sonata IX in F major from *Sonata's in Four Parts* (1697)
Sonata VIII in A minor from *Sonata's in Four Parts* (1697)

The program offers a coherent set of trio sonatas composed by the finest composers of the late seventeenth century, carefully ordered according to keys and chronology, and based on original sources.

As convincing as this draft program looks, our musical director feels that he arrived at this draft almost too easily. He decides to spend a morning in the library, do some reading, and have another look at what he has so far. He starts by looking at the complete critical editions of both Corelli's and Purcell's works. He is happy to learn that the early Roman prints of the trio sonatas provide the most authoritative sources of Corelli's sonatas. He also learns that the sonatas were reprinted across the Alps, and even in London. The London connection intrigues him, as a possible link to Purcell's world (he quickly finds out that some later English prints, "Revis'd by Dr. Pepusch," are also available online). Some of Purcell's sonatas from the second set also survive, so he reads, in a markedly different version, in autograph, in the British Library.[13] Even if he visits the British Library, he will probably be refused ordering Purcell's unique autograph to the reading room, but he might also realize that a high-quality scan of it exists on the library's website, freely accessible to all. He is even more intrigued by a secondary source of the first set, in another manuscript in the British Library—GB-L*bl* R.M. 20.h.9 (henceforth *20.h.9*). Manuscript *20.h.9* was copied by a composer named John Reading, and is supposed to contain many more works from Purcell's time, some of them even Italian, hence fitting the concept of his program.

After obtaining a scan of *20.h.9*, he sees that it is varied indeed: alongside Purcell's twelve modern sonatas (published as *Sonnata's of III Parts* in 1683), it contains earlier works from Giovanni Battista Vitali's (1632–1692) Sonatas Op. 5 (Bologna, 1669) and earlier still, from William Young's second set of sonatas (Innsbruck, 1659) (Morris 2004). Also, in terms of scoring, *20.h.9* contains Purcell's 5-part Overture (scored for two violins, two violas, and bass) alongside two 4-part overtures (scored for two violins, one viola, and bass), his *Three Parts upon a Ground* (three violins and bass), and Young's Sonatas, which follow a northern European model of trio sonata (scored for violin, viol, and bass).

Our musical director finds interest in aspects irrelevant to the prints—who was this John Reading and why did he copy this extremely varied manuscript? A quick look in the encyclopedia gives him dry facts concerning

Reading's marriage or the circumstances of his dismissal from Winchester Cathedral, but these do not reveal much about his musical personality. Then he reads that at least some of the works in the manuscript seem to have been introduced to Reading by members of the King Charles II's Musick, most probably during the court's visits to Winchester in 1682–1684 (Shay and Thompson 2000: 145). Evidence for the contact with the royal musicians may be gathered not only from the works themselves, being written by celebrated members of the King's Musick such as Blow and Purcell, but also from two of the titles Reading attached to them, titles that betray childlike enthusiasm for celebrity gossip: "This piece of Musick was Christ'ned Draggon at New Markett 1679," probably after the name of one of the King's racing horses (Holman 2001: 252); and "Seignor Givano Battista [illegible word] Symphony w[hich] M[r] Nich. Staggins produced as his owne May 29th 1679," referring to the Master of the King's Musick (the most prestigious musical post in the kingdom). What did Reading try to achieve by writing down these unimportant pieces of trivia? Is it possible that, perhaps like young Mozart's famous act of writing down Allegri's *Miserere* from memory in his 1770 visit to Rome (Mozart 1962: 333–336), the act of reproducing a copy of a musical piece was an act of conquest? Was it a proof to one's access to a piece of music identified with a privileged group of professionals, be it His Majesty's Musick or the papal choir?

These hints to Reading's enthusiasm about the privileged repertoire (as well as what seems to have been his taste for sophisticated counterpoint) bring our music director to focus the concept of his program on a more specific aspect of the Italian-English connection—namely Italian music in England—now through the eyes of a real seventeenth-century musician. He decides to replace some of the Corelli sonatas with other works from *20.h.9*. Comparing Corelli's early Roman prints with their later English engraving, he observes that there are no blunt errors in the English edition, that the bass figuring is more complete, and that the later printing style and the score format of the English edition would be far easier for his colleagues to read from. Purcell's sonatas in *20.h.9* also show no major difference from the printed edition, while in the single sonata he now chose from the second set (which by now he realized was written more or less at the same time as the first) the version in the print seems to him as convincing as that in the autograph. The program has changed considerably:

Arcangelo Corelli (1653–1713)
Sonata IV in A minor from *Sonate a tre … Opera Prima* (1681)
Sonata VII in C major from *Sonate a tre … Opera Prima* (1681)
Source: *The Score of the Four Setts … by Arcangelo Corelli* (London, c. 1730)
Henry Purcell (1659–1695)
Sonata VII in E minor from *Sonnata's of III Parts* (1683)
Sonata VIII in G major from *Sonnata's of III Parts* (1683)
Source: British Library MS R.M. 20.h.9

Anonymous
"Dragon" in D major
Source: British Library MS R.M. 20.h.9
Arcangelo Corelli
Sonata V in D minor from *Sonate a tre . . . Opera Terza* (1689)
Source: *The Score of the Four Setts . . . by Arcangelo Corelli* (London, *ca.*1730)
Giovanni Battista Vitali (1632–1692)
Sonata "La Guidoni" in F major from *Sonate . . . Opera Quinta* (1669)
Source: British Library MS R.M. 20.h.9
Henry Purcell
Sonata III in A minor from *Sonata's in Four Parts* (1683?)
Source: *Sonata's in Four Parts* (1697)

But our musical director may justly feel that the concept is now richer, the program more varied, the sources more unified by their English provenance, and the program notes likely to be far more engaging.

This chapter sought to demonstrate several problems encountered by the performer who uses primary sources. First, and most fundamental, is a set of late concepts that modern performers bring with them to the performance of music past. Examining the music "from an abstract catalogue entry down" results in grouping sources together as belonging to the same piece, hence confronting the performer with problems that were inconceivable for the original performers three or four centuries ago. However, thinking like a seventeenth-century performer, "from the physical sources up," essentially goes against one's twenty-first-century vantage point—we know which sources are more reliable than others; we know who the best composers were (at least according to our own tastes)—it is impossible to avoid the application of retrospective knowledge acquired along several centuries.

In cases of conflicting sources, modern performers face several options. On the one hand, if they treat the sources "too critically" and change one according to the other, they might iron out valid differences and narrow their view of past musical styles. It would be a miserable state of affairs if we had a single authoritative text for each entry in a composer's catalogue!

On the other hand, clinging to single sources without collating readings from others (from the physical sources up) may result in performance of supposedly corrupted texts (as in most recordings of Vivaldi's RV439). Although that approach may be close to the state of mind of a faceless eighteenth-century instrumentalist with no academic pretense, historically informed performance aims higher. Pretending to be a faceless eighteenth-century instrumentalist may prove a slippery slope leading to idolatry. The question is therefore fundamental and may be put simply as such: what do performers want to be playing? Is it an idealized text of the work derived from all available sources, carefully weighed? Is it a text that was performed in the past as attested by a specific source, including possible errors that crept into it? The dilemma presented here is at the heart of historically informed performance.

Notwithstanding, in some cases (Purcell's Z. 809), pretending not to have a concordance may lead to fresh examination of textual problems. It is recommended that, before weighing the relative authority of each source with regard to each textual problem, one should consider each source for itself. For that matter, uncritically scoring up Vivaldi's Opus 10 or Purcell's *Ten Sonata's* and grappling with the textual problems that surface along the way would be an essential first step in any responsible engagement with these works, even prior to the consideration of concordances.

Working with primary sources surely has its advantages, but there is no simple method that guarantees that such work will yield a good scholarly (not to mention artistic) result. There is no substitute to the proper scholarly study of the sources and perhaps not every amateur editor understands this, but musicologists should embrace the recent changes in the availability of facsimiles and recruit new students among those who, following the immediate contact with the digitized historical documents, become curious and intrigued.

Chapter 4

"The ear must be chief umpire" (Intuition and Critical Editing)

The previous chapter highlighted the influence, implicit or explicit, that scholarship holds on the text of a performed piece. After scholars have established the various versions of a piece and identified the sources for each version, performers often accept these scholarly decisions—embedded in catalogue numbering, editions, and recordings. Performers always explore blind spots in research with almost every performance decision they reach (after all, many aspects of historical performance practice, like tempo or dynamics, are undocumented and must be hypothesized). They rarely rebel against facts that have been argued and supported empirically by scholarship. It would be naïve, however, to think that the performers' power is limited to perpetuating scholarly decisions, be they right or wrong. In fact, they usually exert their own influence on both their audience and scholarship.

As a preliminary example in which performers (not necessarily historically informed) affect audience knowledge, we can explore the issue of attribution. Let us take one example, representative of many popular musical hoaxes—the famous "Toccata by Frescobaldi." This cello showpiece favorite, composed by Gaspar Cassadó (1897–1966) in a style significantly later than Girolamo Frescobaldi's, is all too often the only piece "by Frescobaldi" that cellists outside the early music circles know.[1] While the situation is essentially similar to Fritz Kreisler's use of the names Pugnani and Padre Martini in the early twentieth century (Haynes 2007: 126–127), no one nowadays would consider programming Kreisler's pastiches in a recital of eighteenth-century music,

A Performer's Guide to Transcribing, Editing, and Arranging Early Music. Alon Schab, Oxford University Press.
© Oxford University Press 2022. DOI: 10.1093/oso/9780197600658.003.0005

whereas Cassadó's work is not only often presented as a genuine Frescobaldi in cello recitals, but sometimes even features in cello recitals dedicated to baroque music,[2] decades after its status as pastiche had been revealed (Schenkman 1978).

Baroque scholars might spot Cassadó's lie from miles away, even if that lie is told very convincingly with superb musicianship, and even if it brings listeners to tears. But even the most critical scholars are not immune to performers' influence, if not in matters of attribution then in matters of style. Being exposed to performances, either during their training or later in their careers, scholars' notion of style is often shaped by the recorded legacy of performers' decisions. The present chapter is therefore a cautionary one: it shows in what ways editors and, in later generations, recording artists, are symbiotically related to scholarship, and it highlights performers' indirect responsibility to scholarship.

Many baroque scholars of my generation grew up on the wonderful recordings of the English Concert from the early 1980s, including that ensemble's recordings of both Bach's fourth Brandenburg Concerto and the F major harpsichord concerto—two works discussed in the previous chapter.[3] Repeated listening to the two recordings may have led these scholars to accept that a certain passage could work with one note in the Brandenburg Concerto and with a different note in the harpsichord concerto. Future students might grow up on the Academy of Ancient Music's more recent recordings of Handel and, similarly, assume that a certain passage could work with one note in the Trio Sonata Op. 5, no. 6 HWV401 and with a different note in the organ concerto in F HWV 295.[4] In both cases (the English Concert and the Academy of Ancient Music), the same performers recorded, at roughly the same time, two works with different variants, hence implying that the two readings are interchangeable. Scholars who listen to these recordings, enjoy listening to them at home or playing them to their students in class, often accept such implications unknowingly. In other words, performers also have the power to argue what sounds may be considered "in style" and "out of style." This becomes even more crucial in issues like musica ficta in recordings of renaissance music—Josquin's "harmonic" style and "melodic" style would be quite different, when learned from recordings of different ensembles. In order to avoid the plethora of problems that arise from renaissance musica ficta, the following chapter will focus on late seventeenth-century music and, more specifically, on the way in which the so-called false relations idiom, with its distinctive dissonant sound, is negotiated between scholars and performers throughout generations.

The aim of the chapter is to highlight the important role that intuition plays in performers' decisions about the text they play. The use of intuition should not be discouraged in any way, and yet performers must be aware of the difference between resolving a textual problem by referring to the sources, and resolving that problem using intuition. It is important to remember that, as I will show, the sources do not always give a proper solution to textual problems, and therefore performers should try and offer their own solution, and be aware that it is their own solution. In the long run, their decisions may play a part in the decisions of following generations.

False Relations and Changes in Taste

Baroque specialists often know a great deal about the instrumentation of the music they study or perform. They have a wide range of treatises on which they base their performance practice. They use simple (and standard) rhythmic notation, and they are almost free of the bounds of hexachordal theory, and therefore also from the confusing issue of musica ficta. Purcell scholars, for example, are often under the illusion that their situation (at least with regard to pitch) is closer to that of Beethoven scholars than of Josquin scholars. At least with regards to Purcell's instrumental music, our understanding of the composer's style and pitch organization is incomplete. In some cases, performers apply their interpretation to a text that is hardly more than a tentative approximation of the composer's intentions.

In his analysis of Purcell's musical style, J. A. Westrup puts considerable weight on the "principle of independent movement" and, more specifically, on "the use of both the flat and the sharp seventh in different parts, either simultaneously or in succession." This idiom, often called "false relations," while not absent from continental renaissance music, is usually identified with English music, and Westrup refers to it as "a survival of Elizabethan practice" (Westrup 1937: 247–250). False relations continued to be abundantly employed well into the second half of the seventeenth century, even after the popularity of that idiom across the channel waned, and despite the objection of some English theorists to it (Herissone 2000: 153). The sound of false relations is distinctive indeed. The fact that false relations appear so frequently in Purcell's music contributes to the idiom's reputation as "English." It is to be found in many different contexts in Purcell's music, ranging from opening formulae to strong final cadences.

While nowadays false relations are accepted as an idiom within the style of seventeenth-century English music, nineteenth- and early twentieth-century musicians found some instances of that idiom either erroneous or merely in disagreement with their own taste. Two such passages, which involve false relations and were received hesitantly over the centuries, appear in the Almand from Purcell's keyboard Suite in G minor Z.661 (mm. 21–23 and 28–29), published by the composer's widow in 1696. These two passages were later modified in numerous later editions (Example 4.1) (see discussion of the suites' editorial history in Hogwood 2003). In the second volume of *Le Trésor des Pianistes* (1861), the editors Aristide and Louise Farrenc modified both instances of false relations: in measure 22 by avoiding the natural seventh (c‴♮) altogether (it is changed to a″), and in measure 29 by postponing the sharp seventh in the left hand, thereby avoiding its clash with the natural seventh in the right hand. It would be interesting to know if in that early stage of their work on the multivolume *Trésor*, Aristide and Louise Farrenc were aware of the significance of false relations in English keyboard style.[5]

Similar modifications appear in Ernst Pauer's edition in the fifth volume of his *Old English Composers for the Virginals & Harpsichord* (1879). Pauer, unlike the Farrencs, explicated the ornaments, but otherwise his treatment of false relations is identical to that of the earlier French edition. Pauer's outlook on English keyboard music was certainly broader than the Farrencs'. Having

EXAMPLE 4.1 a. H. Purcell, Suite Z661, Almand, a) mm. 21–23. Comparison between various editions' treatment of false relations: 1. Frances Purcell (1696); 2. Farrenc (1861) and Pauer (1879); 3. Barclay Squire (1895/1912); 4. Ferguson (1964). b. mm. 28–30

EXAMPLE 4.1 Continued

(b)

edited not only the works of Byrd, Bull, and Gibbons, but also of John Blow in other volumes of *Old English Composers* (all volumes were published at the same time), Pauer knew English keyboard music too well to have considered false relations a textual error, and may have based his decision to edit them out on matters of taste—either his own or his supposed audience's (adherence to the style of the composer was not always editors' top priority). It is safe to assume Pauer understood that false relations were within Purcell's style but also found that they were in disagreement with late nineteenth-century style.

William Barclay Squire, in his two editions of the suite,[6] treats the two passages differently, reflecting a shift either in the way editors understood

Purcell's style or in the way late nineteenth- and early twentieth-century taste adapted and contained some of that style's archaisms. Barclay Squire made a distinction between the two passages—in exactly the same way Farrenc and Pauer did before, he modified the unorthodox leap into a dissonant escape note in measure 22. However, he avoided the modification of the false relations in measure 29 and reverted to Purcell's original reading of the passage. Unlike in measure 22, the dissonance (diminished octave) in measure 29 can be justified by its voice leading circumstances (the f″♮ is prepared in the previous measure, tied over the bar line, and resolved downwards by a step). Thus, one of the two readings that were deemed "wrong" in the 1860s and 1870s was now acceptable.

Only as late as 1964, when Howard Ferguson prepared his "newly transcribed and edited" complete edition of Purcell's harpsichord works, was the passage in measure 22 returned to its original state. Moreover, aware of the unusual sound of the two passages and of the long tradition of modifying them, Ferguson added several cautionary editorial accidentals, reassuring skeptical performers that Purcell indeed meant to enter a diminished octave with a leap in measure 22 and to apply voice-leading procedures to a diminished octave in measure 29, as if it was an ordinary dissonance like a perfect fourth or minor seventh.[7]

Having restored the original readings, many harpsichordists nowadays tend to relish these two passages once deemed wrong and "take their time" on the dissonances. The question is whether harpsichordists do so because they know Purcell's style better than the aforementioned editors at the end of the nineteenth century, or perhaps it is only a matter of taste and intuition—they like the distinctive sound of false relations. Perhaps our generation's knowledge of seventeenth-century works, sources, and treatises has broadened over the past century, but this does not exclude the possibility that performers have merely become accustomed to the sound of false relations. Unlike early twentieth-century musicians, performers nowadays must have heard false relations in countless recordings of Purcell's music. The disturbing possibility is that, unlike Farrenc, Pauer, or Barclay Squire, twenty-first-century harpsichordists do not even ask themselves if those readings are right or wrong. There is nothing easier than mistaking taste and intuition for acquaintance with style.

Ambiguous Accidentals and False Relations

The identification of false relations is more complicated in the Poco Largo movement of the Trio Sonata in G major Z.797. Here, four consecutive cadences (mm. 37–38, 41–42, 45–46, and 49–50) challenge the readings of one another (Example 4.2). One should observe that each cadence ends a dance-like four-measure phrase; that all four phrases and four cadences are of comparable type and of comparable part writing; and that even prior to any discussion of false relations, the cadence type is intrinsically dissonant, containing both final and the seventh degree of the scale on the downbeat of the penultimate measure.

EXAMPLE 4.2 Sonata Z.797, Poco Largo, false relations or similar formulae marked with dashed line.

123

Purcell's way of notating the false relations cadence seems to be irregular. In phrase #1, the first violin's c″ in measure 37, with no accidental attached to it and with no C♯ in the key signature, implies a c″♮, which creates false relations with the second violin's explicit c″♯. If one assumes that a c″ with no accidental is necessarily a c″♮, then one also assumes that all the accidentals that should be in the score are really there, despite the fact that a missing accidental is one of the most common notational errors. However, for the time being, let us suppress any editorial intervention, read exactly what is written, and assume that the cadence in measure 37 does contain false relations. Now let us proceed to phrase #3. Phrase #3 is clearly based on phrase #1—it transposes phrase #1 from D major to G major, and the violin parts are exchanged. Here, however, an F♯ is given in the key signature, hence there are no false relations between the first and second violins, with the first violin's f″♯. The previous assumption—that no accidental in the score means that no accidental was intended—rules out false relations, and that is within a phrase that would otherwise be an exact transposition of a phrase that *does* feature false relations. Indeed, not all performers accept this, and infer that a natural sign is missing from the second violin's downbeat in measure 45.[8]

Assuming a difference between two almost identical phrases, based solely on the lack of accidentals, must be founded on the trustful reading that very few seventeenth-century prints deserve. Phrase #2 poses a similar problem as phrase #3: no accidental is attached to the bass viol's f in measure 41, making it an f♯, which avoids potential false relations with the first violin's f′♯ in the same measure.

The cadence at the end of phrase #4 is the only one that is notated in a way that unanimously rules out false relations. The second violin has a d″♯ in m. 49, which avoids potential false relations with the first violin's d″♯. But phrase #4 is different from the rest in other respects as well. For example, it is the only phrase where the cadence itself is preceded by suspected false relations (the second violin's explicit c″♯ and the bass viol's c, which is supposedly a $c_♯$ as there is no C♯ in the key signature).

The editorial problem here is therefore more complicated than in the Purcell Almand. In the Almand, the voice-leading differences between only two instances of false relations allowed one of the editors, Barclay Squire, to reach a rational decision—only false relations that can be supported by voice-leading considerations should remain unmodified. But here, the similarity of the four phrases makes any decision regarding where to allow false relations harder. It is possible to make a radical decision and add editorial accidentals so that phrases #1–#3 all contain false relations (mm. 37, 41, and 45) along with measure 48 that precedes the cadence of phease #4, and thus to create an unusual concentration of that idiom. Conversely, it is possible to use editorial accidentals to eliminate all these instances of false relations, and thus to wash the movement clean of one of the emblems of the English style. An important reservation that should be stated is that one cannot be sure that an idiom that was employed in one phrase should automatically be inferred in the next—Purcell and his contemporaries modified even repetitions of the same passage.[9]

As in the Almand, the available recordings of the sonatas prove that most performers nowadays read the 1683 print "literally" (false relations appear in mm. 37 and 48, while mm. 41, 45, and 49 remain diatonic). Thus, they use modern conventions (accidentals are valid only until the next measure, the only accidentals that should be inferred by the performer are those of the key signature) for interpreting music written in the late seventeenth century. Depending thus on bar lines and on the key signature, despite the fact that only a few decades before Purcell, English music still relied on ficta mechanisms and was being written without bar lines—clearly has its disadvantages. An issue that complicates "literal" reading further is Purcell's inconsistent addition of cautionary accidentals: in some cases his use of accidentals indicates that accidentals remain valid only until the next bar line (second violin, mm. 48–50, indicating d''♯ and d♮'' in alternation), but in other cases he added cautionary accidentals as if those accidentals remain valid for longer than a measure (second violin, m. 43, f''♯ canceling the f''♮ in m. 42). In yet other cases he added repeated accidentals on repeated notes (second violin, m. 47, sharp sign on second c''♯ is redundant), a phenomenon apparent also in other early works by the composer. At least some of the complication stems from the fact that Example 4.2 is a literal scoring-up of the four printed partbooks, each containing accidentals that cannot be inferred unless one consults the other parts. We do not have Purcell's score of the sonata and therefore cannot know which accidentals he would have thought unnecessary to add if all four parts were seen synoptically.

The literal reading of the passage in the trio sonata gives the impression that Purcell's application of false relations is arbitrary. No stylistic rule of thumb regarding where in the musical grammar they should or should not appear can be extracted from the passage, at least when interpreted according to modern conventions. There are but two other options for reading the passage: one way is to replace the modern "literal" reading with a newly formulated policy as to the application of false relations.[10] Otherwise, addition or modification of accidentals must be founded, in one way or another, on intuition. Thus, relying on our insufficient understanding of the false relations idiom and on our intuition, it seems that we have progressed but little from the days of Farrenc and Pauer, with the exception that we are less willing to admit that intuition plays a significant part in our historically informed decisions.[11]

The unease of the historically informed about the use of intuition, especially in weighty issues such as pitch, does not mean that Purcell's contemporaries were also expected to suppress their intuition. On the contrary, Christopher Simpson, Purcell's antecedent, wrote that it is "hard to determine, what a composer may approve, or disapprove, in diverse cases concerning flats, and sharps" and claimed that in such cases, "the ear must be chief umpire" (Simpson 1659:

27). Because we do not have seventeenth-century ears, we must restrict the range of possible readings via an informed theoretical and intellectual understanding of the syntax of earlier styles.

The Range of Editorial Interpretation

The textual ambiguities discussed thus far belong to the common idiom of false relations. Therefore, despite the different contexts in which the idiom was observed, all these instances could be reduced into a general question of policy—*are false relations within the style and in what cases do they appear*—which the performer (or the editor) may answer using a rule of thumb. The situation becomes more complicated when accidentals cannot be labeled as belonging to false relations. The Fantazia in D minor Z.743—dated "August the 31st, 1680"—supplies many textual ambiguities that cannot be labeled and therefore, when performed, require ongoing decision-making.[12]

The transcription in Example 4.3 reproduces the score of the Fantazia's second section (mm. 58–99) as it appears in Purcell's autograph Add. MS 30,930: all accidentals are original and therefore follow seventeenth-century standards, no editorial accidentals (except Purcell's own) are added, and the number of measures per system remains as in the autograph, allowing us to evaluate the probability of cautionary accidentals that sometimes characterize the beginning of a system. The most immediate feature of the editorial policy employed here, more faithful to the source yet far less critical than a modern critical edition, is that it conveys the somewhat archaic feel of the score. The work (and especially its first section, not reproduced here) "looks" as if it were written some time before the Restoration. Musicians previously acquainted with any of the available modern editions of the score may find this transcription strangely antiquated. Modern editions not only fail to capture this strangeness, but also give the wrong impression of the extent to which we understand the text.[13] The heavy chromaticism of the piece, which attracts performers, listeners, and scholars alike, also poses formidable textual problems. Moreover, unlike the Almand or the trio sonata, whose primary source is printed, here we have a piece whose primary source is the composer's private autograph book. This means that the composer's application of cautionary accidentals may be even less consistent than in the works he offered to the public. As the accidentals here appear outside the context of false relations as well, the fact that Purcell did not use the natural sign (not yet in standard use in England in the early 1680s) poses additional problems. For example, there are numerous cases wherein the meaning of the accidental sign is context-related and two notes are spelled the same but indicate different pitch: the note D, with the sharp sign applied to it, probably indicates D♯ in measure 61 (viol I) and D♮ in measure 86 (viol I); the notes A and E, with the sharp sign applied to them, indicates A♮ and E♮ in the first section (mm. 37 and 34 respectively) and A♯ and E♯ in the second section (mm. 63 and 64 respectively).

EXAMPLE 4.3 Transcription of H. Purcell's Fantazia Z. 743 (second section). Accidentals and number of measures per system, as appear in GB-*Lbl* Add. MS 30,930 (hence the blank space at the beginning of the first system).

EXAMPLE 4.3 Continued

As was the case with the placement of false relations, modern editors simply cannot be certain how Purcell's accidentals should be translated into modern notation. Even when an editor is confident enough with regard to the intended accidentals, it is often the case that other editors would disagree.

By examining how many and which accidentals are regarded as ambiguous by each editor, one can estimate how wide the interpretative range of a passage may be. Measures 58–99 in Purcell's autograph contains 122 accidentals, 107 of which are essential (altering the default pitch indicated by the key signature or a previous accidental in the same measure) and 15 are cautionary (reinforcing a pitch already indicated by the key signature or a previous accidental in the same measure). Purcell's autograph was in no way conceived as a scholarly edition and the composer did not commit himself to a rigorous editorial policy. Thus, modern editors often find it necessary to add accidentals that they think are missing from the autograph (editorial accidentals), and to eliminate some of the composer's cautionary accidentals that they find redundant in light of their own editorial policy. The same passage, in Thurston Dart's scholarly edition, contains 128 accidentals, 14 of which are cautionary.[14] By using small typeface, Dart explicitly indicates 12 accidentals to be editorial. Other editors seem to have found even more ambiguities in the passage: Peter Warlock, in the first modern edition of Purcell's Fantazias, applied 131 accidentals, 22 of which are cautionary (and 15 are indicated as editorial by brackets).[15] Anthony Ford applied no fewer than 143 accidentals, 28 of which are cautionary (and 20 are indicated as editorial by brackets).[16] An average of one editorial accidental in every two measures (as in Ford's edition) implies that the notational convention reflected by the source differs significantly from the convention of those who are expected to read a modern edition of the text it transmits. More important, the disagreement between editors is a reminder that these conventions change over time and from one editor to another.

Evidently, there is considerable variety in the ways in which professional musicians today (be they performers, musicologists, or editors) understand Purcell's style and, consequently, the ways in which they interpret ambiguities in the text. In order to examine the variety of opinions on the interpretation of accidentals, let us examine the text of the final six measures of the piece (mm. 94–99, see Example 4.3), as interpreted in several editions and recordings from the last century. Lowercase Roman numerals (in square brackets) indicate notes that, as one may learn from modern recordings and scores of the piece, often require an editorial accidental.

This passage alone contains two editorial accidentals in Herbert Just's edition ([ii] ♭; [iii] ♯).[17] Dart gives these and two additional accidentals ([ii] ♭; [iii] ♯; [v] ♭; [vi] ♮). All four notes requiring editorial accidentals in Dart also received treatment by Ford, but not only did Ford add two accidentals of his own, one of his editorial accidentals (no. vi) disagrees with Dart's ([i] ♮; [ii] ♮; [iii] ♯; [v]♮; [vi] ♭ (!); [vii]♮). Thus, an editorial accidental does perhaps eliminate an ambiguity, but it does so by suggesting a plausible reading, sometimes just as valid as other readings.

If one collates readings from Jordi Savall's recording with Hespèrion XX, the conflicts become even more marked: in one case, Savall prefers Ford's version ([vi] ♭) over Dart's ([vi]♮); in another case he gives his own reading ([iii]♮) that differs from Dart's and Ford's ([iii] ♯); and in yet another case he goes further to suggest a reading ([iv] ♭, as in the key signature) that contradicts Purcell's own indication ([iv] ♯),[18] and this is shared with a contemporaneous copy, US-NY*p* Drexel MS 5061, hence is also stylistically viable. Nonetheless, it would be impractical to criticize performers for not looking at the autograph—historically informed performers often trust critical editions, and if they choose to contradict the composer's intention, they may be doing so either because they feel entitled to do so, or because the edition they use does not give them enough information.

Purcell's own cautionary accidentals are, again, revealing. In measure 66 (viol II), for example, Purcell adds a flat sign to ensure an F♮ after a significant F♯ in the previous measure (this is a clear case of a cautionary accidental, as there is no F♯ in the key signature). A similar case may be observed in the flat sign in measure 70 (viol II), ensuring a C♮ after a C♯ in the previous measure (indeed, the copyist of Drexel MS 5061 did not add this "editorial" accidental.) More telling is measure 86 (viol I), where Purcell adds a sharp sign to the note d′, in order to ensure that it is played D♮ (leading note to E♭). It is hard to say why Purcell found it necessary to specify this accidental, two whole measures after the previous D♭ in that part. Perhaps he chose to specify the accidental because of another D♭ that occurred in viol II in the previous measure, although it was already canceled in that part.

The fact that Purcell had his own view regarding when cautionary accidentals were required creates further problems when modern editors superimpose their own editorial policy. Indeed, some of Purcell's own cautionary accidentals are taken for granted. Editors who omit Purcell's accidentals are doing so according to the policy that they are expected to implement, but also prevent their users from understanding what the composer himself must have found ambiguous—that is valuable information with regard to *any* composer.

Even if performers need not supply an appendix of variant readings or an explicit philological justification for every note, their insight is not less significant than the most authoritative edition in reflecting the way in which Purcell's musical language is understood today. In measure 69, where the natural sign is assigned to the note F (viol IV, fourth quarter note) in all editions, the La Gamba ensemble plays an F♯. In measure 71, the ensemble Les Voix Humaines changes the note d′♯ (viol II, fourth quarter note) to d′♮ (which contradicts Purcell's explicit sharp sign, but follows the imitative subject more faithfully). In the same recording, in measure 72, the f′♯ (viol III) is read as f′♮.[19]

These are but a few of many conflicts in this short second section of forty-two measures, and they demonstrate a fundamental problem in the way musicians nowadays understand Purcell's idiom, at least when it comes to his consort music. In spite of Christopher Simpson's liberal approach, allowing the performer to decide whether a flat or a sharp should be added to a note, Purcell probably knew exactly what he wanted to hear, even if each editor has a different opinion about what that was.

There are other features of Purcell's use of accidentals that are often modernized, although their full implications are unclear. In the Fantazia in G minor Z.735 and the Fantazia in E minor Z.741, the use of enharmonic spelling contradicts modern conventions. Its use even contradicts the way in which we understand seventeenth-century tonal and modal theories, to the extent that enharmonic spelling may be seen as enharmonic *misspelling*. Enharmonic misspelling is characteristic of highly chromatic consort repertoire from the earlier seventeenth century (for example, Thomas Tomkins, John Ward, or Alfonso Ferrabosco II).

What should performers do with such passages? Christopher D. S. Field shows concern that modernizing accidentals (and not only in Purcell), a procedure normally applied to an entire editing project in order to keep the critical commentary to a minimum, blurs those excerpts that transmit this anomaly. As Field argues:

Even the most scholarly and meticulous modern editions often conceal such anomalies by tacitly "modernizing" the notation and synchronizing the enharmonic changes. . . . Nevertheless such evidence ought not to be suppressed, for it may have relevance both to issues of performance practice (such as tuning and temperament) and to our understanding of a crucial period in the history of harmonic thought. (Field 1996: 18–20)

A crucial period in the history of harmonic thought it indeed was, and composers' fascination with the freedom offered by chromaticism was manifested all over Europe, in vocal as well as instrumental music. In English consort music, passages of enharmonic misspelling are limited in scope, and only occasionally occur for several measures. Purcell's autograph Add. MS 30,930 has two such cases, and they are not always reported by editors.[20] In Fantazia Z.735, measure 23 (Example 4.4a), viol III plays the leading note of the cadence, e♯, but the note is written as an f♭. In measure 32 of Fantazia Z.741 (Example 4.4b), the same pattern is assigned to viol II. A relatively simple explanation can be offered for Fantazia Z.735: with no standard "natural" symbol

EXAMPLE 4.4   a. H. Purcell, cadence on F♯ minor from Fantazia Z.735 (mm. 21–24). Notation follows Purcell's autograph GB-*Lbl* Add. MS 30,930 f67r INV. In m. 23, Viol III plays the leading tone of the F♯-minor cadence (e♯) but the note is enharmonically misspelled as an f♭. b. H. Purcell, cadence on F♯ minor from Fantazia Z.741 (mm. 30–32). Notation follows Purcell's autograph GB-*Lbl* Add. MS 30,930 f61r INV. Viol II plays the leading tone of the F♯-minor cadence (e♯) but the note is enharmonically misspelled as an f♭.

(b)

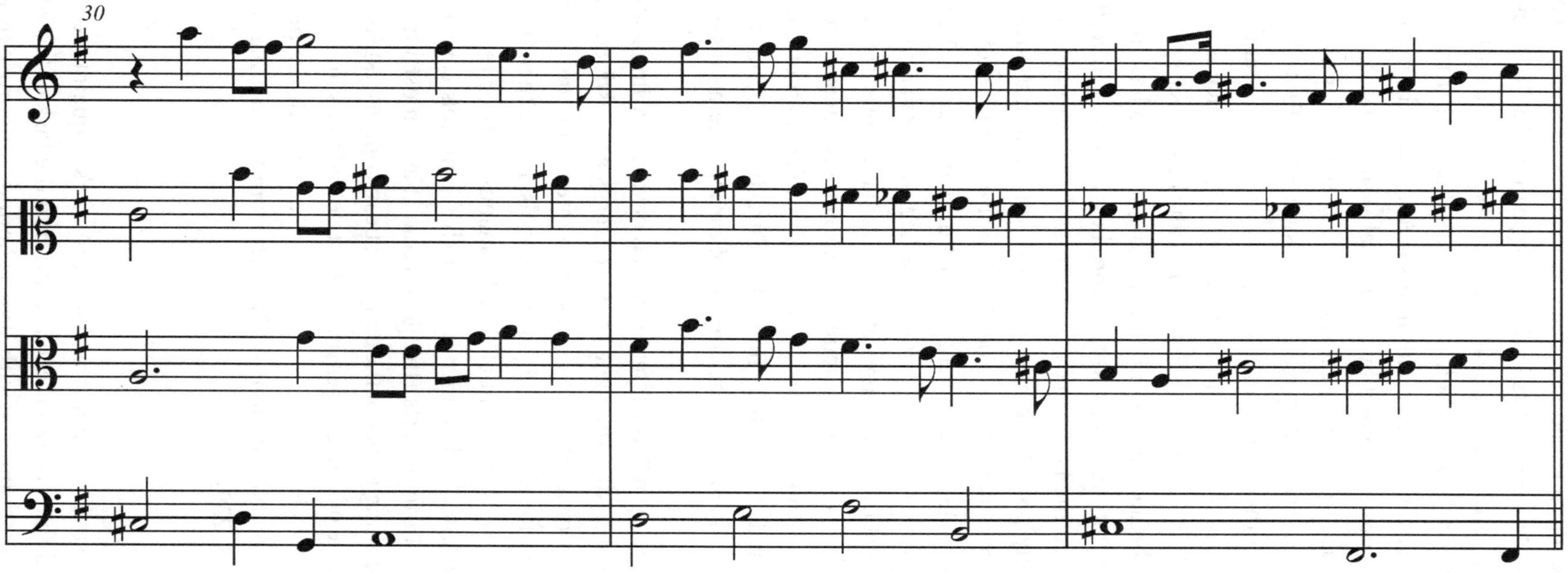

for canceling an accidental, f♭ would have yielded the desired pitch, f natural (=e♯), whereas a written e♯ with two flats in the key signature (that is, B♭ and E♭) would have resulted in an e♮. The irrelevance of this explanation in Fantazia Z.741, written with one sharp in the key signature, indicates that the reason for the enharmonic misspelling is different in this piece. Evidently, it does not stem from a theoretical obstacle posed by any modal system that Purcell had used. No theoretical reason prevented cadencing on a "sharp" key such as F♯ minor. After all, a similar cadence appears in measure 64 of Fantazia Z.743 (see Example 4.3). Yet another similar cadence appears on folio 43v, at the very outset of the first sonata copied into the manuscript (Z802), which is set in B minor. There, also, Purcell cadences on F♯ minor, with the correct spelling of e″♯. The practice of deliberate enharmonic misspelling seems to have been idiomatic to viol music notation. It should therefore be asked why Purcell was not consistent and spelled the E♯ correctly in Fantazia Z.743 (Example 4.3, m. 64). I cannot confidently provide an answer to this question, but additional parameters should be consulted. Can it be that the use of a C1 clef for the higher viol in Fantazia Z.743, the only fantazia that does *not* use a G2 clef for its top part, implies a different notational *ductus*, perhaps more renaissance and vocal in character (the first thirty measures of this fantazia are rather restrained harmonically and might as well be inspired by earlier seventeenth-century motets)? As Field implied (noted earlier), a thorough explanation of the phenomenon cannot be founded on a study limited to Purcell's time, and requires in-depth inquiry into the intellectual background of earlier generations of consort music.[21]

The notational anomaly in Purcell's fantazias may have several implications. First, it may serve to contradict the view of these works as "abstract," either as compositional studies or as abstract essays in counterpoint, and confirms the composer's intention for them to be played on viols, rather than by other types of consort.[22] Second, it may hint at specific manuscripts or repertories that Purcell was exposed to, and confirm the search for models earlier than Locke for the fantazias in four parts (the generation that is most identified with enharmonic misspelling is that of the early Jacobean composers). Third, it serves as another example of Purcell's sensitivity to style and to its implications for notation, shown most clearly by Adams in connection with the peculiar rhythmic notation of *Laudate Ceciliam* Z.329, also from the first half of the 1680s (Adams 1990: 238–239).

Conclusions

The ability to identify stylistic idioms is central to one's acquaintance with a composer's style, and this acquaintance is central to the task of the editor. Moreover, the editor's acquaintance with style is bound to improve through the process of editing when, for example, an unusual reading reappears and assumes the status of an idiom with which other passages can be compared. When performing music of the seventeenth century, performers are often required to act as editors, or at least to read the same primary sources that the editor uses, and to do so critically (which enables them, for example, to spot an error). Thus, the circular process of editing applies also to performers, who crystallize their stylistic acquaintance with the composer while working toward any specific performance or throughout their professional life.

The editorial history of the Almand from Suite Z.661 shows that, in the same way that individual editors or performers may improve their acquaintance with a composer's style over a limited period of time (a few hours of editing a work, a few decades of performing a certain repertoire), so the scholarly world may improve its acquaintance with style over very long periods—it took more than a century to fully accept the validity of two passages containing false relations within Purcell's style. As we have seen, this ideal progressive trajectory is hindered in two ways. First, the process is no longer based solely on research and hard evidence, but also on audience's acquaintance (fortunately, performers and editors are exposed not only to critical editions but also to music making that prioritizes the aesthetic result over the sterility of text). Second, new errors might appear in the text at any time.

Once recognized as an inherent part of Purcell's style, false relations must be kept in their proper place in the musical grammar: one must make sure that they are identified even when not properly notated and, by the same token, one must make sure that they are not imposed on passages that are meant to be diatonic. As demonstrated on the Trio Sonata Z.797, editors' and performers' decisions—where false relations should appear and where they should not—are often based on intuition. The decision is complicated further in cases where ambiguities regarding accidentals cannot simply be labeled as belonging to a certain stock-type, as was the case in the Fantazia Z.743. The policy of critical editors—as reflected in their addition of cautionary accidentals, deletion of original cautionary accidentals, and modernization of original accidentals— sets the range of possible future errors. The general conclusion from the discussion may therefore be that any editorial intervention potentially blurs a significant element in the score. Even the few liberties taken by the present author in typesetting the examples for this chapter—standardizing the order of the flats in the key signature in Example 4.1; and scoring up a set of part books in Example 4.2—may iron out some details that may prove meaningful for another discussion.

When engaging in the study of early music, a highly critical approach to the sources is crucial. Especially at the present time, when it is so easy for one to develop one's own understanding of earlier styles based on available modern editions and recordings, scholars should stay on guard and keep grappling with the primary sources. Performers should be encouraged to enjoy the ever-growing availability of primary sources over the Internet, to not sink into the passivity of students whose scores are edited for them and performance practice preached to them without any need of exploring things themselves.

Historically Informed Arrangement

Notation, Genre, and Idiom

In his commentary on the recorder's early repertoire, Anthony Rowland-Jones describes that repertoire as "[running along] a continuum ranging from the most specific . . . to the most far-fetched arrangement." That description is applicable to most other instruments identified with early music. Rowland-Jones offers a rough division of the continuum into four types: designated repertoire, probable repertoire, extended repertoire, and "arranged" repertoire (Rowland-Jones 1995: 26–27). The applicability of these categories, at least to some periods in music history, requires some caution: much of the sixteenth-century repertoire is "probable" repertoire simply because no explicit instrumental designation appears in sources, or because it is designated for a class of instruments rather than for a specific instrument. For example, the posthumous publication, in score format, of Rore's madrigals (Gardano, 1577) was designated not for a specific instrument, such as organ, harpsichord, or harp, but "for performance on all sorts of perfect [i.e., polyphonic] instruments" ("*accommodate per sonar d'ogni sorte d'Istrumento perfetto*"). On the other hand, in such early repertoire, the lack of an explicit designation does not necessarily mean that the composer, arranger, or copyist did not have a specific instrument in mind.

As far as renaissance and baroque repertoires are concerned, Rowland-Jones's four categories also represent four different kinds of relationship between the source (that is, the historical document that transmits the music) and the musical piece. Works "designated" for a certain instrument are likely to survive in a state that allows them to be played on that instrument without

A Performer's Guide to Transcribing, Editing, and Arranging Early Music. Alon Schab, Oxford University Press.
© Oxford University Press 2022. DOI: 10.1093/oso/9780197600658.003.0006

substantial editorial intervention; thus, when a source does not require that substantial editorial intervention, it is often considered "probable repertoire" for that instrument.[1] In contrast, "extended" repertoire and "arranged" repertoire *do* require considerable editorial intervention.

Adaptation of music from one medium to another, or from one social function to another, has been ever-present in music history, and does not conflict in any essential way with the historically informed approach.[2] When examined from the perspective of sixteenth- and seventeenth-century practice, some adaptations may seem more than probable, while others might seem harder to justify. Sources identified with, and collected for, groups of professional musicians, such as the *ministriles* of the Duke of Lerma in the early seventeenth century (E-LER*c* ms mus. 1), or the band employed by the English princess (later Queen) Anne around the close of that century (GB-L*bl* add. MSS 30,839; 39,565–7, henceforth *Engloisse*), are often both coherent enough and varied enough to allow performers who perform from them to add material that, although not included in the sources, would fit the same implied requirements and preferences of those historical groups. Just as very few in Handel's London would have found anything wrong with arranging an orchestral overture for the harpsichord, modern harpsichordists should likewise in no way feel limited to playing only those overtures for which contemporary arrangements survive. Rather, they should feel free to transcribe other overtures at their pleasure. Of course, it is best to follow concrete models of "Handelian" keyboard arrangements in order to make sure that the translation from the orchestra medium to the keyboard medium takes place along the lines accepted in Handel's time. The same general guidelines may be applied to turning late seventeenth-century trio sonatas into concerti grossi, or to writing new *harmonie* (woodwind) arrangements of late eighteenth-century Viennese opera numbers. Adaptations of these kinds do not always require working from scratch; sometimes it suffices to add new parts to existing material. For example, when arranging a concerto grosso, one may use the original parts of a trio sonata as the *concertino*, adding new parts for the *ripieni*.[3]

Rowland-Jones is cautious when addressing the concept of "arrangement," putting the term in scare quotes. He warns the reader that, when applied to early repertoire, the term implies more than a hint of anachronism. The term usually not only describes a substantial adaptation, but also assumes the existence of a fixed text as a point of reference. The first canonic composers were also those who first attempted "arrangement" in a more modern sense— for example, Geminiani-Corelli, Bach-Vivaldi, and Mozart-Handel. None of them attempted an arrangement of a piece older than one generation. Similar sensitivity is required with the use of terms like "improvisation." It requires an improvisational effort to play diminutions to a madrigal or to realize a basso continuo part. From a modern point of view, we might regard the two activities as related skills under the blanket category of "improvisation" (see, for example, Ferand 1961). Early seventeenth-century musicians, by contrast, probably regarded the performance of diminutions and the realization of basso continuo as unrelated activities.

For those who intend the music they perform to sound as it did centuries ago, it is only natural, at least initially, to greet the topic of arrangement with skepticism. They might embrace some arrangements, for new instruments or new combinations of instruments, as profound works of art, but they will inevitably find them flawed for being historically improbable. For example, performing "The Art of Fugue" with a piano trio, a saxophone quartet, a cello ensemble, or a synthesizer can produce a profoundly musical and pleasing result, even if it has no historical "justification."[4] However, historically informed does not necessarily equal historically verifiable, and one has to apply a historically informed stance not only to performance, but also to theory (Tatlow 2013), analysis (Schubert 1994), and arrangement (Cypess 2020)—even if such a holistic view evokes resistance and, for some, is even "linked to ideology and fundamentalism."[5]

The following chapter does not attempt to cover general aesthetic considerations applicable to both historical and non-historical approaches to arrangement. Nor does it deal with the simple reallocation of parts (as when an ensemble takes a five-part motet and simply assigns the vocal parts to various melodic instruments, or when one plays the solo part of Schubert's Arpeggione Sonata without modification on an instrument other than the arpeggione). Instead, this chapter demonstrates historically sensitive re-setting of works according to historical practices that can be extracted from surviving arrangements.[6]

Such a process of re-setting must be done in a way that is sensitive to the structure and function of the music. For example, players of melodic instruments often feel that Bach is at his most inspired in some of the cantata arias, and wish to play those vocal solos on their instruments. While arrangements may work perfectly as far as range and rhetoric are concerned, structurally, the types of ritornello forms employed by Bach in his cantatas have no real instrumental parallels to justify such transcriptions. Thus, assembling a "sonata" or a "concerto" from movements that are utterly uncharacteristic of those genres may result in a mere compilation of wonderful music that the composer and the composer's contemporaries would never have defined as a "sonata" or a "concerto." Alternatively, any of Bach's ritornello-based preludes for keyboard may easily be "translated" into a concerto movement, provided that one properly analyzes the prelude and correctly determines which sections should be allocated to the *ripieni*, and which to the *concertino*. I will describe several processes of analysis and re-setting. In so doing, I will demonstrate how an arranger who wishes to follow a historically informed approach can distinguish between those characteristics of the work that may be tampered with (in a historical fashion), and those that should be left alone. For example, if one rescores a Bach fugue for solo violin for four-part ensemble, one must ensure that the four parts function just as equally as in a fugue originally written for four parts.

Let us consider the possibility of transcribing Bach's French Suites BWV 812–817 for two viols, or for viols and continuo. While one may freely criticize the violation of the composer's "intention" in a narrow sense (Bach probably never intended the suites to be arranged for viols), one may also cite numerous examples, from Sainte-Colombe's *Concerts* to Boismortier's *Sonates* of 1725, of the use of two-viol scoring in roughly comparable circumstances and with comparable musical structures, at around the same time and place. The sound of such an ensemble would not have been foreign to the composer, nor to the musical aesthetic of his time. Indeed, Bach himself frequently experimented with unusual scorings in the Brandenburg Concertos. In some of his cantatas, Bach experimented with instrument combinations he had never used before and was never to use again. The question of whether the composer would have "liked the sound" or not is as fascinating as it is impossible to answer, and it is therefore beyond the scope of the present study.[7]

Basic Reduction Procedures

Let us begin our exploration of historical arrangement technique with two arrangements from the 1690s. The two arrangements discussed here demonstrate relatively simple procedures of adaptation from one scoring to another. Both pieces are taken from the aforementioned *Engloisse* partbooks that may have belonged to the band of Princess Anne.[8] *Engloisse* may have served various smaller groups from the princess's band, for it is made up of discrete sections, each intended for a different scoring. The recto side of each partbook contains mainly four-part pieces, and the verso, three-part pieces for treble I, treble II, and bass. Although they were probably intended for a group of wind instruments (Anne's band was largely modeled after the German "Hoboisten" model), many of the pieces in *Engloisse* show little regard for the sonic properties of the instrumentation for which they were composed or arranged.[9]

Indeed, we have some arrangements from that period that, despite their unquestionable historical authority, are far from satisfactory. Some of the three-part pieces in *Engloisse* seem to be arrangements of pieces that survive in other sources as four-part pieces. In such cases, comparison allows us to reconstruct and study the process of arrangement. In the case of Paisible's Prelude on folios 79r–78v INV, the arrangement was done clumsily (Table 5.1). The texture of the original piece (Magdalene Partbooks, Set XXV, no. 4) is essentially that of a Roman concerto grosso, alternating between *tutti* sections in four parts (treble

Table 5.1 J. Paisible, Prelude: outline of arrangement from four parts (Magdalene Partbooks) to three parts (*Engloisse*)

	Magdalene partbooks	*Engloisse*
Tutti	Treble I	Treble I
	Treble II	Treble II
	Tenor	
	Bass	Bass
Soli	Treble I	Treble Ia
	Treble II	Treble Ib
	Bass (played high)	Treble II

I, treble II, tenor, and bass) and *soli* in trio texture (treble I, treble II, and bass, the last playing in high register). We do not know how many musicians played this four-part music, nor the exact instruments they used. In *Engloisse* the piece is in three parts throughout. The *tutti* sections, apparently played two per part, simply omit the tenor part, thus losing much rhythmic interest and intensity (see Example 5.1). In the *soli* sections, treble I and treble II are both written in the treble I partbook, apparently played one per part, while the high-playing bass is reallocated to treble II.

While arrangements like this one do retain some distinction between *tutti* and *soli*, the way in which the tenor part was simply discarded generates countless problems: missing chord notes, missing imitative entrances, and unbalanced calls and responses. While no performer should feel obliged to follow such precedents today, it is important to remember that such arrangements existed and surely were performed, even by the most professional bands, of which the princess's band was surely one.

Other arrangements from the verso side of *Engloisse* are more resourceful. Take, for example, the tune in G minor from Paisible's music for the play "Love's Last Shift" (folio 74v INV). In what appears to be its original version, London Royal College of Music MS 1172 (folio 6r), the tune appears in four parts. In *Engloisse*, the original tenor is not simply omitted. Instead, parts of the tenor are subtly merged with parts of treble II to create a new hybrid treble II part. Example 5.2 gives the score of the outer parts (treble I and bass) (almost identical in both versions), and between them the inner parts of both versions—the merged treble II from *Engloisse* and the separate treble II and tenor from the Royal College Manuscript.

For most of the piece (mm. 5–10 and 13–20), the original treble II moves in parallel thirds below treble I. Let us consider the harmonic implications of this parallel motion, mainly on strong beats, by looking at the first two

EXAMPLE 5.1 J. Paisible, Prelude, mm. 1–8 (*tutti* section). The tenor part (marked 'viola' in the example) appears in the Magdalene Partbooks (four-part arrangement), but not in *Engloisse* (three-part arrangement).

columns of Table 5.2. When the bass plays the root of a triad and treble I plays the fifth above it, treble II plays the third. When treble I plays the third above the root, treble II doubles the root. But when treble I doubles the root, which happens less often, treble II cannot add a sixth above the root (as this would change the chord), and so it may either double the root as well, or add

EXAMPLE 5.2 J. Paisible, tune from "Love's Last Shift" (from GB-*Lcm* MS 1172) with two sets of inner parts: an arranged treble II part taken from the *Engloisse* MS (second staff, indicated "*Engloisse*"), and the original treble II and tenor (third and fourth staves, indicated "*Lcm* MS 1172").

EXAMPLE 5.2 Continued

144

EXAMPLE 5.2   Continued

Engloisse

the third or the fifth. This method of extensive parallel motion in thirds was advanced by Henry Purcell as the preferred method for composition in three parts (Purcell 1694: 115–116). When we look at the right-hand column of Table 5.2, however, an inherent problem to the method becomes apparent. As a rule, whenever treble I plays the third above the bass, treble II doubles

Table 5.2 Structure of chords in root position, when treble II is parallel thirds with treble I

The note played by Treble I above the root in the Bass	Treble II (mainly in parallel thirds)	Notes missing (in three parts) or given to the Tenor (in four parts)
5	3	None (tenor may double the root)
3	1	5
1	5	3
	3	5
		5
	1	3
		1

the root, which means that the fifth of the chord is absent—a compromise indeed.[10] Had the arranger in *Engloisse* applied to the tune from "Love's Last Shift" the method we observed in the Prelude discussed earlier, and simply omitted the tenor, a perfectly valid three-part arrangement would have resulted. Instead, at least in some sections (we can see it most clearly in mm. 18–21), the arranger chose to deviate from Purcell's method by breaking the parallel motion—precisely in order to achieve the missing fifth. The arranger took short segments from the treble II and the tenor (marked with rectangles in Example 5.2, third and fourth staves) and combined them into the new treble II in *Engloisse* (Example 5.2, second staff).

The choice between striving for "full" harmony and for "smooth" part writing (both adjectives taken from Purcell's aforementioned discussion of the subject) pertains mainly to pieces where chords in root position predominate and the music thus lends itself to parallel thirds between the trebles. In the music of Purcell himself, however, inversions and dissonances abound. As a consequence, Purcell's treble II parts are often quite intricate, and the result tends toward "full," rather than to "smooth," harmony. In fact, had Purcell attempted to reduce any of his four-part theater tunes to three parts, he himself would have been forced to employ the same merger technique we observed in the *Engloisse* arrangement of Paisible's G minor tune. In the Slow Aire from Purcell's music for "The Married Beau" (Example 5.3), the harmonic progression goes through numerous inversions and seventh chords, which do not facilitate parallel thirds. The example is laid out like Example 5.2: treble I and bass are given as they appear in *Ayres for the Theatre*, the posthumous anthology of Purcell's theater music. The inner parts include treble II and tenor, as they appear in *Ayres for the Theatre*, and a suggested treble II part that merges segments from the original inner parts. The result is a possible three-part arrangement.

EXAMPLE 5.3 H. Purcell, Slow Aire from "The Married Beau" (from *Ayres for the Theatre*) with a new treble II part by the author (indicated "New Part"), as a substitute for the original treble II and tenor (indicated "*Ayres for the Theatre*").

EXAMPLE 5.3 Continued

Sound and Specific Instrumentation

The pieces and the arrangement procedures analyzed in the previous section might give one the impression that seventeenth-century musicians did not care for the sonic attributes of specific instruments or instrument families, but rather thought in abstract functions like treble, tenor, or bass. While it is true that few comments by theorists or composers on issues like timbre and balance survive from before 1700, early awareness of instrumental idiom is clearly reflected not only in the abundance of treatises on specific instruments but also in the repertoire itself. One of the clearest and earliest examples of such awareness is a piece for vihuela by Alonso Mudarra: the "Fantasia que contrahaze la harpa en la manera de Luduvico."[11] Unlike much of the sixteenth-century "probable" repertoire mentioned at the outset of this chapter, Mudarra's piece is not merely designated and idiomatic, but could even be considered "doubly" idiomatic. First, it is written in tablature and so it fits the tuning, the size, and the sustain of the vihuela. Second, it tries to imitate the idiom of another instrument, namely the harp (and more specifically, the idiom of a harpist called Luduvico). The piece contains an early example of the "campanella" technique—the use of fingerboard positions that allow adjacent notes to sound simultaneously, like bells or like the unstopped strings of the harp. While the piece is notated in impeccable vihuela idiom throughout, toward the end it starts to sound less idiomatic of the vihuela and more idiomatic of the harp (or at least improvisational to the point of using risky dissonances). So confident was Mudarra in players' acquaintance with their instrument's idiom that, at that one point in the piece, he added a textual remark reassuring the players that the resulting dissonances were indeed a part of the effect he was after.[12] Mudarra's fantasia shows the importance of idiomatic notation for the message of the piece: the idiomatic notation of the vihuela allowed Mudarra to clearly notate the campanella effect, and thus to achieve the idiomatic sound of the harp. Achieving this effect in staff notation would have been immeasurably harder.

Idiom can be conveyed in staff notation, too, by using instrument-specific symbols and notation style. Let us fast-forward two centuries to Rameau's collection of five concerts—his *Pièces de clavecin en concerts, avec un violon ou une flûte, et une viole ou un deuxième violon*. The cover page openly suggests alternative instrumentation ("a violin *or* a flute, and a viol *or* a second violin"), and Rameau adds detailed instructions in the Preface about the modifications one needs to make in order to realize the alternative instrumentation.[13] In this publication Rameau juxtaposed parallel versions, for solo harpsichord and for ensemble, of several movements. Comparison of these versions reveals markedly different instrument-specific notational styles.[14] In the opening strain of "La Livri" (the harpsichord version), for example, the right-hand part calls for four types of ornaments (*agrémens*): *cadence* ("⌇"), *pincé* (")"), the *port de voix* and the *coulez* (both marked with "("), and the combined *pincé et port de voix* (" () ") (Example 5.4, top staff). Rameau refers, in his introduction, to a detailed explanation of these *agrémens* that he published in a book of harpsichord pieces some fifteen years earlier.[15] When he notates the same melody for the violin or the flute (Example 5.4, middle staff—an octave higher if played on the flute), Rameau does not use the *pincé*. The other three ornaments—the *cadence*, *port de voix/coulez*, and *pincé et port de voix*—remain, but are notated differently. The *cadence* is marked with a "+" sign, a standard sign in music for the flute (Hotteterre 1968), rather than with a "⌇" sign. The combined ornament *pincé et port de voix* (which appears twice on the note A♭ in mm. 1 and 5) he changes to a *port de voix* alone. The *port de voix* and the *coulez* were described by Rameau himself as two notes tied in exaggerated legato (resulting in simultaneity)—the *port de voix* going upward and the *coulez* going downward.[16] In the flute or violin version of "La Livri," however, Rameau marked these ornaments as slurred appoggiaturas.[17] Rameau also changes the rhythm of an ornament in measure 3 by adding an *accent*, and adds a dotted rhythm to measure 7.

As he did with many of his keyboard pieces, Rameau chose to rework "La Livri" for the stage. Eight years after he published his *Pièces de clavecin en concerts*, he wove it, transposed into A minor, into Act III of his opera *Zoroastre*. Under the title "Gavotte en Rondeau[,] gracieux sans lenteur," the piece is arranged for three parts: first violins and flute, second violins, and bass. To facilitate comparison, I have transposed it back to C minor (Example 5.4, bottom staff).[18] In this version as well, Rameau does not use the *pincé*, notating the other types of ornaments as he did in the earlier flute/violin version.

EXAMPLE 5.4 J. Ph. Rameau, "La Livri," principal melody, mm. 1–8, in three versions: harpsichord version from *Pièces de clavecin* (1741), flute/violin version from *Pièces de clavecin* (1741), and orchestral version from *Zoroastre* (1749).

From the comparison of the three versions of "La Livri" we may conclude that, when Rameau "translated" an excerpt from one idiom (that of the harpsichord) to another (that of the flute or the violin), he changed not only rhythmic and ornamental subtleties but, even when rhythm and ornamentation remain the same, he changed the set of notational symbols with which he wrote down the same musical ideas. Above all, we can see that, while the existence of ornaments is embedded in the structural level of a piece (as are the notes of a basic melody), sometimes the type of ornament is instrument-specific, and sometimes it is only notated with an instrument-specific symbol.

One may look at the three versions of "La Livri" chronologically. First came the original harpsichord version of "La Livri," followed by two successive arrangements. But one may look at "La Livri" in another way, too. It is possible to view the essence of the original version as an abstract idea that was merely realized in the shape of a harpsichord piece. Thus, in this view, while the notation and harmonization gave the original a certain character that Rameau regarded as fitting for a harpsichord piece, that character was an accident occasioned by the essentially arbitrary choice of instrument. Then, when Rameau set out to write a trio version, he peeled off the harpsichord layer to expose the abstract underlying idea, and then deployed the very different approach to notation and harmonization required to realize that idea in the shape of a trio.[19]

The model of an abstract idea and its possible realizations may become clearer if we take the issue from the individual miniature to well-defined genres. Bach's sonatas for viola da gamba and obligato harpsichord are, on the surface, sonatas for a solo instrument and accompaniment. However, even a cursory look at their score shows that they are essentially trio sonatas: the viola da gamba plays one solo part, the harpsichord's right-hand part plays another solo part, and the harpsichord's left-hand part plays the bass. Once the arranger decides to read them as trio sonatas for which Bach chose one of several possible realizations, he is free to choose a different realization, be it a proper sonata à trè (as in Hille Perl's rendition of BWV 1029 for violin, viola da gamba, and continuo) or a solo sonata with some modifications in the division of the parts between the viola da gamba and keyboard (as in Anner Bylsma's rendition of the first movement of BWV 1028, where the viola da gamba part and the right-hand part are swapped for half the movement).[20]

Borrowing Rameau's Borrowing Strategies

We have seen that Rameau had little problem with printing two different versions of the same piece, in two different scorings, in the same publication, let alone to reuse an earlier piece in a new opera. This is not to imply that, when he chose to rework a piece, he did it without discretion or creativity. In fact, Rameau is among those composers whose approach to arrangement may serve a good model for musicians nowadays—his attention to the fine details of instrument-specific notation echoes his even greater attention to musical details of part writing and, indeed, harmony (as befits his role as one of those who laid the foundations to the study of harmony).

The three versions of "La Livri" discussed earlier show that the composer rethought musical and expressive contents while arranging a piece. Let us observe the three arrangements in their entirety (Examples 5.5, 5.6, and 5.7) and compare three basic aspects that give each arrangement its unique character: ranges and instrumentation, the use of low and high registers, and details of

EXAMPLE 5.5 Rameau, "La Livri" (harpsichord version) from *Pièces de clavecin en concert* (1741).

EXAMPLE 5.5 Continued

EXAMPLE 5.6 Rameau, "La Livri" (trio version) from *Pièces de clavecin en concert* (1741).

EXAMPLE 5.6 Continued

EXAMPLE 5.6 Continued

EXAMPLE 5.6 Continued

EXAMPLE 5.6 Continued

harmony and counterpoint. For the present discussion, we shall refer to the three structural sections of the piece as refrain, 1st reprise, and 2nd reprise.

Instrumentation and Ranges

Arrangers often start working on a piece by examining the available instruments and their ranges, in terms of bottom and top limits, paying, for the moment, only limited attention to the way in which the ranges themselves can be exploited most effectively. Later in the process, as we shall see, the arranger must think about how each instrument sounds in specific areas of its range. Considering the instruments' range is also an important first step toward appreciating arrangements made by others.

The range of the solo harpsichord version of "La Livri" (Example 5.5) is G′–g′′ (four octaves), although most of the piece uses a more limited range— E♭–e′′♭ (three octaves). Within that range, the texture is mostly in three parts. While the top part is largely an independent melody, the character of the middle part and the bottom part is defined less clearly. The latter two parts sometimes combine into an arpeggiating texture, sometimes proceed more independently, and sometimes take turns in shadowing the top part in parallel thirds (see 1st reprise).

In the trio version of "La Livri," from *Pièces de clavecin en concerts* (Example 5.6), the harpsichord is much more "bottom heavy": the refrain explores the range G′–g′, particularly the lower part of that range. The 1st reprise extends the range up to b′♭, and even climbs up to f′′ for a short passage. The 2nd reprise reaches g′′ just before its end. The violin part goes up

EXAMPLE 5.7 Rameau, "Gavotte en Rondeau[,] gracieux sans lenteur" ("La Livri") from *Zoroastre* (1749), 98–99.

EXAMPLE 5.7 Continued

EXAMPLE 5.7 Continued

to the same f″ and g″ as the harpsichord—rather moderate for a violin part (Rameau's violin part reaches d‴ and e‴♭ in other movements of the set)—and uses the bottom G string in double stops at the beginning of the 1st reprise. When played on the flute, the refrain is transposed up an octave, resulting in the overall range of d′–c‴. Despite all the transpositions, the 1st reprise is bound to sound rather pale on the flute. The note e′♭ is certainly not the strongest and clearest note of the baroque flute. The viol part spans a very wide range: C–g′. When the flute approaches its lowest note at the beginning of the 1st reprise, the viol is at its brightest. The passage in question works far better with the violin, as the viol's part actually lies between the two notes of the violin's double stops—an unusually rich "blend" of string sound.

The flute part of the later orchestral arrangement (Example 5.7) puts the instrument to immeasurably better use than does its parallel in the trio arrangement. This suggests that Rameau intended the top part of the trio version for violin, and that the flute was, at best, second choice. On the whole, Rameau uses the instruments' range in the orchestral arrangement effectively. The range of the first violin and the flute parts in this version is narrower (a′–e‴) than in the trio version. Considering the key of A minor, this range is also far more effective for the flute. The second violins' range is g♯–g″, and the bass range again spans almost three-octaves: C–a″.

Low and High Registers

We have seen that the overall range of the solo harpsichord version is G′–g″. This is valuable information if one wants to reallocate parts to different instruments. However, it still does not tell us much about how Rameau explores this range as the movement unfolds. When does he reach the highest note? Is the bass always predominant? The gradual ascent to the highest notes, f″ (in the 1st reprise) and g″ (in the 2nd reprise), gives perhaps an overall shape. Yet although a rise to a climax is an important consideration in counterpoint, it is not the sole one. No less important for the overall shape of the piece is how Rameau reserves the two bottom notes (G′ and C) for the end of each refrain, and how the left hand otherwise plays higher, thus creating an overall lighter sound. Indeed, for most of the refrain the bass moves within a "middle" range B–g. Each of the two reprises begins lower than that middle range and climbs higher—the climax of the melody in each reprise coincides not with the heaviest moment of the bass but, on the contrary, with the moment when the bass gives way, so to speak, to the melody.

In the trio version, the bass exhausts the bottom register for most of the refrain, releases the tension of that register in the middle of the 1st reprise for one measure only, and again for several measures in the 2nd reprise. In other words, the special sonic effects that Rameau carefully paced at structural moments in the harpsichord version are harder to perceive in the trio version. Also the gradual ascent in the melody, first to f″ and then to g″, is lost in this arrangement, since the flute transposes the refrain and reaches the climactic c‴ already in the second note of the piece, putting the f′ and the g″ in the middle of the instrument's range.

In the *Zoroastre* version, however, the well-shaped melodic curve of the harpsichord version is reinstated. The refrain goes up to a″, the 1st reprise to d‴, and the 2nd reprise to e‴. The transposed bass is manipulated wisely here: the range of the bass in the refrain of the harpsichord version (G′–g), when transposed a sixth higher (E–e′), allows Rameau to differentiate the two halves of the refrain by means of bass register: the "antecedent" phrase is played higher than the "consequent" phrase that resolves it. In the 1st reprise the transposed bass part can, for the first time, offer its bottom note (C) on the C major chord, immediately before the flute goes up to its first climax (d‴).

Of the two arrangements of "La Livri" in *Pièces de clavecin en concerts*, the solo version is immeasurably more focused and clearer to the ear than the trio version. Later on, in the *Zoroastre* version, Rameau is able to fix the problems he encountered in the trio version. Through the transposition of the piece, he is able to exploit the melodic instruments much more effectively.

Details of Harmony and Counterpoint

We mentioned in the previous paragraph that the "antecedent" phrase of the refrain is played higher than the "consequent" phrase that resolves it. This is not the only achievement of the modified bass in the refrain of the *Zoroastre* arrangement. It is also interesting that the arrangement makes extensive use of root positions in the refrain, one byproduct of which is a short contrapuntal imitation of the head of the flute's melody (e″–a″) at the beginning of measure 5 (e–a). In other words, Rameau creates the impression that the refrain was conceived contrapuntally by introducing an imitation that was not there in the previous versions of the piece.

In itself, the use of root position, as well as more sparing use of eighth notes, somewhat changes the character of the bass part, making it more harmonically driven. For the reasons discussed earlier, this also allowed Rameau to make more extensive use of parallel thirds in the second violin part.

The most interesting differences between the versions are in the subtle re-harmonizations of the melody. First and foremost is the harmonization of measures 3–4, where a reduction of the harmony (Example 5.8) shows that each of the versions takes a markedly different approach. The harpsichord (Example 5.8a) and *Zoroastre* (Example 5.8c) versions both reach a half-cadence through a prolongation of the tonic, but the former adds a certain "spice" through the use of the sharp sixth, while the latter creates interest through the use of an augmented chord. The trio version (Example 5.8b) is the only version that

EXAMPLE 5.8 Rameau, "La Livri," three harmonizations of mm. 3–4. a) harpsichord version from *Pièces de clavecin*. b) trio version from *Pièces de clavecin*. c) orchestral version from *Zoroastre* (1749).

introduces a real subdominant in the cadence, and it amplifies that subdominant with two dissonances.

The three versions of "La Livri" demonstrate that Rameau permitted himself considerable liberties in reworking a piece, and that, in the process of adapting the piece to a new scoring, he rethought character, textural intensity, and harmonization. In his many arrangements (Girdlestone 1958: 52–56; Sadler 1979: 18–24), he sometimes took his most private music, even music that he had written decades before, and turned it into effective music for the stage. It is interesting to observe some of his counterintuitive decisions, especially in recasting the left-hand accompaniment. An earlier rondeau for the harpsichord that Rameau adapted to *Zoroastre* is a case in point: "Les Tendres Plaintes," published in 1724, long before the production of *Zoroastre* in 1749, or indeed before Rameau started to compose operas.[21]

Let us first try to understand the composer's compositional decisions by creating a simple, almost mechanical, arrangement as our point of departure. The refrain is based on a characteristically ornamented melody in the right hand, accompanied in the left hand by two-part arpeggiation. Also the high "antecedent" phrase in the bass and the low "consequent" are familiar from "La Livri." The translation of the ornaments from those accepted in keyboard music to those accepted in music for the flute or the violin is done along the lines described earlier in the chapter. Disentangling the left-hand part should also be relatively simple, and the refrain could be easily arranged for flute or violin, a second violin, and a cello or bass viol (Example 5.9).

While the hypothetical arrangement proposed in Example 5.9 is valid, and would hopefully preserve some of the elegance of Rameau's original, it fails to preserve the flow of the original ongoing eighth-note motion. When Rameau, in 1749, attempted his own arrangement of this old harpsichord piece, his approach was markedly different (Example 5.10). First of all, he transposed the piece up a fourth, to G minor. This transposition allowed Rameau to rethink his choice of bass instrument. In this case, he chose not the bass, and not even the viola, but the violin.[22] The idiomatic harpsichord arpeggiation is not divided between the two violins, but rather given more or less unchanged to the second violin, while the first violin is free to play a new melody, some of it in parallel sixths with the principal melody in the flute. Needless to say, theater acoustics can hardly preserve the accumulative reverberation of the harpsichord arpeggios when those arpeggios are played by the violins, and yet that is the effect that Rameau sought, and that one should perhaps take from Rameau as a possible accompaniment texture for new arrangements.

To conclude our short discussion of Rameau's arrangement technique, let us try to borrow Rameau's technique and attempt an arrangement of a harpsichord piece by Rameau's older contemporary, François Couperin. Couperin

EXAMPLE 5.9 Rameau, "Les Tendres Plaintes," refrain (mm. 1–16). Staves 1–3: hypothetical arrangement for flute, violin, and cello; staves 4–5, original harpsichord version from *Pièces de clavecin avec une méthode . . .* (Paris, 1724)

EXAMPLE 5.9 Continued

published the short piece "Les Rozeaux" as a part of his *Troisième Livre de pièces de Clavecin* in 1722, two years before Rameau published his own book with "Les Tendres Plaintes." The two pieces share the same division of roles between the hands: the right hand plays an ornamented melody, while the left hand plays a quicker, arpeggiated texture. They also share the high "antecedent" and low "consequent" pattern. Thus, it would take little effort to produce again, as a preliminary step, a simple "mechanical" arrangement. In this case, our preliminary arrangement gives up the flow of sixteenth-note motion (Example 5.11) similar in essence to the one suggested in Example 5.9.

However, if we want to adopt Rameau's way of handling "Les Tendres Plaintes," we could begin by considering a high instrument for the bass. The range of the bass part in the refrain is exactly two octaves (B–b′). If we transpose the piece by a minor second or a minor third, the resulting range (c–c″) could be accommodated by the viola. A slightly bolder transposition by a sixth (g–g′) can also be considered (Rameau transposed "Les Tendres Plaintes" by a fifth), in which case the second violin could accommodate the arpeggiated bass, the right-hand part would lie comfortably within the range of the descant recorder (not unheard of in operatic scores), and a new melodic part could be given to the first violin, shadowing the recorder (Example 5.12).

EXAMPLE 5.10 Rameau, "Les Tendres Plaintes," refrain (mm. 1–16) from *Zoroastre* (1749), 19–20.

EXAMPLE 5.10 Continued

Arrangement Case Study: From Lute Song to Consort Song

To this point, we have seen how arrangers exercise their artistic freedom mainly with regard to the instrumentation and scoring of a piece, and, in Rameau's case, also concerning harmony and counterpoint. In none of the cases discussed so far, however, have we observed any change in the timeline of the piece through the addition or removal of music, even when the music was shifted from the domestic sphere of intimate harpsichord music to the public sphere of opera.

EXAMPLE 5.11 F. Couperin, "Les Rozeaux," refrain (mm. 1–8). Staves 1–3: hypothetical arrangement for flute, violin, and cello; staves 4–5, original harpsichord version from *Troisième Livre de pièces de Clavecin* (Paris, 1722)

EXAMPLE 5.11 Continued

EXAMPLE 5.12 Couperin, "Les Rozeaux," refrain (mm. 1–8). Staves 1–3: hypothetical arrangement for recorder and violins, based on Rameau's arrangement of "Les Tendres Plaintes" (see Example 5.10); staves 4–5, original harpsichord version from *Troisiéme Livre de piéces de Clavecin* (Paris, 1722)

EXAMPLE 5.12 Continued

The surviving corpus of John Dowland's works, however, demonstrates that even a slight modification of genre may result in a modification in the way the melody and the counterpoint evolve, changing the length of phrases. Dowland was constantly recasting his own works in different media. His arrangements are often so idiomatic that scholars who attempt to spot which version of a piece is "the original" usually have no internal musical evidence to rely on, and must therefore resort to paleography and circumstantial evidence to work out chronology.[23] For example, Dowland's most famous piece, "Pavane Lachrimae," survives in sources both in A in G. So far, scholars have been unable to determine which is the original (Gale and Crawford 2004). By contrast, arrangements of Dowland's works made by other musicians, although of varying quality, prove rather telling in terms of the arrangement process simply because we know that they are arrangements and therefore postdate the originals.

Let us examine Dowland's lute song "Sorrow, stay" and two contemporary attempts to transform it into a consort song. Philip Brett's description of the consort song gives an idea of the generic features the consort song:

The accompaniment fluctuates between a simple chordal, and a freely contra-puntal, style; it derives and develops some material from the slower-moving voice part but rarely stages a regular set of contrapuntal entries upon one theme. The solo part is not always the top voice of the quintet; sometimes it is the second or even the third, but it can always be sung by a boy, either a high treble or an alto. There is no attempt at word-painting in the madrigalian sense and the text is treated syllabically, although the penultimate syllable of a phrase is sometimes briefly extended. (Brett 1961–1962: 74)

Two sets of part books in the British Library, Add. MSS 17,786–791 and Add. MSS 37,402–406, offer an interesting comparison. The first transmits an arrangement made by William Wigthorp with modified lyrics ("Sorrow, come"), and the second, an anonymous arrangement, retains the original lyrics while taking much more liberty with the music.

Wigthorp's part-writing avoids some of the dotted-rhythm ornaments that are characteristic of the original lute part. The clearest way in which he turns the lute song into a proper consort song is in creating imitative counter-point. This he does by rhythmically echoing or foreshadowing the voice part and adding a newly composed treble part above it. Example 5.13 gives the beginning of Wigthorp's arrangement (mm. 1–7) in score, superimposed over a transcription of Dowland's original for ease of comparison (note that Example 5.14 gives the final measures of the song, mm. 29–36, in similar format). The new part reacts to the lyrics almost as closely as the original, for example in the descent down to d′, the lowest note in that part, at "But down, down I fall" (Example 5.14, m. 33).[24]

The anonymous arrangement in Add. MS 37,402–406 is similar to Wigthorp's in that it adds a new treble part. The arranger does, however, take a bigger "risk" by adding short interpolations to accommodate tighter contra-puntal imitation between the parts, significantly modifying the timing with which the lyrics are delivered, their rhythm and the barring (Example 5.15; compare with Example 5.13). Although it omits the extended repetition of the

EXAMPLE 5.13 J. Dowland, "Sorrow, Stay," mm. 1–8, in two versions: arrangement by Wigthorp (British Library Add. MSS 17,786–91) and Dowland's original from *The Second Booke of Songs*.

EXAMPLE 5.13   Continued

lend   true re-pen-tant teares   to a woo-full

lend   true re-pen-tant   tears   to a woe-full,

true re-pen-tant teares,   lend   true   re-pen-tant re-   pen - - - tant

EXAMPLE 5.13 Continued

EXAMPLE 5.14 Dowland, "Sorrow, Stay," mm. 29–36, in two versions: arrangement by Wigthorp (British Library Add. MSS 17,786–91) and Dowland's original from *The Second Booke of Songs*.

EXAMPLE 5.14 Continued

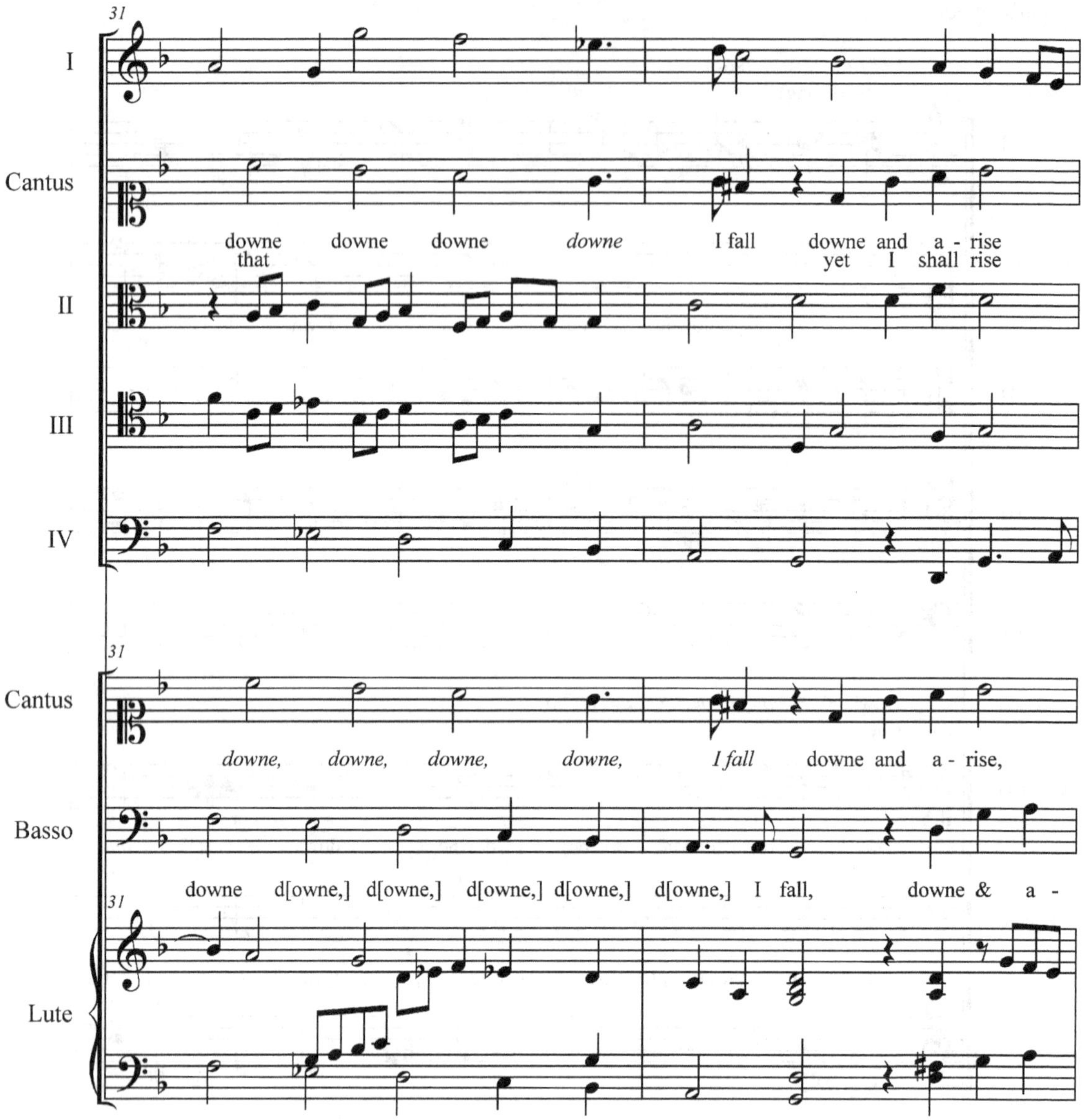

EXAMPLE 5.14 Continued

EXAMPLE 5.14 Continued

final verse, and with it one of Dowland's master strokes,[25] the originality and the generic sensitivity of this arrangement are worthy of careful study, and perhaps even imitation. Both arrangements have been recorded. In some recordings, the performers revert back to variant readings from Dowland's printed book, whether in the lyrics or the music—creating hybrid texts of the kind discussed in detail in Chapter 3.[26]

EXAMPLE 5.15 Dowland, "Sorrow, Stay," mm. 1–8, anonymous arrangement (British Library Add. MSS 37,402–406).

EXAMPLE 5.15 Continued

Not every lute song lends itself easily to polyphonic arrangement. Some of Dowland's later songs, like "In darkness let me dwell," are closer in style to early baroque monody, whereas many of Thomas Campion's songs are not only syllabic but also clearly divided into short phrases separated by pauses. Thus, imitating the techniques observed in the arrangements of "Sorrow, stay" requires serious intervention on the side of the arranger.

Let us take, for example, Campion's "The Sypres curten of the night is spread" from his (and Philip Rosseter's) 1601 *Booke of Ayres* (Example 5.16a). As a first stage, it is recommended to transcribe the original print into staff notation (few non-lutenists would be able to work directly from a lute tablature). Detailed instructions as to the translation process might vary from one lute tuning to the other, and are therefore beyond the scope of this book. However, some interpretative aspects embedded in the process will be overviewed in this chapter's final case study, in the discussion of Huwet's Fantasia. At this stage, let us begin with a simple transcription of the first strain of the song (Example 5.16b).

In essence, the process of transforming this lute song into a consort song requires that one replace the lute part with three or four viol parts and manage to make them sound contrapuntal, along the lines described by Brett (see earlier). The bass part is likely to remain unchanged, and therefore one should simply try and rewrite whatever is played by the lute above the bass (Example 5.16c).

Although the first section has only seven numbered measures, measure 6 is a double measure that accommodates a cadential hemiola. Thus the first strain of the song is essentially a symmetrical phrase of eight dotted whole notes, a symmetry more characteristic of the lute song than of the consort song. By adding two measures that foreshadow the melody of the first phrase, and another measure that foreshadows the melody of the second, it is possible to achieve three characteristics of the consort song at once: continuity without rest between phrases, asymmetry of phrases, and imitative counterpoint (Example 5.16d). Apart from these changes, the only modification that was required was a minor rhythmic change in the tenor viol part (m. 4 in Example 5.16d, corresponding to m. 2 in the Examples 5.16a–c)—again, in order to give the various parts the rhythmic independence characteristic of the contrapuntal texture.

Rather than simply being pragmatic transcriptions, some re-settings appear as a site for the display of one's originality. One classic example is Frans Brüggen's fragmentary recording of a "concerto" after Bach's B minor Sonata BWV 1030 for flute and harpsichord. In the provocative act of recording only fifty-six measures of a possible arrangement, Brüggen pointed out that an entire concerto based on the sonata is a possibility, but also that the act of noting that possibility does not necessitate recording the complete arrangement. This is an example of a fragment at its most powerful. Had he recorded the "concerto" in complete form, listeners and critics might well have been tempted not to deal with questions of historical probability. By recording a fragmentary arrangement, Brüggen put his stamp on an excellent idea and left it for future arrangers to pursue, thus ensuring that the credit for the idea will forever remain his.

Music is often "trapped" inside its instrument-specific realization, a problem nowhere more marked than in music for the lute. The fact that lute music is notated in tablature makes it almost inaccessible to scholars outside the lute-playing community. For this reason, composers who wrote almost exclusively for the lute, such as Alonso Mudarra and Francesco da Milano, in many ways among the finest composers of their age, do not receive as much

EXAMPLE 5.16 a. T. Campion, "The Sypres curten of the night is spread," transcribed from *A Booke of Ayres . . . by Philip Rosseter* (1601). b. Campion, "The Sypres curten of the night is spread," first strain. Lute part transcribed into staff notation. c. Campion, "The Sypres curten of the night is spread," arranged for voice and three viols. d. Campion, "The Sypres curten of the night is spread," arranged for voice and three viols, with added imitative material.

(a)

The Syp - res cur - ten of the night is spread,
The wea - ker cares by sleepe are con - quered,

and o - ver all a si - lent dewe is cast,
but I a - lone with hi - dious griefe, a - gast.

In spite of Mor - phe-us charmes a watch doe keepe

o - ver mine eies to ba - nish care - lesse sleepe.

EXAMPLE 5.16 Continued

(b)

The Syp - res   cur - ten of   the night   is   spread,
The wea - ker   cares   by__ sleepe are   con - quered,

and o - ver   all   a si -   lent dewe is   cast,
but I   a - lone   with hi - dious griefe, a - gast.

EXAMPLE 5.16 Continued

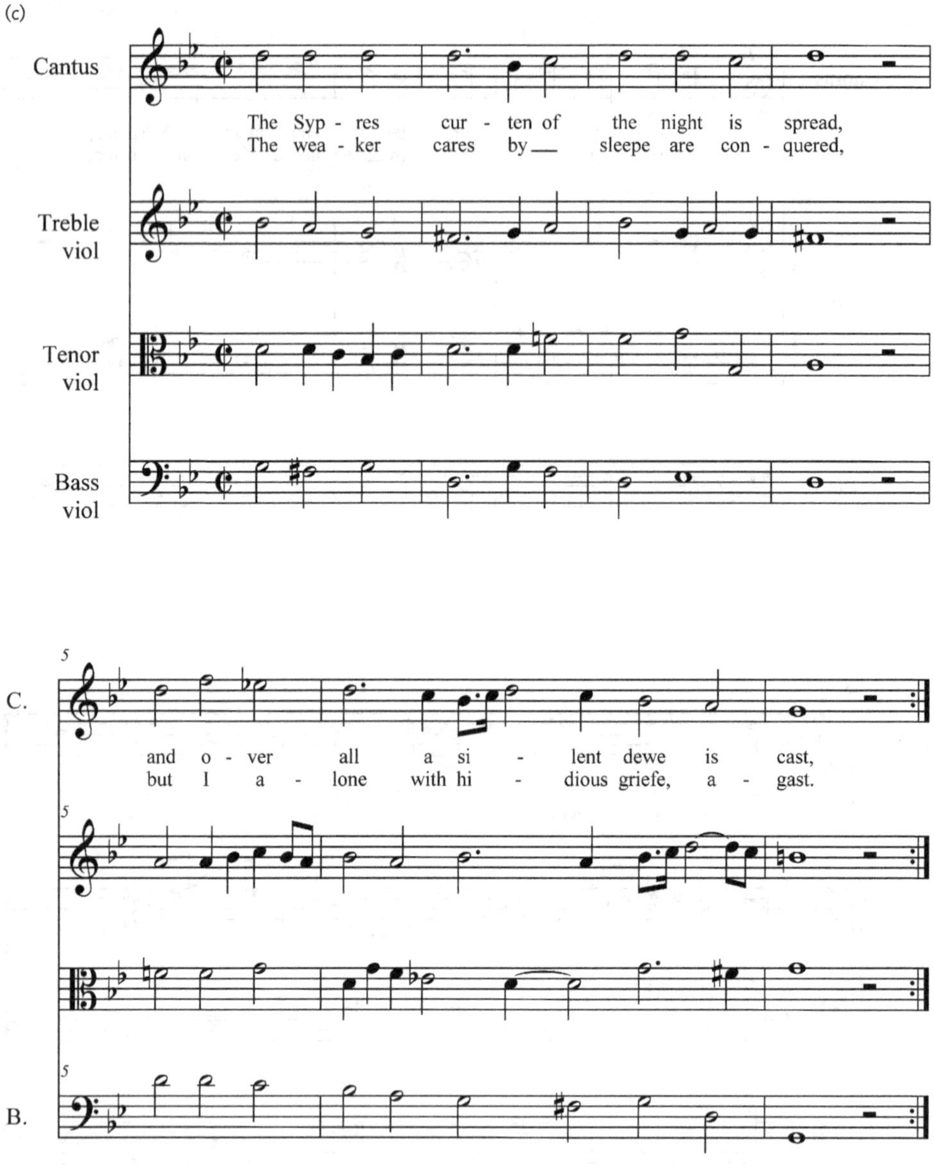

EXAMPLE 5.16 Continued

(d)

Cantus:
The Syp-res cur-ten of the night is spread,
The wea-ker cares by sleepe are con-quered,

C.:
and o-ver all a si-lent dewe is cast,
but I a-lone with hi-dious griefe, a-gast.

attention in history books as they deserve. Scholars interested in contrapuntal technique who want to study a polyphonic piece for lute usually have to work from a transcription, which is itself an interpretative work. In some cases, such as works written to be played on the piano with a single hand, the instrumental designation seems to preclude even the possibility of transcription. Audiences might justly frown upon any attempt to play such works on the piano using two hands because it might seem like "cheating," as if the work came with certain "terms of use." Does orchestrating Erwin Schulhoff's Suite no. 3 for Piano Left Hand somehow breach the work's terms of use? Would it be considered cheating to treat it as the basis for a work without any comparable technical limitation? And what about Paganini's "Caprices"? If one takes a caprice that is essentially written in three parts (such as Op. 1, no. 6), and which seems to be founded on a single technical principle of violin playing, will an arrangement for three melodic instruments lose its *raison d'être*? Does Paganini's music exist only to be played on the violin? Liszt's answer, reflected in his *Études d'exécution transcendante d'après Paganini*, also uses the concept of an abstract idea and its instrument-dependent realization. Here Liszt took an abstract model, defined not only by structural notes, but also by a certain level of virtuosity, and translated into a different instrumental dialect—that of the piano. Within the context of Renaissance and baroque music, such "trapped" music appears sporadically from the mid-sixteenth century on, for example in idiomatic toccatas written either for the harpsichord or the lute. Arrangement of such music requires serious contemplation: Is there substantial essence beneath the instrument-specific details? Is it even possible to recast the music for another instrument? One must remember that, at times, it was the profit motive, rather than artistic curiosity, that triggered problematic transcriptions from one instrument to another. Thus, even if much of Corelli's violinistic flair is bound to be lost in translation when arranged for the recorder, the publisher John Walsh must have made a tidy profit on *Six Solos for a Flute and a Bass by Archangelo Corelli*. Yet even "bad" arrangements are sometimes faithful to old practices, and one can learn a good deal from analyzing them.

Arrangement Case Study: From Organ to Recorder Consort

For the next few examples, let us examine arrangements for a type of ensemble that, on the one hand, is very common, but, on the other, requires considerable originality in solving problems of range and dynamics: the recorder consort. The recorder, like the harpsichord and the viol, was revived after more than a century of disuse. Like the harpsichord and the viol, its revival was promoted by two schools of performers—activists and historicists. The activists sought to place their instruments on an equal footing with any other modern instrument (hence their promoting of new music, struggling for equal opportunities and requirements in competitions, and embracing of innovative models and techniques). The historicists, by contrast, celebrated their instruments' belonging to a specific time in history and saw the revival of those instruments mainly as means of performing early music.

How historical is the recorder consort? There is some iconographical evidence of the existence of recorder ensembles (and specifically quartets) around 1500. The most celebrated evidence is a quartet (apparently SATB) played by angels, among a multitude of angelic and biblical musicians, in an engraving on the cover to Michael Praetorius's *III. Polyhymnia Panegyrica* (1618).[27] However, the fact that there are about forty-five identifiable instruments depicted in the engraving, of all sizes and volumes, hints at an encyclopedic idealization rather than a realistic depiction of performance practice (no one could have heard the recorder quartet or the clavichord among the timpani, sackbuts, and other loud instruments depicted). There are, of course, explicit references, as early as in Attaingnant's *Vingt et sept chansons musicales à quatre parties* (1533) (where Attaingnant alternately specifies four-part flute and recorder consorts). But even when recorders are not mentioned explicitly, SATB consorts were common in the sixteenth century (as evidenced, for example, by Virdung's *Musica getutscht* of 1511 and Martin Agricola's *Musica instrumentalis deudsch* of 1529). Thus there is some degree of historical justification for transferring SATB scoring to a recorder consort. For the present discussion of historically informed arrangement, let us consider the recorder as a historical instrument. We will avoid climbing to its (incomplete) third octave or using accidentals too extensively, sticking instead to its baroque idiom.

The most common motivation for arranging a piece is that an ensemble desires to engage with it using the forces at its disposal, even if those forces do not meet the requirements of the original. Thus, during the nineteenth century, popular symphonies were arranged for the piano not because anyone believed that such an arrangement could transcend the artistic achievement of the original, but simply because the piano offered the only way to engage with that repertoire outside a symphonic performance.[28] One may also sense that the act of arrangement acquires some significance as an act of homage (see, for example, Hummel's chamber arrangements of Beethoven's symphonies, written and published after the Beethoven's death) (Kroll 2012). In this case, it is no accident that the rise of arrangement coincides with the creation of the classical canon.

Many performers of melodic instruments (like the oboe, bassoon, clarinet, or saxophone) want to engage with Bach's solo music. Unfortunately, Bach wrote only thirteen suites, sonatas, and partitas for solo melodic instruments, a rather meager output compared to the vast corpus of his keyboard music, which are impossible to play on a melodic instrument. As a result, performers have arranged the same thirteen works hundreds of times, and for every possible instrument. Outside the "literal" transcription—simple transposition—of a piece, however, it is possible to "unpack" some or all of its movements. The fugue in Bach's G-minor Sonata for solo violin BWV 1001 can be seen as the surface manifestation of an abstract model that could also be realized, as it indeed was, as a five-part fugue for the organ (BWV 539). It could potentially be recast for several melodic instruments. The analysis and decision-making entailed in the arrangement process might, in some cases, lead to contrapuntal and harmonic conundrums that cannot be resolved by the mechanical process that is often mistakenly identified with transcription.[29]

Indeed, in contrast to solo oboists or saxophonists, ensembles of melodic instruments have slightly more varied repertoire from which to choose because they are not limited to the thirteen aforementioned works, and because, at least in theory, many of Bach's works for keyboard could be arranged for them. Wishing to retain the basic properties of wind instruments, recorder ensembles are often attracted to Bach's works for the organ.[30]

Before attempting a translation of Bach's works—compositions that consistently push the technical limits of the North German organ—into the medium of an ensemble, let us begin with the works of Jan Pieterszoon Sweelinck, in whose music the challenging passages are more limited. I have always been fascinated by Sweelinck's music, and I have long found it frustrating that no ensemble music by him has survived. A collection of his fantasias composed by him (*Fantasien mit 3 Stimmen der alle 8 Tonos*) may have been published, by Samuel Scheidt, in Halle around 1630. If it was indeed published, it has since been lost. The bulk of his music for the keyboard is fantasias and toccatas, which are hard to arrange for ensembles. (His variations, of which he wrote only a few, are more "arrangeable," and some recorder ensembles do play them.) Despite the fundamental affinity between the sound of the organ and that of a consort of wind instruments, transcription poses several challenges. Organ works often lack convenient pauses for breathing. They often exploit the full range of the organ, while the maximum range of an SATB recorder ensemble is less than four octaves. And registration is often fundamental to the structure of the original, sometimes even within a single passage of running scales (at least in the North German school of organ playing).

As a first example, let us take Sweelinck's "Fantasia auf die Manier eines Echo" (from D-Bgk HB 103 fols. 10r–11v, also identified as SwWV 275 or a3). Even from the title of the piece, one may anticipate that it explores some features of the organ that are hard to reproduce with an ensemble which essentially has only a single 4′ stop. One must distinguish between sections that lend themselves to polyphonic transcription and those written in the idiom of a multiple-stop instrument. Thus, the *exordium* of the piece (up to the cadence on m. 25, roughly a quarter of the whole piece) requires almost no modification when transcribed to an SATB recorder quartet.[31] Challenges for the transcriber begin in the second section (mm. 25–61), where there are phrases that are repeated *piano*, intended to be played on a second manual; and in the third section (mm. 62–106), where a similar effect is sought by exploiting the full range of the organ and by transposing motifs and blocks of chords from one octave to another.

Before proceeding to the arrangement of the second and third section, two general remarks are needed. One of the problems that might occur when arranging an organ piece for melodic instruments is that, in some cases, the part-writing is not continuous. Composers for the organ, when writing for a specific number of parts (for example, a fugue in n parts), often employed reduced textures for considerable stretches of music. While that is perfectly workable on the organ, when arranged for an ensemble it results in very long periods in which one or more ensemble members are idle. For example, if one wanted to arrange for five players Bach's C minor fugue BWV 546, in which fewer than 30 of the 159 measures of the fugue feature genuine five-part writing, the bass player would have to sit silently for most of the piece. In Sweelinck's music, the 247-measure "Aeolian" Fantasia (a2) is written for four parts, but begins with only two; a third part joins after about a third of the piece, and the fourth part joins only well into the second half.

Thus, at times, one may wish to enhance a reduced texture by adding a part. This can be done in several ways. One way is by "orchestrating" the part-writing and doubling one or more of the parts up or down an octave. This texture is very unusual in Renaissance compositions for ensemble. More in the style would be the addition, if possible, of imitative material. In contrapuntal music, however, much of the contrapuntal potential is likely to have already been exhausted by the composer. In some cases, the addition of imitative material may be the most elegant way to add a part. This technique was known to Sweelinck—see, for example, the masterly imitation of the song melody "Fortune my foe" in the opening measures of his setting of that song for the keyboard (Example 5.17).

Let us now return to the "Fantasia auf die Manier eines Echo" (henceforth Echo Fantasia). Within the context of Sweelinck's fantasias and toccatas, passages over a pedal point are likely to invite the addition of material. For example, measures 48–52 (Example 5.18a) contain a two-part canon over a pedal point, but the addition of a third part is possible (Example 5.18b). It is most probable that Sweelinck knew that the thematic material he had chosen (in this case, stock material in the keyboard music of his time) allowed for such an intensification, and that he decided against including one because a stretto canon in the unison is not very effective on a single keyboard (try to play the alto and the tenor from Example 5.18b on the keyboard and note the frequent part-crossing). Undoubtedly, arranging the work for an ensemble of melodic instruments allows additions that cannot be accommodated by the hands and feet of an organist. The cadence in measures 60–61 is a case in point. An ornamental two-note figure appears in an inner part in measure 61; its limited scope is dictated by the left hand having to hold the bass note A (Example 5.19a). When played on recorders, the ornament could be elaborated to include a diminution of a predominant motif from the preceding measures, something that would be very difficult to achieve at the keyboard (Example 5.19b).

There are two, equally immediate, ways of transcribing the short passage (mm. 30–34) from the second section (Example 5.20a). One is to give the second part (the echo) to the alto recorder and the third part (supplying

EXAMPLE 5.17 J. P. Sweelinck, Setting of "Fortune my foe," mm. 1–4.

EXAMPLE 5.18 a. Sweelinck, Echo Fantasia, mm. 48–52. Original version for the organ. b. Arranged for SATB recorder quartet.

harmonic support) to the tenor recorder (Example 5.20b). Another is to do it the other way around (Example 5.20c). Here, the specifics of the recorder ensemble are important: while both recorders can play both parts, they differ considerably in terms of register. If the tenor recorder plays the echo, it sounds in the second octave of the instrument, which has the same kind of projection as in the soprano recorder. Alternatively, if the alto recorder plays the echo, it will sound mainly in the first, quieter, octave of that instrument. Thus, the arranger's ability to imitate the *forte-piano* effect that Sweelinck wanted depends on the allocation of material to each recorder. Although seventeenth-century composers who wrote for recorders may or may not have been concerned about the balance of the various instruments in the ensemble (it is hard to say to what extent they were), relative dynamics can certainly have a crucial influence on the success of an arrangement.

The third section in Sweelinck's Echo Fantasia (Example 5.21) attempts a different echo—this time without the explicit change of manual, but with shifting the octaves of one of three parts (resulting in an effect similar to changing the combination of stops). Within the "single-stop 4′ organ" at our disposal, this change of blend is rather subtle. An arranger might want to enhance it by using

EXAMPLE 5.19 a. Sweelinck, Echo Fantasia, mm. 58–61. Original version for the organ. b. Arranged for SATB recorder quartet.

the different timbres of the various recorders. The two upper parts may be exchanged between the soprano and the alto, and the bottom may be exchanged between tenor and bass, or played solely by the tenor.

It is often the case that opening and ending sections in organ music are those that make an arrangement for melodic instruments difficult. They tend to present the wildest quasi-improvisational runs, the longest organ points, or the most sudden increase in the number of parts. The section that is arguably most challenging in Sweelinck's fantasia is the final twelve measures (mm. 95–106, Example 5.22a). Although the composer avoids explicit *piano* or *forte* instructions, his use of the wide range of the organ offers an effective substitute. In this passage, Sweelinck does not exchange individual parts, but rather the player's hands—a device that, like a scale running across the entire keyboard, does not naturally lend itself to ensemble playing. Thus, a four-part transcription may work effectively, but will inevitably retain some awkward octave leaps (Example 5.22b).

It is possible, however, to imagine that the composer was after a texture even more ambitious than the idiomatic organ texture, namely that of polychoral music, which developed across the Alps around Sweelinck's time.[32] If we reimagine the passage as a polychoral texture (with two SATB recorder quartets), we can now interpret the Sweelinck's use of different octaves as a

EXAMPLE 5.20 a. Sweelinck, Echo Fantasia, mm. 29–34. Original version for the organ. b. Arranged for SATB recorder quartet. c. Arranged for SATB recorder quartet (alternative: alto and tenor parts exchanged).

necessity associated with writing for the keyboard—one that we can circumvent by creating an alternative juxtaposition between two choirs (Example 5.22c). In such a case, as we try to transcribe the "gist" rather than every detail in the text, we might want to interpret some running passages (for example mm. 103–104) in a polychoral context, but discard others (such as m. 105) if we do not find convincing polychoral equivalents.

EXAMPLE 5.21 Sweelinck, Echo Fantasia, mm. 63–68. Original version for the organ.

We have seen that, unlike what one might expect, the arrangement of organ music for recorders does not always require the *thinning* of a dense five- or six-part organ texture. On the contrary, in momentary textural reliefs, and at moments where the composer has already reduced an idealized dense texture to work idiomatically on the keyboard, it sometimes requires *thickening*. Conversely, an arrangement of Van Eyck's "Fantasie & Echo" for solo recorder, discussed extensively in Chapter 1, may be based on its reinterpretation as a three- or four-part contrapuntal fantasie, perhaps even in the style of Sweelinck (Wind 2004: 19).

The opening section of Van Eyck's "Fantasie & Echo" may at first be interpreted as an antecedent-consequent pair of phrases (one of two-and-a-half measures, another of three) (Example 5.23a). However, if one imagines an imitative exordium in the style of Sweelinck, further imitation may be introduced, and the clear division between the two phrases eliminated (Example 5.23b).

Because the medium of a solo fantasie dictates a rather formal echo repetition (in which there is no room to overlap the voices of the dialogue), transferring the piece to the medium of consort music allows the arranger to rethink such passages, and even to manipulate the timing of the dialogue. For example, measures 15–20 (Example 5.24a) present two five-beat "calls," each answered by an equal-length "response." The five-beat unit in itself is uncharacteristic of early seventeenth-century style.[33] By using more than one melodic instrument, the arranger can preserve these calls and responses without sacrificing the clarity of the dialogue (Example 5.24b). Indeed, when performed by an unaccompanied recorder, the five-beat phrasing does not feel at odds with any audible duple or triple meter, and may, at worst, sound as unmeasured as a recitative. If five-beat phrases are imposed on other parts in polyphony, however, the result may sound at odds with the style of the period. Moreover, if the arranger were to choose to transfer the *essence* of the gesture, rather than insisting on its specific, scoring-dependent manifestation, then, as we saw in the example from Sweelinck (see Example 5.18b), he or she could enhance the counterpoint with additional imitative parts (Example 5.24c), thereby making the counterpoint more interesting, and may even recall material from the opening section.

The preceding examples all sit rather comfortably within the range of the recorder consort, and in Sweelinck's keyboard idiom, which often maintains

EXAMPLE 5.22 a. Sweelinck, Echo Fantasia, mm. 95–106. Original version for the organ. b. Arranged for SATB recorder quartet. c. A polychoral arrangement for a double SATB recorder quartet

(a)

EXAMPLE 5.22 Continued

(b)

EXAMPLE 5.22　Continued

EXAMPLE 5.22 Continued

(c)

EXAMPLE 5.22 Continued

EXAMPLE 5.22 Continued

EXAMPLE 5.22 Continued

the fundamentals of vocal polyphony (Dirksen 1997: 517–552), each individual part usually fits within the limited range of a single recorder. However, other composers for the organ, even when writing passages for a single "part," often exploit the full range of the instrument. Arranging some of Bach's virtuoso preludes and fugues, for example, poses serious challenges.

The first twenty-five measures of the Prelude and Fugue BWV 543 challenge both arranger and performer in several ways. First is the continuous melodic line that stretches over more than three octaves and explores various registers (it reaches f″ in m. 1, A in m. 9, and b″ in m. 22). Transferring it verbatim to a single instrument is impossible. Breaking that line into sections, each allocated to a different recorder, might create an uncharacteristic relay race, with instruments forced to stop abruptly on a sixteenth without a close to their melodic phrase. (Even in a relay race, a runner usually slows gradually after

EXAMPLE 5.23 a. J. van Eyck, Fantasia in Echo, mm. 1–6. b. Van Eyck, Fantasia in Echo, mm. 1–6. Suggested 3-part arrangement.

(a)

(b)

passing the baton to the next runner.) The second challenge is a continuous pedal point on A (or often A′ when performed on the organ with a 16′ stop) that, stretching over fourteen whole measures, must be broken more than once for the sake of breathing. Additionally, the fact that, at least in the first section of the piece, the texture alternates between one, two, and three parts, means that one or more recorders might remain idle for substantial periods of time.

Arranging the Prelude for an SATB recorder ensemble might at first seem doomed to failure. Not only can the bass recorder not produce the 16′ doubling of the pedal point (A′), it cannot even produce the 8′ pitch a. Even a great bass

EXAMPLE 5.24 a. Van Eyck, Fantasia in Echo, mm. 15–20. b. Van Eyck, Fantasia in Echo, mm. 15–20, parts condensed and overlapped. c. Van Eyck, Fantasia in Echo, mm. 15–20, parts condensed and overlapped with additional imitative entrances.

(Großbass) recorder in C cannot play that note. Moreover, since the tenor recorder cannot produce a proper a (it can only produce a′ and a″), it is impossible to split the pedal point between the tenor and the bass. Such alternation would require using two bass recorders, two great bass recorders, or a bass and a great bass.

As the problem of the pedal point can only be solved efficiently by letting the bass player take rapid breaths, let us first try and solve the problem of the run of sixteenths that sometimes acts as a single part and sometimes as a combination of two parts. My suggested solution for measures 1–25 (Example 5.25) is based on four premises: first, that the two-part polyphony implied by the arpeggios (and their underlying 7-6 progressions) may be unfolded so that two recorders play two independent parts, neither of them exclusively dominated by sixteenths. Second, that the use of two instruments allows smoother transitions from register to register by replacing only one instrument at a time. Third, that introducing another instrument in measure 15 is an easy way to make the intensification more gradual. Fourth, that in genuine polyphony (in contrast to the hidden polyphony of the original), when none of the parts is solely responsible for maintaining the harmonic progression, the arranger may introduce genuine melodic fragments (as I added in the soprano in m. 10 or in the alto in m. 19). Other idiomatic keyboard gestures (like the tremolo in m. 23) may be replaced by equivalent gestures (like trills) suitable for melodic instruments.

Arrangement Case Study: From Lute to Recorder Consort

Lute music occupies a peculiar place in early music, largely because of the characteristic tablature notation in which its repertoire is "trapped." While music historians weave plenty of vocal music and instrumental music (especially for the keyboard) into their narratives, all too often they simply omit lute music altogether. The original musical thought of composers like Milan, Kapsberger, and even Dowland is rarely analyzed; their contributions to the development of style, harmony, and counterpoint are regularly overlooked. Although lute music was probably always isolated by its notation, it was often at the forefront of fashions, such as the *style brisé*, and theoretical progress, such as equal temperament. At the very least, much rich music is hidden from musicians and audiences—simply because it is notated in tablature.

Let us examine the various challenges entailed in arranging, for a recorder quartet, a work originally written for lute. The opening of a fantasia by Gregory Huwet, which was published by Robert Dowland in *A Varietie of Lute Lessons* (1610) (Example 5.26), shall serve for purposes of demonstration.[34] Even before assigning the music to each recorder, the arranger is likely to begin by translating the tablature into staff notation—an act that already entails interpretation, most immediately in the unavoidable decisions regarding the duration of notes when the texture is polyphonic (see also Example 5.16b). In Example 5.26, system i gives a "literal" transcription of the tablature notation into staff

206

EXAMPLE 5.25 J. S. Bach, Prelude and Fugue BWV 543. Staves 1–2 give the variant from manuscript Mus. ms. Bach.P. 288. Staves 3–6 offer a possible arrangement for SATB recorder quartet.

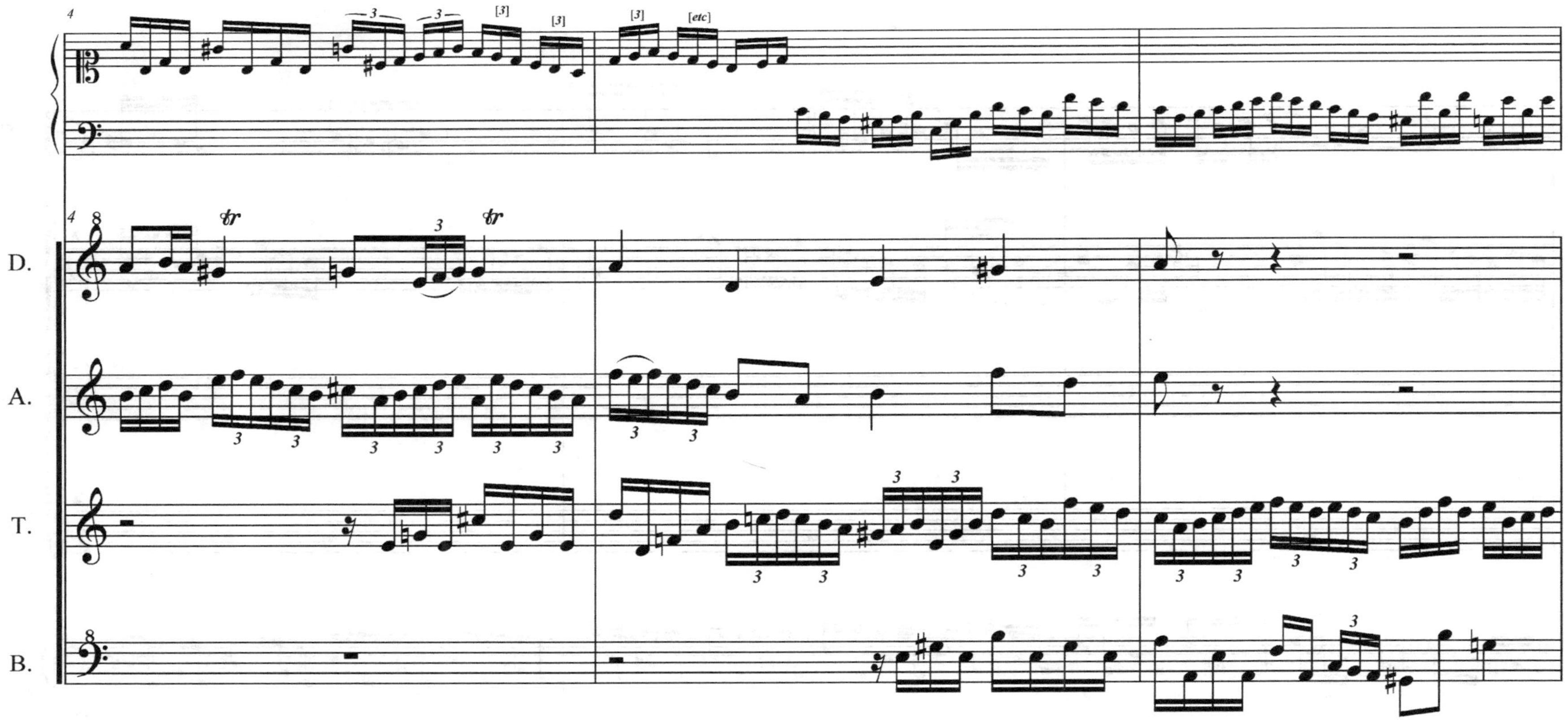

4
[3]
[etc]
D.
A.
T.
B.

EXAMPLE 5.25 Continued

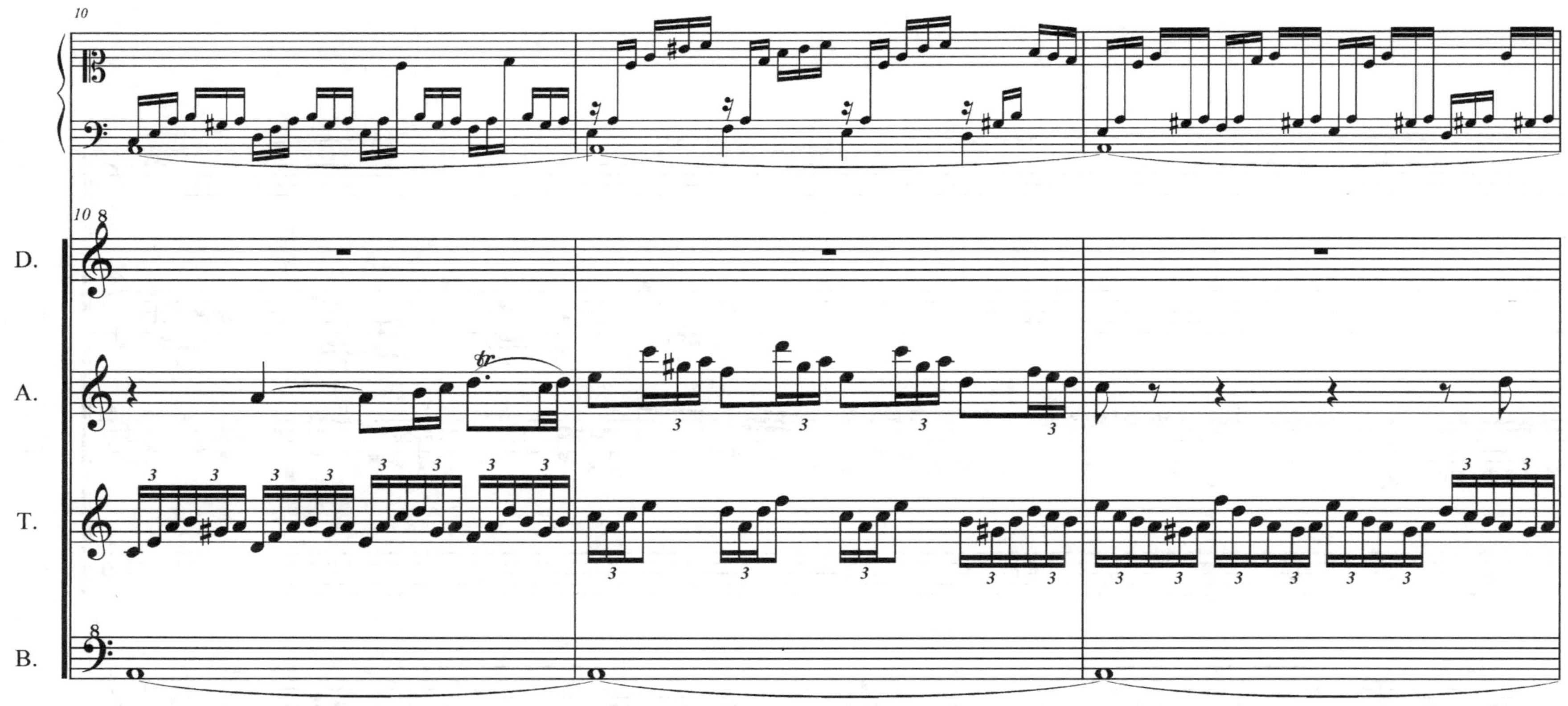
10
10
D.
A.
T.
B.

EXAMPLE 5.25 Continued

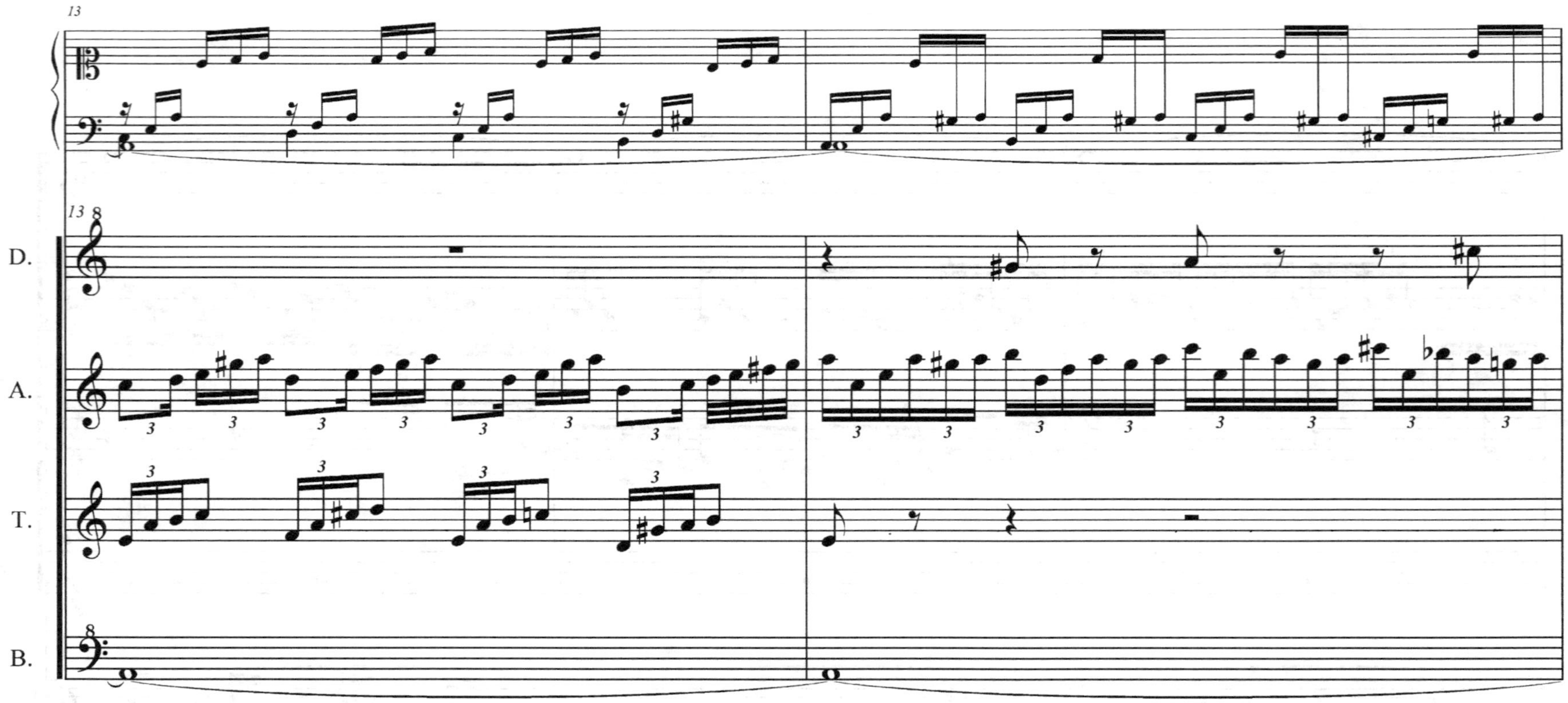

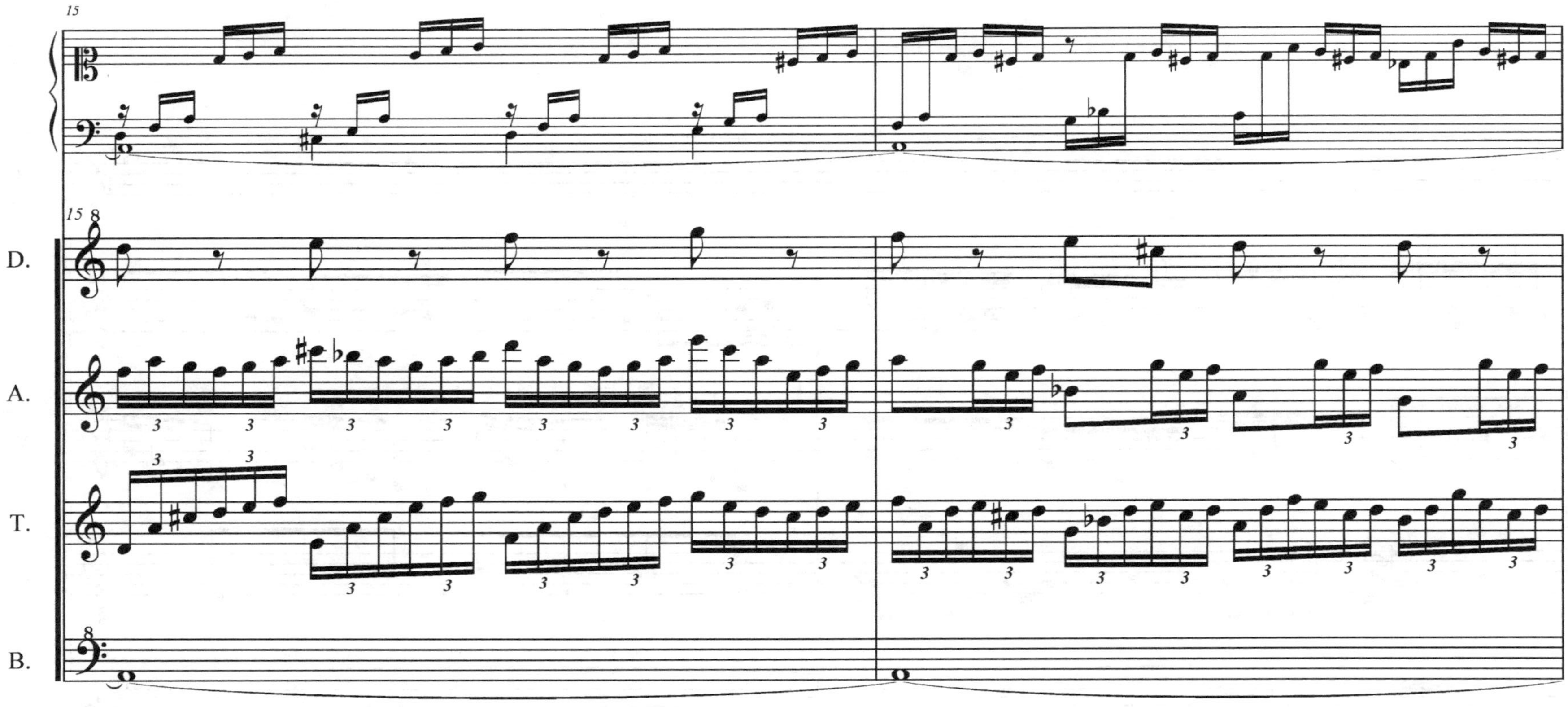
15
D.
A.
T.
B.

212

EXAMPLE 5.25 Continued

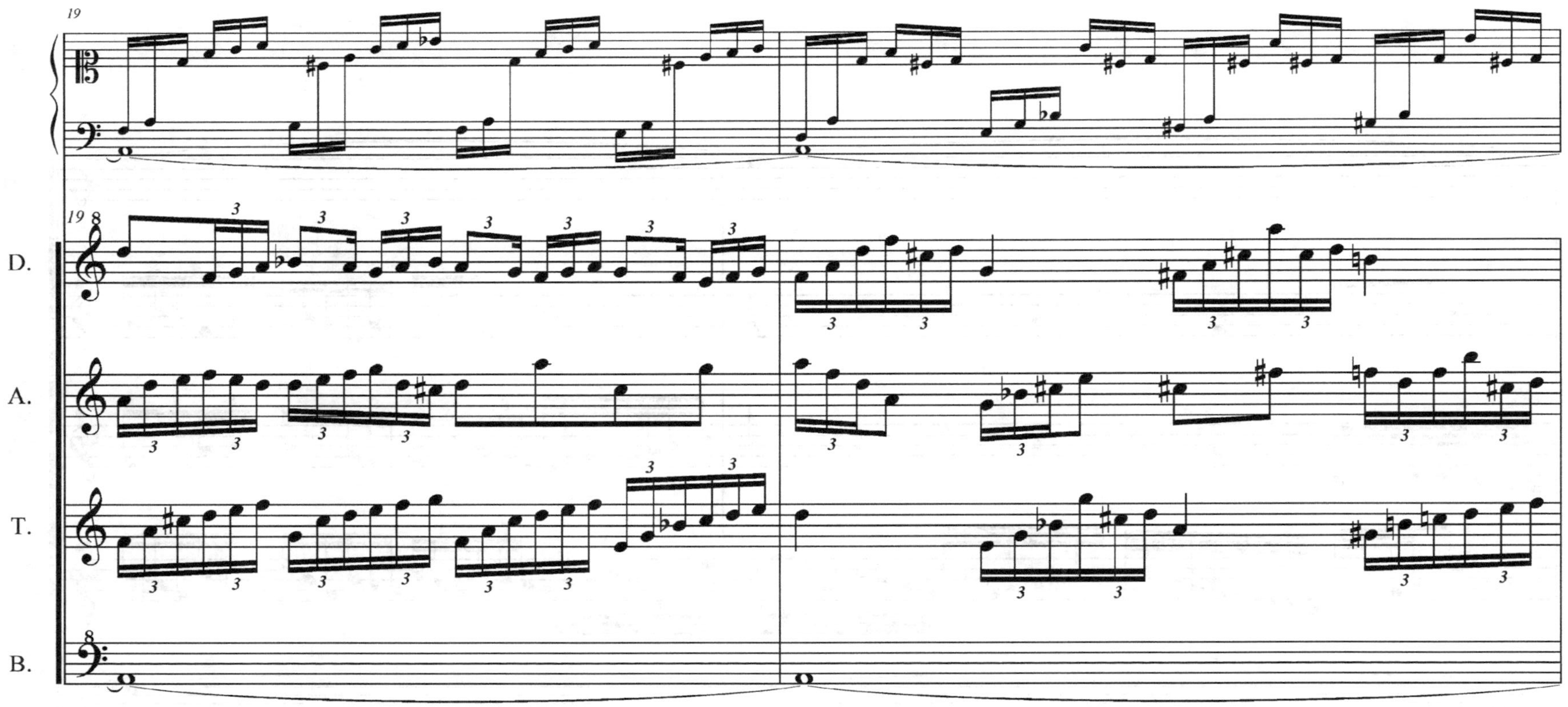

19
D.
A.
T.
B.

EXAMPLE 5.25 Continued

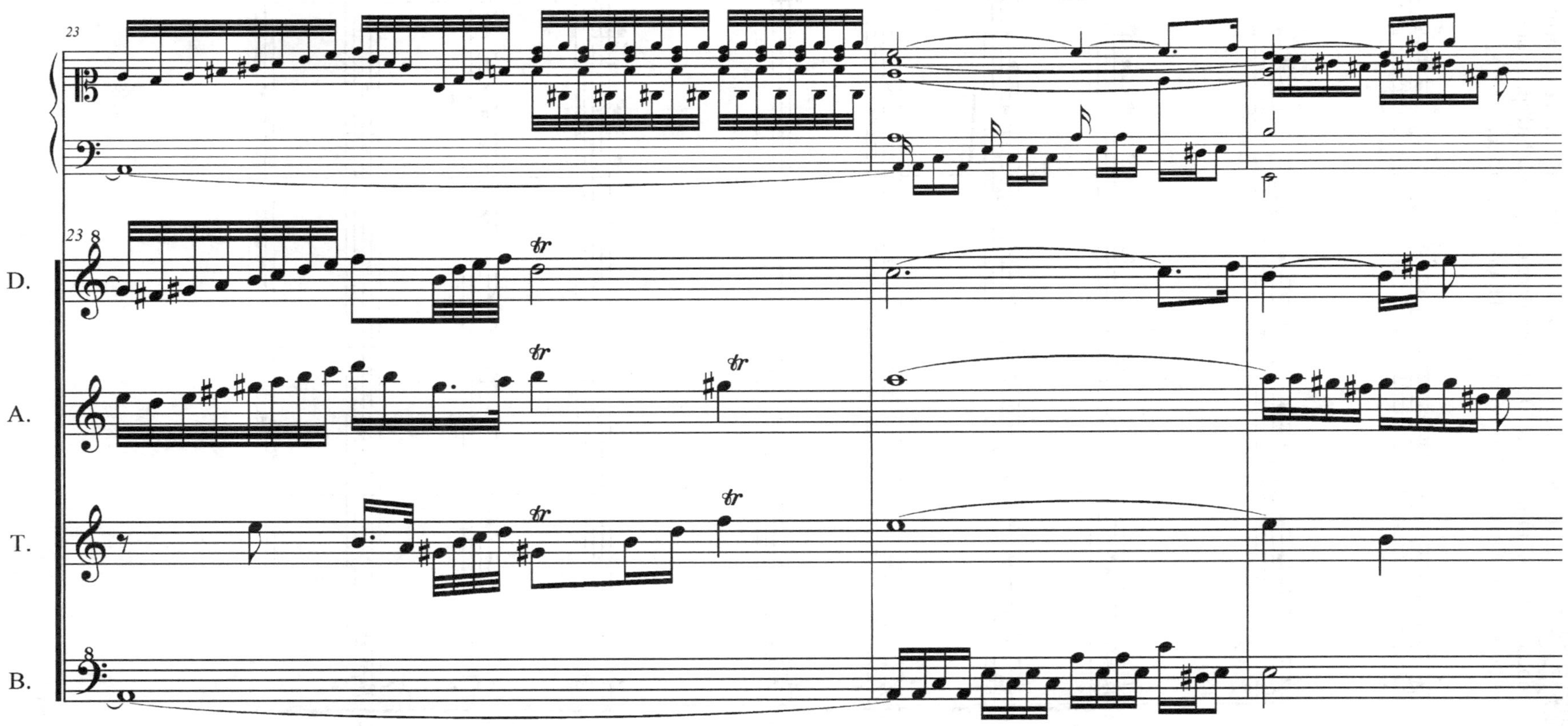
23
tr
D.
A.
T.
B.

EXAMPLE 5.26 Gregory Huwet, Fantasia, mm. 1–27. i) a "literal" transcription of the tablature notation into staff notation; ii) a preliminary polyphonic interpretation; iii) division into consistent SATB scoring; iv) improved four-part scoring.

EXAMPLE 5.26 Continued

EXAMPLE 5.26 Continued

EXAMPLE 5.26 Continued

EXAMPLE 5.26 Continued

EXAMPLE 5.26 Continued

EXAMPLE 5.26 Continued

EXAMPLE 5.26 Continued

EXAMPLE 5.26 Continued

notation. Reading two or three independent parts in this single system (or, indeed, in a tablature) means that the performer or the arranger should identify which notes belong to which part, decipher which notes should be held longer than what is written, and give each part its own character. Lutenists often do all that on the spot, even when sight-reading a piece. The lutenist's hands, accustomed to playing other works in the same style, might do some of the thinking, as it were, simply extending notes by instinct. In some cases, lutenists have the privilege of holding a note beyond its natural short decay (dictated by the physics of the lute), thus exempting themselves from deciding when to stop it. For the arranger, however, the same decisions are both more cerebral and more obligatory. The arranger's decisions must result in playable, independent parts that tell the wind players not only when to start each note, but when to stop it, too.

System ii provides such a preliminary interpretation of system i. Note that while measures 1–10 adhere to one-, two-, and then three-part texture, occasional deviations may occur, as in the four-part chord in measure 9. Also of an interpretative nature is the extension of several notes to the point when they become dissonant suspended notes (systems i–ii, mm. 10, 18–19). As the texture becomes denser, it becomes more difficult to know how to separate the parts.

Composers of lute music did not always conceive of four-part polyphony in a way that suits a four-staff score. Occasional chords with "too many notes," extensive passages with only a single part playing, sometimes even awkward part-writing that derives from comfortable hand positions—all these are frequent in lute music. System iii nonetheless attempts to divide the polyphony into a consistent SATB scoring (here designed for an AATB recorder quartet). System iii is not a finished four-part score suitable for performance, for it contains several contrapuntal problems and small-scale inconsistencies (including, a two-part passage in mm. 9–10 that is unplayable on a melodic instrument). The allocation of two simultaneous notes to any one instrument is useful when those notes clearly do not belong in any other part. In such cases, one must find a suitable compromise, either deciding that one of the notes is more important than the other, or finding a creative way to include both.

In system iii, measures 9–10, one solution might be to sacrifice the e″–f#″ ascent, instead finding an alternative route up to the g″ (system iv, mm. 9–10). Other solutions for the reduction of two (and sometimes even three) parts allocated to a single instrument may be seen in measures 17–18 and 23–27. Only system iv provides a playable arrangement, suitable for performers and ready for the extraction of parts.

When turning polyphonic lute tablature into staff notation, one may easily translate written-out trills into abbreviated signs such as ⁓ (mm. 11, 27). Idiomatic cadential figures (m. 16) may also be simplified. Other idioms may prove more challenging.

The omitted third in measure 7, first beat, does not stem from any instrumental limitations of the lute. It does, however, sound empty when played by a consort of melodic instruments. An elegant solution would be to add an imitation of motif x (system iv: A. Rec. 2, m. 6, is imitated by A. Rec. 1, mm. 6–7). The all-quarter-note motion (systems i–iii, m. 8) is more idiomatic of the lute than the consort; the ornamental eighth-note motion (system iv, A. Rec. 2) helps to soften the otherwise mechanical effect (see also system iv, A. Rec. 1, m. 18). The momentary transition to a thick, four-part texture (systems i–ii, mm. 9–10) prior to the entrance of the "real" fourth part (m. 11) is also acceptable in lute music, but not in strict contrapuntal writing.

The entrance of the fourth part brings with it several lute-derived problems, like parallel octaves (systems ii–iii, mm. 11–13), discontinuous line-writing (system ii, mm. 11–17), and overuse of the higher register by a single part. With minor modifications to the melody, the arranger can avoid the parallel octaves (systems iii–iv: T. Rec., mm. 11–12; A. Rec. 2, m. 13). By dividing melodies between the parts, the arranger can increase the level of imitation, relieve some of the exhausted registers, and allow proper phrase endings (system iv, B. Rec., mm. 14–15: the added notes in the bass part make it possible to avoid an a″ in A. Rec. 1, allow a rest in A. Rec. 1, and provide better continuity). Added material can serve to foreshadow motifs and improve the counterpoint (system iv, mm. 14–15: the added motif *y* in T. Rec is manipulated into A. Rec. 1). Adding notes may sometimes force further alteration, which is ideally kept for ornamental material (system iii, m.15: T. Rec. note g would clash with the added a in B. Rec. and is therefore changed into e). It is important to use added material in order to avoid the sudden entrance of several parts (system iv, A. Rec. 2, m. 16). As a rule, the more problems a single modification can solve, the better. Merely adding a dot may sometimes serve both to avoid all-quarter-note motion and to explicate an implicit suspension (system iv, T. Rec., mm. 18–19).

As we have seen in the Bach prelude, wide-ranging sixteenth-note scales are essentially a virtuosic element, and they require some modification when arranged as consort music. While in the Bach prelude this was solved by making plain the slower two-part texture that lies behind the arpeggiated sixteenths, here the scalar movement must be broken into short excerpts to allow a more equal distribution of material among the parts and a better use of the various registers. Just as running sixteenths on the lute usually imply a one- or two-part texture, the addition of running sixteenths in parallel thirds may help to make the arrangement more idiomatic of consort texture (system iv, A. Rec. 2, mm. 23–24; T. Rec., m. 26; A. Rec. 1; m. 26). As before, added material is invaluable if one wants to maintain a three- or four-part texture and improve the continuity of part-writing (system iv, T. Rec., m. 25).

Conclusion

We have seen that extending repertoire by borrowing compositions from various genres and media requires, first and foremost, certain sensitivities. Early music performers must be sensitive to those aspects of the piece that are idiomatic of a specific instrument, and to those details of notation that stem from idiom and must be altered if the piece is transferred to another instrument. To transfer a piece from one medium to another, we must deploy some compositional devices, which, in turn, require some creative invention. Yet the surviving music from the sixteenth to the eighteenth centuries offers countless models of arrangement for borrowing and imitation.

In this chapter I have examined several examples taken from various genres. Starting with examples of simple alteration of scoring (from four- to three-part ensemble) in the works of James Paisible, I went on to discuss Rameau's arrangements of his own keyboard works, which are not only more sophisticated than the Paisible arrangements, but also demonstrate great sensitivity to the characteristic sonic properties of each instrument and the correct way of notating music for each instrument. Then I surveyed some examples from the repertoire of lute songs that showed that transforming a lute song into a consort song requires the addition of short imitative phrases, the elimination of rests, and sometimes, as the result of those two modifications, the creation of asymmetry as well. The examples from the organ works of Sweelinck and Bach showed that imitative counterpoint often requires modification, and that timbral contrasts may require some rethinking, especially if one attempts to arrange organ music for a small ensemble such as a recorder quartet. Writing for larger ensembles offers alternatives, such as polychoral textures. The challenges posed by lute music are many, beginning with the tablature (which is often counterintuitive for non-lutenists) and ending with the necessity to interpret, rather than transcribe, the duration of each and every note.

As this book proceeds from chapter to chapter, the skills I discuss require more and more intervention by the performer, culminating in this and the following chapter, and their extensive discussion of arrangements. Indeed, it is the act of arranging performance material that early music performers most clearly display the same versatility that was so characteristic of musicians in the baroque era and before. In my opinion, that versatility is inseparable from the ideal toward which early musicians should strive. The exhausting routine of concertizing does not encourage performers to experiment, or to sit down at their desks and arrange or compose. Those who do cultivate an individual approach to repertoire, however, will very likely arouse the interest of audiences, thus generating, in turn, more concert engagements.

Some performers, to be sure, may feel "threatened" by the suggestion that they should intervene with the musical text in ways that are traditionally identified with professional arrangers and composers. It is worth remembering, however, that all the examples discussed in this book are based on concrete models. Performers are acquainted with these musical texts no less intimately than any researcher. Many of the approaches to arrangement offered here required little compositional skill (in its modern sense), but merely some command of counterpoint—a subject that is, in many conservatories, an integral part of the general curriculum. Fifty years ago, the variety of good counterpoint textbooks available for performers was much more limited than it is today. It is mainly the courage to dare to write one's own score which early music departments today do not always supply. Precisely this courage should be nourished as early as possible in a musician's career.

Chapter 6

Writing for Early Instruments Today

Orchestration, the systematized study of instruments and the sounds they produce, emerged in the nineteenth century. While much of the framework for such study evolved slowly throughout the preceding century (Dolan 2013: 53–89), the first classic work on the subject (still in demand today) was published only in 1844—Berlioz's *Grand Treatise on Modern Instrumentation and Orchestration*. It is important to note that Berlioz's treatise, like many treatises that follow it to this day (for example, the books by Gordon Jacob, Walter Piston, or Samuel Adler), leans on master examples from the past, but is otherwise preoccupied by contemporary concerns and with writing for contemporary instruments (the adjective "modern" is sadly omitted from the title of most English translations of Berlioz's work). While writers today do not resort to evocative and lyrical descriptions of sound as often as Berlioz did, very little has changed in the way writers gather information about orchestration—their knowledge about what "does work" and "does not work" in orchestral writing is usually based upon years of composing, arranging, and, above all, listening to music.

For the present discussion on orchestration and arrangement, let us deviate from these accepted traits in two aspects: first, I will focus on early instruments and, to some extent, on the way they were used in the past. Second, I will attempt to base some of my arguments on empirical examination of the sound produced by early instruments, using digital methods that were unavailable to Berlioz (and barely available even to Adler when he first published his orchestration book). As Boulez warned us (in the context of discussing contemporary music), a quantitative discussion of timbre sometimes neglects "the quality of integration of sound and timbre in the structure of a composition" (Boulez 1987, 161). That approach, however, still has much to offer within the context

A Performer's Guide to Transcribing, Editing, and Arranging Early Music. Alon Schab, Oxford University Press.
© Oxford University Press 2022. DOI: 10.1093/oso/9780197600658.003.0007

of historically informed performance. After discussing some of the historical and technical aspects of orchestrating for early music instruments in general, I will offer two case studies that highlight the various considerations one might encounter when orchestrating new music for early instruments.

Neoclassicism and Early Music

Musical neoclassicism, as a concept, evolved rather naturally from nineteenth-century historicist tendencies. However, its rise as a sweeping fashion in the world of contemporary music is usually identified with its adoption by the influential modernists in the 1920s, mainly Stravinsky in his Octet and Schoenberg in his Suite for Piano, both in 1923.[1] Alongside pieces with telling titles like Malipero's Ricercari per undici istrumenti (1925) and Bloch's Concerto Grosso (1925), the neoclassicist fashion showed a sudden shift in composers' approach to musical form, genre, textures, melodic character, and harmonic language. A related process that occurred concurrently was a surge in interest in early music—unprecedented in scale until the 1960s (Haskell 1988: 75–85).

The growing fashion for early instruments—that is, for the instruments themselves and for the sounds they produce—developed somewhat independently of the formal and generic aspects I have listed. While Stravinsky expressed genuine interest in Bach's instrumentarium (Stravinsky and Craft 1979: 31), neither he nor any of the aforementioned composers thought that the revival of the concerto grosso or of the ricercar is dependent on the revival of the instruments that participated in these genres originally. Various early instruments, or modern variants thereof, started to reappear in the early twentieth century, in disconnected pockets and by independent individuals. Arnold Dolmetsch and Wanda Landowska, for example, went in very different paths, appealed to different audiences, with different repertories, but both are recognized nowadays as pioneers of the same early music revival. Each of the composers who composed for these pioneer-performers developed their own individual approach to composing music for early instruments.

Although not an avid revolutionary or self-claimed enfant terrible, as Stravinsky and Schoenberg were, Paul Hindemith made some pathbreaking attempts in the composition for early instruments, even before Stravinsky's aforementioned Octet and Schoenberg's Suite. In 1922 Hindemith composed his Kleine Sonata Op. 25, no. 2 for viola d'amore and piano. While the viola d'amore was not entirely forgotten during the nineteenth century,[2] Hindemith's interest in that instrument formed part of his general interest in early music and in his proto-HIP approach (Butt 2002: 3). Hindemith's writing for the viola d'amore in that piece, in clear neo-baroque style, celebrates the early instrument's characteristic fourths- thirds-based accordatura: it contains parallel fourths in quick succession (which is much harder to execute on the violin), seven-note chords, and frequent D-major open-string chords (albeit out of tonal context).

With his head leaning on the instrument's chin rest, Hindemith must have been impressed by the reverberation effect of the viola d'amore's sympathetic strings. In his Kleine Sonata, however, he did not yet fully exploit the instrument's unique resonance. In concert setting, the accompanying piano would probably overshadow most of the viola's reverberation (with the possible exception of a few solo passages in the second movement). Hindemith's approach to "orchestrating" the viola d'amore, at this stage, was largely conservative, only slightly bolder than Vivaldi's.

By 1927, Hindemith had taken a new approach to the instrument. As he set to write his Kammermusik No. 6 (Op. 46, no. 1) with solo viola d'amore, he took the challenge to blend the instrument with a much larger ensemble. Hindemith's thoughts about the fundamental properties of the viola d'amore are reflected in the scoring of this piece, especially when compared to the scoring of Kammermusik No. 4 (Op. 36, no. 3) with solo violin, which he composed two years prior (Table 6.1). In both cases, Hindemith chose not to include violins in the orchestra, probably to avoid rivalry with the soloist. However, knowing that the projection of a solo viola d'amore is weaker than that of a solo violin, in the later piece Hindemith reduced the accompanying ensemble significantly. In addition, he reverted from two piccolos and clarinet in E♭ to the more standard flute and oboe; he "made room" for the lower register of the viola d'amore by omitting the violas; and he further emphasized the instrument's alto-tenor register by weakening the lower bass register of the ensemble (two double basses instead of four, no contrabassoon, and no bass tuba). The score starts with a forceful tutti but soon recedes to a lightly orchestrated second movement (without the trumpet and trombone); the third movement starts with an extensive solo for the viola d'amore and, although the tutti gradually returns, the piece ends surprisingly with just the

Table 6.1 Comparison of scoring in Hindemith's Kammermusik Nos. 4 and 6	
Kammermusik No. 4	**Kammermusik No. 6**
Solo Violin	Solo Viola d'amore
2 Piccolos	Flute
Clarinet in E♭	Oboe
Clarinet in B♭	Clarinet in B♭
Bass Clarinet in B♭	Bass Clarinet in B♭
2 Bassoons	Bassoon
Contrabassoon	Horn
Cornet à pistons	Trumpet
Trombone	Trombone
Bass Tuba	3 Cellos
4 Violas	2 Double basses
4 Cellos	
4 Double basses	
4 drums (Tom-toms)	

bassoon and the viola d'amore playing below it, on the open bottom string. Thus, Hindemith contrived those few possible combinations that allowed the audience to hear (and enjoy) the resonating sympathetic strings of this curious instrument.

Concurrently with Hindemith's experiments with the viola d'amore, another early instrument made its way back to the concert hall—the harpsichord. The harpsichord is undoubtedly a more prominent instrument than the esoteric viola d'amore. However, perhaps because it sounds almost antithetical to the piano and despite its historical significance, it was adopted first outside the German mainstream.

The pioneering concertos by De Falla, Poulenc, and Martinů could not explore the sonic properties of a historical instrument, if only for the reason that historical instruments were not available to the composers. De Falla and Poulenc wrote their concertos for Wanda Landowska, who played a Pleyel instrument that had astonishingly little in common with the baroque harpsichord. Martinů wrote for Landowska's student, Marcelle de Lacour. Both Poulenc and De Falla published their works as concertos for harpsichord *or piano*, but both showed great concern for issues of balance that could arise from the harpsichord scoring specifically.

De Falla wrote his concerto as a chamber piece—a sextet. In the performance instructions, he requests that the harpsichord be placed before the other instruments,[3] that all the dynamics should be adjusted so that the instruments do not cover the harpsichord, that the harpsichord should use its maximum volume, and that the string parts should not be doubled. Poulenc was more optimistic about the instrumental blend: he hoped that, if he orchestrated the piece properly, Landowska's Pleyel could compete not only with five instruments but with a full orchestra. The score of his "Concert champêtre" shows several passages where the composer "helps" the harpsichord. For example, Poulenc asks the harpsichord to join the orchestra's fortissimo chords a thirty-second note after the rest of the orchestra, so that the percussive attack of the harpsichord is heard separately from the orchestra.

De Falla, who was more alert to the instrument's subtleties, labored over every note in his concerto (he began composing it in October 1923 and finished in June 1926). As he did not wish to explore anything softer than the fullest harpsichord sound throughout the piece, most of the composer's attention to detail went to other aspects. Only three measures in the first movement have alternative notation for performance on the piano (Example 6.1a), and these hint that De Falla did not find doubled octaves in the left hand on the harpsichord as convincing as on the piano. Most of the attention went to indicating, as accurately as possible, the kind of arpeggiation required on every chord. A short cadenza toward the end of the first movement shows several kinds of arpeggiation in quick succession (Example 6.1b).

EXAMPLE 6.1 a. Falla, Harpsichord concerto, first movement, mm. 127–129 (the composer's alternative left-hand part for performance with piano is given in small typeface). b. Falla, Harpsichord concerto, first movement, mm. 141–146, showing variety in arpeggio figurations.

While the harpsichord concertos of the 1920s and 1930s reimagined the baroque harpsichord as a massive instrument, experiments to revive its more intimate relative, the clavichord, were more historically sensitive. Herbert Howells wrote his "Lambert's Clavichord" Op. 41 in 1927. As the clavichord (even when it does not follow a historical model) is too soft to combine with any other instrument, Howells had no choice but to explore the subtleties that were characteristic of sixteenth- and seventeenth-century virginal music. In a way, Howells's collection (as well as his later collection, Howells's Clavichord, of 1961) reconstructs the social context of the genre (Howells's miniatures convey friendly tributes and in-jokes relevant the composer's social circle) and, as a part of that larger project, shows valuable insight into the sound of the clavichord.

An important turning point in the early music revival, and specifically in its use of historical models of instruments, came about in the mid-1960s. As Haskell notes, this period saw the rise of a new kind of early music professionals, of unprecedented technical ability (especially in the revived instruments) and of an insatiable appetite for innovation—tendencies that yielded a tight bond between these early music virtuosos and the avant-garde scene (Haskell 1988: 75–85). There is one more development that affected the rise of this new type of early musician, and that was the change of mindset with regard to the use of genuine historical instruments, or copies thereof (Haynes 2007: 43–45). In other words, the search for new sounds manifested itself both in growing awareness to the subtleties of historical instruments and their copies, and in a new approach to exploring the sounds of early instruments. Unlike Landowska's Pleyel, which was a product of its time (the early twentieth century), the instruments that featured modern music festivals from the 1960s onward were genuine baroque recorders, renaissance lutes, and viols. These instruments were often handmade copies of museum instruments and bore the names of the builders whose instruments they were modeled after (like Rottenburgh, Bressan, and Norman)—labels that suddenly became household names among professionals and amateurs alike. The modernized harpsichords gradually went out of fashion, replaced by copies of original harpsichords on museum display. In some cases, as that of Skowronek's "Harpsichord of Nicholas Lefebvre 1755," instrument builders went a long way in imitating original building techniques (Skowronek 2002).

One of the iconic compositions of these watershed years is Mauricio Kagel's Music for Renaissance Instruments (1966). The piece is somewhat self-contradictory in its notation: on the one hand, it contains very detailed instructions with regard to pitch (for example, the accordatura of the lute and theorbo) and rhythm, and, on the other hand, it uses "extended techniques" (like using a violin bow on the lute or manipulating the pipes of the regal) and it gives its performers almost unlimited freedom with regard to fundamental issues like the number of performers (from two to twenty-three), the inclusion and omission of entire sections of the score, and the beginning and ending points of the piece (which is written as a continuous cycle). For Kagel, the composition of the work was motivated not so much by historical curiosity as by the search for innovative sound material, a search that he soon pursued further with Acustica (for experimental sound generators and loudspeaker) and Exotica (for "außereuropäische Instrumente"). Nonetheless, Music for

Renaissance Instruments broke all known boundaries of the playing technique of old instruments.

Performer-composers like Hans-Martin Linde went on to explore extended techniques even further in their solo music (like "Music for a Bird" and "Amarilli mia bella" for recorder or the later "Anspielungen" for traverso). After the 1960s, historical instruments and copies (and close-mic studio recording of these instruments) increased the sensitivity of performers and audiences alike to the subtleties and even to the "imperfections" of old instruments. Notes and registers with uneven volume or different timbre, for example, were embraced in the performance of both early music and avant-garde.

Paradoxically, instruments like the early twentieth-century Pleyel harpsichord became, at the same time, obsolete for performing seventeenth-century music, and "authentic" for performing works from the 1920s. Even the most superb copy of a late-seventeenth-century Ruckers harpsichord will prove disappointing if used for performing Poulenc's concerto.

The Spectral Study of Early Instruments

Recording technology revolutionized every conceivable aspect of music making. For the study of music history, however, recording has one principal barrier—no recordings exist before the very end of the nineteenth century. Through the study of mechanical instruments, one can gather valuable information about tempo, ornamentation, perhaps even dynamics, from as far as the early eighteenth century, but nothing on what singing voices sounded like, and very little about how instruments were played by musicians, combined with other instruments, and how they sounded in venues. Few studies of recorded performance seek to generalize about what instruments sounded like in the past, what sounds instrument builders in the past tried to achieve, or what people in the past actually heard (Tai and Chung 2012; Caselli, Cecchi, Malacarne, and Masetti 2020). All the rarer are cases where the results of such studies return to the domain of music performance and inform performance practice.

Study of the sound produced by early instruments and their copies can nonetheless shed light on issues of instrumentation. Studying the spectrum of instrument sounds can provide a solid basis for making decisions while arranging music for these instruments. Thus, the differences between the modern flute and the traverso, for example, while often described figuratively and with metaphor, can actually be examined and quantified. Let us examine the spectra of selected notes played on a traverso and on a modern flute (Figure 6.1). The selected notes (forming a two-octave D-minor arpeggio) represent both low and high registers of the instruments and, in the traverso's case, represent both regular and fork fingerings. All the notes in the figure were played by the same player in one session, using the same recording equipment.[4]

(a)

(b)

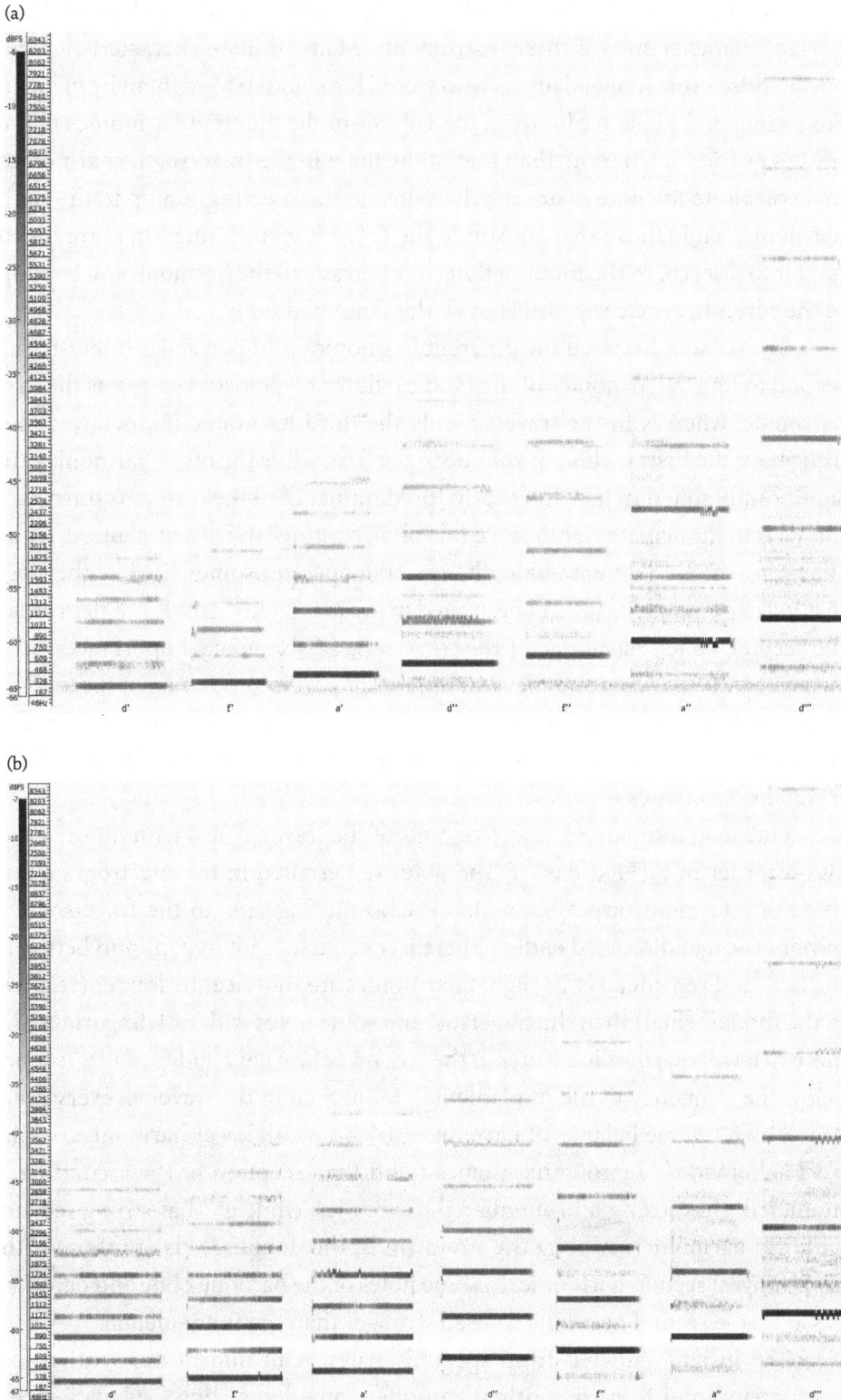

FIGURE 6.1 a. Spectrogram of selected notes played by a traverso. b. Spectrogram of selected notes played by a modern flute.

A comparative analysis of the flute and traverso spectra reveals several important characteristics of these instruments. Many of these characteristics will not surprise professional flautists who would have understood them by instinct. For example, the balance between the volume of the different harmonics in the traverso varies much more than that of the flute: in the traverso, the harmonics that constitute the note d′ are clearly visible in the spectrogram up to the sixth harmonic, while those that constitute the f′ (with its fork fingering) are much harder to discern. In the modern flute, by contrast, all the harmonics, at least up to the seventh, are clearly visible in all the examined notes.

The balance between the different harmonics is of particular interest. The second to fourth harmonics of the modern flute are almost as strong as the first harmonic, whereas in the traverso, only the third harmonic (an octave and a fifth above the first) is close in volume to the first, while the other harmonics are significantly softer. In fact, the relative predominance of the traverso's third harmonic is of immediate significance for "orchestrating" the instrument. As far as "blending in" with an ensemble, the traverso operates somewhat like the clarinet in later ensembles (as will be argued in greater detail). This is not to say that the second, softer, harmonic of the traverso is of secondary importance—it is excited by overblowing and plays an important part in producing of the second octave. Matejová's (2020) recent study on the possibilities the traverso offers for contemporary music shows the irregularities (both in timbre and pitch) of the traverso's harmonics.

One may compare the spectrograms of the traverso also with those of the alto recorder in F (Figure 6.2).[5] The notes represented in the spectrogram are those of a G-minor arpeggio, which is close in fingering to the traverso's D-minor arpeggio discussed earlier. There is, of course, a lot in common between the flute and recorder, yet its higher harmonics are significantly louder (relative to the fundamental) than the traverso's, and some notes with fork fingerings are quite rich with harmonics. Notes in the second octave have audible "airy" sound below the frequency of the fundamental. More than in the traverso, every note has its own unique balance of harmonics: b′♭ has weak lower harmonics, while b″♭ has remarkably strong harmonics (with the exception of the second harmonic); d″ has strong odd-numbered harmonics, while g‴ has strong second and fifth harmonics. Among the woodwinds, the double reeds are those with the strongest second harmonic. In some notes of the baroque oboe and baroque bassoon, the second harmonic is even stronger than the fundamental.

The insight gathered from spectral analysis can inform our writing for instruments, and in early music it can offer some interesting explanations to decisions that early composers made, probably by intuition. Telemann, for example, when combining the flute and recorder, time and again demonstrated awareness of the traverso's third harmonic and its predominance over the second. In his Quatuor for recorder, two traversos, and basso continuo,

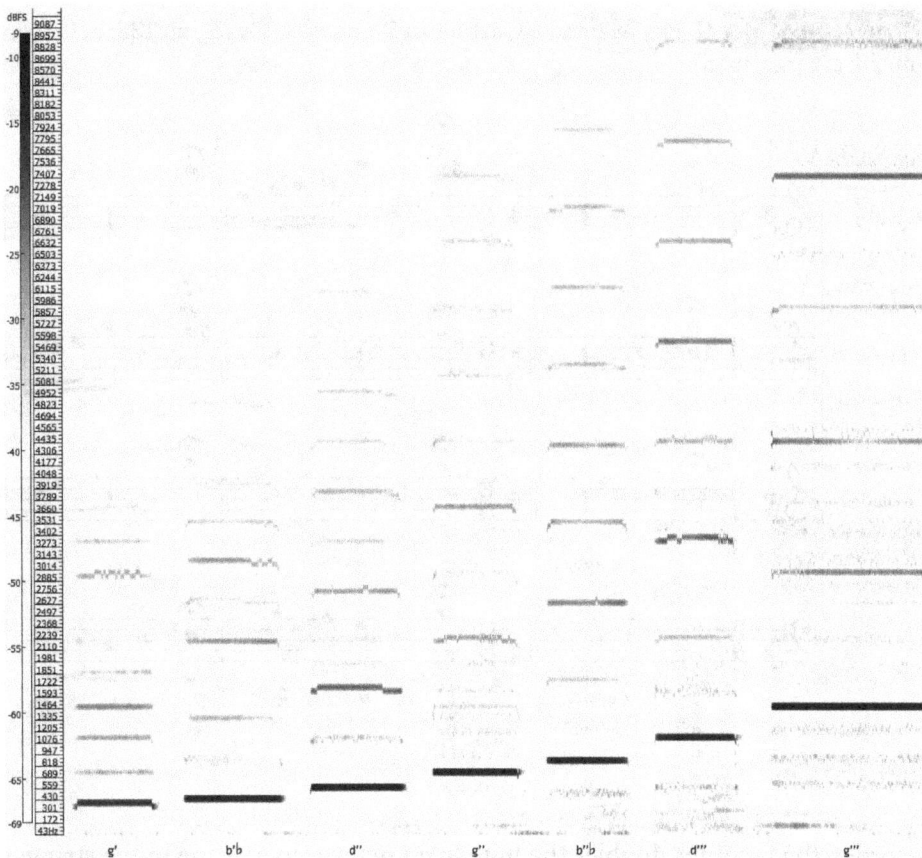

FIGURE 6.2 Spectral analysis of selected notes played by a recorder.

Telemann three times puts the music into halt on a tense seventh chord, once in the second movement and twice in the third (Example 6.2). All three dramatic chords end, quite unusually, when one or two instruments stop before the others. In the two cases from the third movement (marked 2. and 3.), those instruments that resume the music after the fermata also stop earlier, perhaps to allow the players to breath. In the chord from the second movement (marked 1.), traverso I (playing the third of the chord with a trill) stops before the others but, unlike the other examples, here traverso I does not play immediately after the fermata. The reason it stops earlier may be the curious spacing of the chord—A in the bass, g‴ (almost four octaves above the bass) in the recorder, and in between them e″ and the shortened c#″ in the traverso. It is possible that Telemann was sensitive to the spectral properties of the traverso and wanted to avoid the collision of the strong harmonic g#‴ (the third harmonic of traverso I's c#″) and the recorder's g‴, for which reason he shortened the duration of the traverso's note.[6]

If we assume that Telemann considered such issues, then even some of his innocent-looking octave doubling may be more sophisticated than they seem. In the famous "bagpipe" passage from his E minor concerto for traverso and

EXAMPLE 6.2 G. Ph. Telemann, Quatuor in D minor. a. Vivace, m. 135; b. Largo, m. 28; c. Largo, m. 52

recorder, the recorder doubles the flute in an octave (to a drone in the strings), which creates an overall effect that could be compared to that of the organ: if the traverso acts as an 8′ register, then its second harmonic (equivalent of a 4′ register) would be weak, but its third harmonic (equivalent of a 3′ register) would be clearly audible. The recorder thus completes the missing 4′ register and adds a 2′ register to the rich sound mixture.

With some early instruments, discussion of their spectral profile must take into consideration the medium in which the instrument is heard by the audience. The most extreme example would be the clavichord, an instrument practically unusable in concert, but of great expressive powers when recorded. Indeed, combining it with other instruments, while impossible in concert, is possible in the studio, but this would require an unnatural balance between microphones—the clavichord would have to be significantly amplified compared to almost any other instrument. Most record producers would hesitate to create a listening experience so far removed from historical performance practice.

When recorded solo, the sound of the clavichord may be completely redesigned. While some historically informed performers seek to reconstruct the actual standing distance from the instrument (and its implication on the overall volume),[7] some artists take a whole new approach to the instrument—which is most easily done outside of historically informed circles. Arguably the most celebrated example is Keith Jarrett's *Book of Ways* (1987), recorded on two clavichords with close miking (and with some left-right separation), allowing the listener to hear the instrument's sound in a way that is even more intimate than the player would experience.

Similarly, the double-manual harpsichord's ability to simultaneously combine some notes played "single" (one string per key) and some "double" (two strings per key) offers a lot when recorded "inside the instrument," certainly more than in a venue. In robust concert conditions, the harpsichord can be amplified, as for example in Penderecki's Partita (1971).

The early instrument whose spectral subtleties are most challenging to convey through recording is the church organ. The challenge is philosophical, not less than it is technical: for the church organ, the acoustics of the venue, the church wherein the instrument is installed, are usually considered by the organ builder. The sound of the instrument is therefore finalized on-site when the builder has the ability to evaluate the influence of the particular space on the instrument. For that reason, close miking, while it gives the listener an illusion of extreme proximity to an early instrument, also compromises the builder's intentions more than with any other instrument.

Virtual organs are among the most impressive musical instruments invented in recent decades. The virtual organ is essentially a computer program that consists of a very rich library of samples taken from a real organ, with a user interface that imitates that of a real organ—allowing to operate features similar to those of a real organ (choice of registers or combinations thereof, keyboard coupling, control of physical devices such as the swell box or the tremulant) through a MIDI console with multiple keyboards and a pedal keyboard, and without going to the venue where the sampled instrument is installed. For organists specializing in early music, the virtual organ allows not only to play samples of actual historical instruments, but also to experiment with register mixtures, adjust the instrument's basic pitch, and adjust its temperament without effort. As liberating as virtual organs may be for the historically informed, they also challenge the ideology and the aesthetic of the early music movement in every possible aspect: their interface (the MIDI keyboard) is invariably modern and their sound source is digital. In fact, they might intuitively evoke the perennial Bach-would-have-loved-the-synthesizer argument, so often argued against the historically informed cause.

Other questions regarding the virtual organ are slightly more practical: if the sound of the sampled instrument contains not only the sound source (the historical organ pipe) but also the venue where that sound source is installed (including its acoustics), how can that instrument be joined in ensemble that sound in another venue, characterized by its own acoustics? If one managed to sample an organ with close miking, filter out any trace of the original organ-venue's reverberation and reflection, and then recorded that organ with other instruments, adding artificial reverberation of another venue, that might create a pleasingly unified ensemble sound. The philosophical contentions of that venture, however, are not to be dismissed. A specific venue's acoustics are not always an unwanted byproduct imprinted on the resulting sound but rather an integral part of the composer's vision. For example, the score of Vaughan Williams's Fantasia on a Theme by Thomas Tallis (1910) brims with awareness to the long reverberation time of Gloucester Cathedral, where it was planned to be premiered. The lush doublings and accompanying textures of that work might sound too busy if heard from too close to the orchestra or in the sterile, "drier" acoustics of a recording studio. The idea that the addition of "artificial" reverberation to such recording might bring the performance closer to the composer's intentions once again challenges many of the accepted truths about historically informed performance and *Werktreue*.

These questions notwithstanding, some of the most historically informed and historically sensitive ensembles feel that the virtual organ brings them closest to realizing their artistic vision.[8]

The baroque orchestra is another "revived instrument" characterized by the acoustics of the venue in which it plays. In the late 1950s, the Concentus Musicus Wien was virtually the only active baroque orchestra and its unique sound was known to few (the ensemble started recording only in the 1960s). By the mid-1970s there was already a substantial number of baroque orchestras that recorded regularly (and often in churches with rich reverberation), and from whose recordings one could generalize a "baroque orchestral sound."[9] While not many modern works written for baroque orchestras have been recorded, a few famous examples like John Tavener's Eternity's Sunrise (for the Academy of Ancient Music) indicate that, alongside the vibrato-less sound of the 1970s and the 1980s, the reverberating acoustics are a quintessential aspect of what is perceived nowadays as the sound of the baroque orchestra. Similarly, modern composers often experiment with the distinct vocal style identified with early music consort performance. In turn, "early" vocal ensembles' take on vocal repertoire from before the early music revival is often accepted enthusiastically.

Arranging New Music for Old Instruments

After Kagel, both performers and composers felt free to treat the early-ness of early music instruments as secondary to those instruments' sonic properties. Like their colleagues playing "modern" instruments, early music performers today commission new works, and these are very often innocent of "early" influence or themes. Similarly, contemporary composers do not see themselves bound to the traditional instrumentarium of the symphony orchestra. Electronic instruments (both analog and digital), computers, experimental instruments, instruments taken from other genres and cultures, toys, tools, or kitchen utensils—when composers nowadays write for any instrument, they often study its possibilities detached from any historical or social baggage that it may carry.

Modern composers, unlike their renaissance and baroque predecessors, often seem liberated from the obligation to "supply" or "produce" functional music. However, the fact that the number of professional early music performers out in the market is in constant increase also means a relative increase in the number of early music ensembles that demand new repertoire. Even without detailed statistics about the issue, it seems safe to argue that the *recorded* new repertoire for early instruments is but a fraction of a much more substantial repertoire that is written and performed daily by early music ensembles of all ranks. Thus, although they are less "functional" than their predecessors, modern composers do answer a real demand when they write new music written for early instruments.

Even if an ensemble does not perform new music, it can nonetheless attempt to arrange existing music and, unlike the cases described in Chapter 5, that music could be of the twentieth and twenty-first centuries. This opens countless new possibilities in programming a concert.

Arranging new music for old instruments raises the same set of questions that a composer might encounter beginning to write, from scratch, a piece for them: should the players use historical techniques only? Does the instrument signify any historical or social meaning? How can the gap between the renaissance or baroque aesthetics reflected in the instrument's sound (timbre, temperament, tunning) on the one hand, and the modern aesthetics reflected in the music on the other, be bridged?[10] I will examine some of the more practical considerations of arrangement for early instruments on two pieces that represent two stylistic extremes in the music of the 1910s—the first of Anton Webern's Three Little Pieces (1914) and the first of Frank Bridge's Three Miniature Pastorals (1917).

Webern's Three Little Pieces Op. 11 are written for cello and piano. The nine measures of the first one (Example 6.3) allow a brief discussion of the role of sound in arranging modern music (even if, by now, it can hardly be called modern music). Attempting to score the arrangement of the first piece for an ensemble that is close to original—for example a viol and a harpsichord or organ—might yield an unsatisfactory result: the glissando in measure 6 is impossible to execute on the viol, the pianissimo-pianississimo piano part on the harpsichord is unlikely to blend with the viol. A chamber organ might work better than a harpsichord in this case, but it will set rigid limits on the dynamics, a disadvantage in arranging Webern. Moreover, the effect of an organ arpeggio in measures 1 and 4 would be far removed from the gesture Webern must have had in mind. The baroque cello and the fortepiano, although closer to the modern cello and the piano, will inevitably sound like a sorry compromise—their strengths and timbres cannot manifest themselves within Webern's idiosyncratic expressionism.

EXAMPLE 6.3 A. Webern, Three Little Pieces Op. 11, first movement.

In such cases, a scoring concept that is different altogether will allow to distance the arrangement from the original, and to judge the result afresh. An arrangement for traverso, violin, bass viol, lute, and harpsichord (a normal lineup for many a Telemann-based program) will offer the kind of timbral variety that Webern relished in some of his chamber works (Example 6.4).

The traverso's airy sound (resulting, among other reasons, from the spectral structure discussed in the previous section), may achieve an effect that is close to the cello's flageolet in measures 2–3 and 6 (certainly closer than the modern flute)—the last flageolet in measure 7 is bound to sound louder than pianissimo, and the arranger might consider giving it to the violin instead. Yet, in terms of timbre, it could relate to the previous flageolets played by the flute and exploit the timbral variety of the ensemble. The violin is the only instrument in the ensemble that could play the glissando in measure 6, and it is

EXAMPLE 6.4 A. Webern, Three Little Pieces Op. 11, first movement. Arranged for traverso, violin, bass viol, lute, and harpsichord.

EXAMPLE 6.4 Continued

versatile enough to take additional notes in several other contexts. The viol can substitute the cello in the "mit Dämpfer" and "am Steg" passages. The harpsichord and lute, between them, can offer interesting substitutes to some of the gestures in the piano part (and even in the cello). In the example I offer several optional doublings (lute, m. 2, *if* the lute has a low E bass string; violin, m. 2; traverso, m. 3; violin, mm. 4 and 8). These make the melodic gestures of their respective parts more expressive, and make small adjustments to the balance within some of the chords—both considerations are open to debate in the context of arranging Webern, but should be kept in mind when arranging music in general. Indeed, programming Webern's Op. 11 together with Telemann would not, perhaps, be every ensemble's first choice, but it is important to remember that, at least after the spectral experiments of the 1960s, it is possible at least to consider such arrangements.

Frank Bridge's Three Miniature Pastorals are diametrically opposite to Webern's Little Pieces. It is a set of Schumannesque piano miniatures (perhaps reminiscent of Kinderszenen) and, in its first edition, each of the three pastorals is accompanied by an engraved sketch, as naïve as the miniatures themselves. The first sketch is of two rural figures, a boy sitting on a branch of a tree and playing his pipe, and a girl in a simple dress dancing to the boy's tune. Let us take Bridge's cue and take the recorder as the early instrument closest to the pipe. To avoid an all-too-mechanical transcription, we will not take the harpsichord to accompany the recorder but the lute.

The pastoral is written in ABA′ form (Example 6.5). The first question that arises is that of the key—the A and A′ sections are set in F♯ minor and the B section in A major. These keys are slightly too "sharp" to fit the recorder, as well as for the lute—tuning problems could be expected even before the first note was played. A minimal transposition a semitone up will set the piece in a more natural key for both instruments.[11]

Section A lends itself to almost-literal transcription—the recorder plays the melody, which is easily distinguishable and nicely set in the best range of the treble recorder. The accompaniment, in flexible two- and three-part texture, works with almost no modification on the lute (Example 6.6). The inner part in measures 9–14 has to be transposed down—keeping it in its original octave is possible with some effort, but it is important not to exhaust the upper register of the lute so early in the piece, and leave some room for development toward section A′.

Had Bridge written the work for lute in tablature, the duration of many of the notes would have been left for the lute player to decide. Thus, tying notes whenever possible (Example 6.7) would sound more sonorous and idiomatic on the lute, although in A′ Bridge notates ties explicitly. One should decide if the more sonorous accompaniment should not be left for later in the piece.

Section B breaks the continuity of the melody—the left hand maintains the eighth-note motion but without a distinctive melody, while the right hand provides only sustained chords. The instinct to retain the same division of roles

EXAMPLE 6.5 F. Bridge, Three Miniature Pastorals, first movement.

EXAMPLE 6.5 Continued

EXAMPLE 6.5 Continued

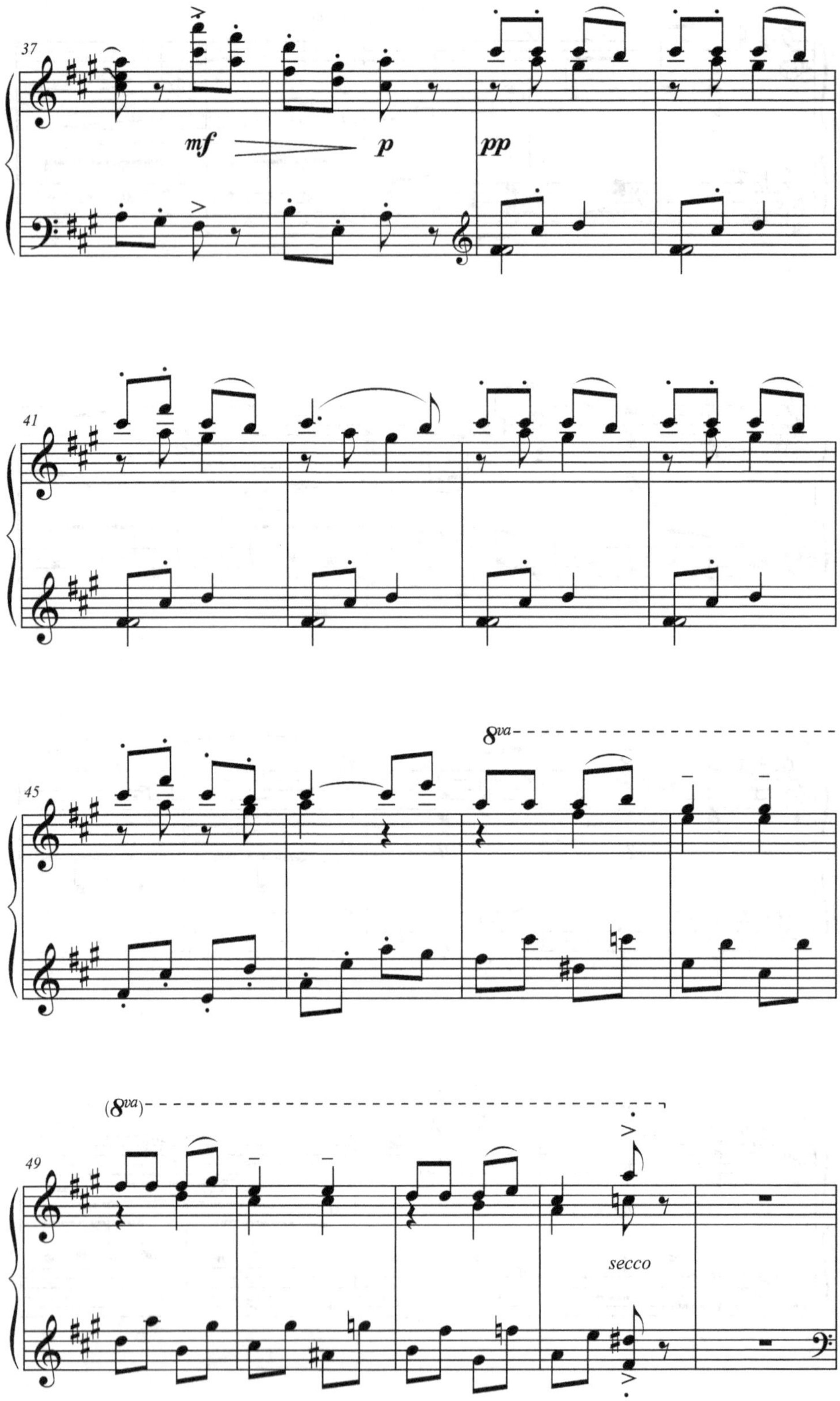

EXAMPLE 6.5 Continued

EXAMPLE 6.6 Bridge, Three Miniature Pastorals, first movement, mm. 1–21. Transcribed for alto recorder and lute (literally transcribed from the original piano part).

as in section A (the recorder playing the melody and the lute accompanying) breaks up the musical phrases somewhat artificially (Example 6.8). Moreover, since the following eight measures (mm. 30–37) transpose the preceding eight up an octave, these would sound far less idiomatic and "simple"—both for the recorder and for the lute. In fact, that the responsibility to convey the harmony falls on the shoulders of the lute part exclusively makes the lute part less idiomatic.

It is therefore preferable to use the melodic fragment in measures 24–25 to start a quasi-improvised part melody where Bridge (who already uses the left hand for the bass and the right hand for sustained chords) simply could not

EXAMPLE 6.7 Bridge, Three Miniature Pastorals, first movement, mm. 1–21. Arranged for alto recorder and lute, lute part adapted to contain tied notes.

EXAMPLE 6.8 Bridge, Three Miniature Pastorals, first movement, mm. 22–29. Arranged for alto recorder and lute.

add one. By doing so, at least from measure 26 onward, the "improvisatory" recorder part can help in conveying the harmony (and water down the lute accompaniment) (Example 6.9). By manipulating the quasi-improvisation, an element that was not in the original, it is possible to convey a sense of climbing up to the top note of the piece (the f''' in m. 36). That is, indeed, an important principle in arrangement—if the composer did not supply enough material to manipulate, bring your own.

EXAMPLE 6.9 Bridge, Three Miniature Pastorals, first movement, mm. 22–37. Arranged for alto recorder and lute (alternative).

Section A′ begins with a transposition of measures 1–13 (with slight changes in articulation). Again, trying to apply the same transposition to the recorder and lute version would result in climbing to the recorder's top register (which is all but the pianissimo that the composer wants here) and, for the lute, even beyond (Example 6.10a). Again, the arranger should seek alternatives for creating a softer sound. One such option is to swap the parts—to let the recorder play the drone bass, and the lute play the melody (Example 6.10b).

Bridge's ongoing involvement with folk music, and the relatively traditional use of the recorder and the lute that our arrangement allows, brings us to another common modern use of early instruments—performance of folk or folk-inspired repertoire. Similarities between early music and folk music stem from the fact that both are, to a large extent, the fruit of revival movements. One cannot rule out the possibility that playing techniques identified with Irish trad music or classical Andalusian music were in use in Europe during the renaissance (Shull 2006)—indeed, some of the most inspiring achievements of the early music revival were inspired by that notion—and yet, any stylistic similarity of that kind is essentially conjectural. Some renaissance and baroque repertoires seem to address contemporary folk idioms (the term "folk" is of course an anachronism in this case), but these might be sophisticated commentaries on, rather than faithful documentation and notation of, genuine early folk music (see, for example, Milsom 2017 on the "Cries" genre).

EXAMPLE 6.10 a. Bridge, Three Miniature Pastorals, first movement, mm. 38–45. Arranged for alto recorder and lute. b. Bridge, Three Miniature Pastorals, first movement, mm. 38–45. Arranged for alto recorder and lute (alternative).

Early music performers, throughout the various "waves" of the early music revival, seem to have modeled their aesthetic on what they *perceived* to be authentic—a notion that had been shaped by the folk each generation had grown up listening to (Upton 2012). It is therefore interesting to see how some repertoires that are notated very loosely (unaccompanied, without specific instrumentation or indication of tempo and dynamics) are often interpreted as "folk" music. The repertoire of Italian saltarello and istampitta and French estampie became an important case for such folk-music influence since the late 1960s, even if, to quote Thomas Forrest Kelly, "[there] is something fishy about these two repertoires—the very fact that they are written down" (Kelly 2011: 26).

An interesting case study is the song "Western Wind"—a sixteenth-century song that survives in what may be an incomplete form and that was used as a basis for several Tudor Mass cycles. From around the time of the late-1950s folk revival, the song has been repeatedly performed and recorded in the style of a folksong, and its many recordings reflect the changing trends in folksong performance: Richard Dyer-Bennet's and Alfred Deller's recordings (both from 1958) use guitar accompaniment and feature free-modal harmonies, while Isla Cameron's (1962) and Maddy Prior and Tim Hart's (1971) recordings opt for "clean" a cappella renditions. That is also roughly when the song was adopted in its folksong guise by early music performers who perform it either in conjunction with the Mass settings based on it or as an independent ballad.[12]

Not only Tudor songs but also later songs are often stripped of accompaniment in order to make them sound earlier. The song "Johnny has gone for a soldier" (or "Buttermilk Hill"), for example, is often identified with the American Revolutionary War although its refrain ("Shule, shule, shule a gra") discloses its earlier Irish origin. Elegantly harmonized in its iconic performances by Pete Seeger (1961) and by Peter, Paul, and Mary (1963), early music ensembles like the Boston Camerata perform it a cappella and with clean, vibrato-less, vocal production very similar to that used in the aforementioned performances of "Western Wind."[13]

The dividing lines between folk music and early music remain blurry to this day. Many artists explore the possible traces of old styles and practices within oral traditions, seek the roots of oral traditions within early notated repertoire, and interpret early sources in light of traditional techniques and style. Thus, the use of folk- and trad-related techniques on early instruments—like the so-called bowed triplets, finger articulation, and drone accompaniment—and trad-related arrangements is a topic that justifies a study of its own.

Conclusions

Music for revived instruments underwent a fundamental change. In the 1920s, it was a few early music pioneers who were active in the foremost musical centers (and mainly in Europe) and who commissioned several masterpieces from the most celebrated composers of their age. Nowadays the early music revival is a global phenomenon, with thousands of active performers (amateurs, students, and professionals) who commission and perform countless new works.

The emphasis I have given, throughout this chapter, on the spectrum of early instruments reflects only one of several approaches and, not by coincidence, an approach that complements the discussion in previous chapters. Some composers today may take different approaches, for which reason I avoided detailed discussion of more recent compositions—the field is simply too rich to be reduced into a set of rules of thumb (how to write for the upper register of the traverso, or which pitched percussion instruments sound best when they double a violone). Moreover, while the Poulenc or Martinů concertos are by now canonic masterpieces, loved by many and accessible to all, more recent works might not be familiar to all the readers of this book.

The richness of repertoire might encourage one to make broad generalizations and division (indeed, not very different from the imaginary Webern-Bridge divide I implied with relation to the music of the 1910s). One could, for example, imply a rough division between "pastiche" and "modern."

The conclusion, however, comes full circle: in the same way that performers should not read a treatise as a fixed canonic text but accept more fluid texts, so should performers resist the temptation to look up to a "canon" of modern works for early instruments. In the same way that the proliferation of "early" improvisation testifies to the fact that early music is once again a living tradition, so does the phenomenon that so much new music for early instruments is being written and performed and then discarded without gaining a "classic" status testify to the fact that this music once again fills a function in modern concert life. Accepting the temporality of this repertoire may even help us better to understand those sixteenth- or seventeenth-century works that no one expected to survive beyond their first and only performance. Should one's recently premiered song cycle for countertenor, strings, and two lutes have longer shelf life than a Purcell court ode performed alongside it in the same concert?

Revivalist tendencies toward early music, ever since their early manifestations in the eighteenth century, have been negotiating the various tensions between historicism and contemporality. Any attempt to *resolve* those tensions, by way of a compromise between the two poles, runs the risk of weakening the relevance of engagement with early repertoire. The path thus leads us to *embrace* that tension: to give the dead composer the same respect we give to our living audience; to strive for an intimate understanding of the performance experience of centuries ago and, at the same time, to convey that understanding with all media that is available to us today. In many respects, the reverence toward the musical text throughout this book may seem, in some quarters, as reactionary if not downright dangerous. That is possibly true, and yet it helps to balance the hazards of self-indulgence.

Performing new music on early instruments provides one possible way of embracing the tension, as it offers new ways of listening both to the instruments and the music. In fact, early twentieth-century repertory has now become, in itself, subject to historically informed practices. The encounter with that repertory occasions a new set of questions: is there any essential difference between a performers' approach when engaging with Monteverdi's modernism and Webern's? Can Bridge's renaissance-like melos serve to liberate contemporary composers from their ages-old obligation to explore new grounds with every piece they write? After all, if we can "create medieval music" (as argued by Barbara Thornton, see Chapter 2), cannot we also create twentieth-century music? Does musical historicism contain the seeds of its own destruction after all?

The skills I have surveyed throughout the book pertain to the crucial challenge of fashioning one's artistic statement through the crafting of one's own performance material. Where appropriate, I aimed to complete the discussion with a historical examination of various traits and trends in order to illuminate the choices made by earlier generations of early music performers. I hope that my admiration of the movement's pioneers will not be interpreted as naïve nostalgia. The message of the book is essentially a forward-looking and optimistic one, for I firmly believe that there is still a lot to contemplate and much need for further innovation.

The tone of this book is an optimistic one. Looking back at several decades of historically informed performance, it seems that performers and scholars found that modus vivendi that allows the philosophical and the practical to inspire, rather than to paralyze, one another. Like the most fundamental forms of human expression, musicianship finds its outlet and defies barriers, real or imagined.

Notes

Acknowledgments

1. Gresham Lecture, 9 November 2010, https://www.youtube.com/watch?v=idqqnG3Q 5xo, accessed March 15, 2018.

Introduction

1. In the years since Rose published his short essay, it became clear that there is more to the digital future than the availability of recordings and sources. The Covid-19 crisis offered even clearer evidence that the digital sphere is, to some extent, the most stable element of the music business. For a pre-Covid analysis of the uses of social media for the promotion of early music performances, see Lee 2016.

2. https://www.bach-digital.de/.

3. Chapters 3 and 4 of my book may thus be seen as complementing Grier 1996. Grier's book is a primary reading in many courses in music editing, and all of its baroque case studies are based on the music of Johann Sebastian Bach.

4. The ensemble The Cardinall's Musick, for example, was led for several years jointly by a conductor (Andrew Carwood) and a musicologist (David Skinner). In a joint interview, Carwood explained that both he and Skinner "get equal credit on the front of our discs because we think the scholarly input is very important. Yes, the singing's very beautiful and the interpretations are important, but it's the academic work that helps to make us different from other groups." (Robbins 2000: 42). Similarly, according to Judy Tarling, "The idea of having the joint sounding directors of The Parley of Instruments, Roy Goodman and Peter Holman, represent the two sides of the coin—performance and research—presented the perfect solution to a problem: the academic attempting to perform or the performer struggling with the research" (Tarling 2020: 481).

5. See, for example, More Hispano, *Glosas: Embellished Renaissance Music*, CD Carpe Diem CD-16285 (2011); Le Concert Brisé, William Dongois, Sylvestro Ganassi: *La Fontegara* CD RIC 395 (2018)

6. Taverner Consort, Andrew Parrott, *Monteverdi: Mass of Thanksgiving* (Venice 1631), CD EMI Reflexe 54886.

7. Gabrieli Consort, Paul McCreesh, Morales: Requiem: Music for Philip II, CD Deutsche Grammophon Archiv 457597-2 (1998).

8. See, for example, The Hilliard Ensemble's 2004 recording of Machaut's motets, where the ensemble added the following note: "New edition of the motets by Nicky Losseff from the Machaut manuscript A, Paris, Bibliothèque Nationale, MS fonds français 1584." Even if Losseff's edition is not accessible online, the note nonetheless clarifies that the ensemble was using a unique edition.

9. The term "file sharing" itself is bound to become an anachronism. Such may be the case with the witty title *American Popular Music from Minstrelsy to MP3*—a textbook that was originally published in 2003 (not long after the Napster revolution), and whose fifth edition was published in 2017. While the MP3 file format is still supported by

most audio devices, it is no longer synonymous with the file-sharing revolution, and advances in storage technology and browsing speed have made its primary merit—data compression—less crucial for most Internet users.

10. One can find various examples, often expressing astonishment at the possibilities offered by information networks, throughout the past two decades. Two representative examples are Zeichner 2000: 6 and Lee 2016.

11. The long-run implication of that is that performers may use good editions but ignore prefaces and commentaries that often offer information that is significant for them.

12. Some examples composed by the keyboard player Henry Hey, as well as a full-length piano sonata by the pianist and composer Avner Hanani (The Trump Sonata), are accessible on YouTube at the time this book is written.

13. The most famous example is Hitler's bunker scene from the 2004 film *Der Untergang*.

14. Note the certain similarity between that approach, which proliferated way into the 1980s (and, in some quarters, also to this day), and mid-nineteenth century Rankean historical positivism. The comparison is drawn here not so much to dim some historically informed players as outdated, as to hint that historical-positivism may still inspire history-related ventures, two centuries after Leopold von Ranke formulated his ideas.

Chapter 1

1. Thus, many enthusiasts whose acquaintance with a piece of medieval music is limited to a single rendition of it might react to the same piece differently when listening to another performance of it, if they recognize it as the same piece at all. Hence the frustration of those who want to use recordings for teaching music history and must commit to a single performance, lest all their students fail their listening test.

2. See Susan Hellauer's insight from her work with Anonymous IV: "We look for both continuity and variety in the music, and for musical texts which help to illuminate the theme in question. . . . We use either our own transcriptions or good modern editions, and prepare the music to our satisfaction. The order of the pieces and their key relationships are crucial, as are variations in texture and voicing." Interview in Sherman 1997: 43–53 (45–46).

3. The number of surviving copies of each part allows us to estimate the original number of performers. For example, if, sometime in the future, a historically informed orchestra attempts to reconstruct the number of violins in the New York Philharmonic's Schubert performances around the year 2000, it will be possible to do so even without recourse to recorded material and office records. In the digital archives of the New York Philharmonic, one can find five pencil-marked copies of the first violin part of Schubert's Symphony No. 3 (Bärenreiter edition, printed in 1992). Given the standard of two players per desk, one may conclude that ten first violinists took part in performances postdating the printing of that part. https://archives.nyphil.org/index. php/artifact/86906f3e-c413-4be5-94d8-1a05be9c7f8c-0.1.

4. See, for example, Donald Greig's account of the early years of his ensemble, Orlando Consort: "Our reasons for approaching [Oxbridge musicologists] was born of the same pragmatism that would lead one to ask an architect to design a house: musicologists knew much more than we did, were close at hand (this was in the days before the internet and email) and were willing to help (and often *pro bono*)." (Greig 2015; see also Everist 2013.)

5. The measures in Figure 1.1 are unnumbered, but the reader may refer to Example 1.1, where the layout follows that of the original and the measures are numbered.

6. Thiemo Wind, "Eyck, Jacob van," in *Grove Music Online. Oxford Music Online* (Oxford University Press), http://www.oxfordmusiconline.com/subscriber/article/grove/music/09151.

7. As I have shown in relation to Purcell's music, printers were also liable to place types upside down. The resulting text, albeit wrong, could look correct, if it somehow fit the harmony (Schab 2010).

8. John Reading's manuscript, GB-L*bl* R.M. 20.h.9 is discussed in detail in Chapter 3.

9. Henry Purcell, *Fantazias and Miscellaneous Instrumental Music*, Purcell Society Edition, Vol. 31, ed. Michael Tilmouth and Thurston Dart, rev. Michael Tilmouth (London and Sevenoaks: Novello, 1990).

10. In rare cases, composers even wrote ricercari for five or six parts, as in Luigi Battiferri's *Ricercari . . . Opera Terza* of 1669.

11. It is within this context that one may examine Bach's choice of the open-score format for his *Art of Fugue*. Bach's choice was perhaps more nostalgic than his choice of German organ tablature for some of his earlier works, but it is not essentially different. Both systems of notation were standard for keyboard music and became obsolete in as late as Bach's youth. Bach's use of open score in *The Art of Fugue* also does not indicate the "abstract" nature of the piece or its composer's lack of interest in issues of scoring or instrumentation.

12. Dowland added "hold lines" in the Margaret Board Lutebook, which may reflect the pedagogical purposes of that manuscript (Gale 2013).

13. See, for example, Gavito's discussion of the song "Vaghi rai" (Gavito 2015: 197–200).

14. The 'Engloisse' Partbooks, GB-L*bl* Add. MSS 30,839; 39,565–567. See Chapter 5.

15. It is on the same page number in all parts—a very effective way to make sure that all members of the ensemble are playing the same piece. They are literally "on the same page," albeit in different books.

16. GB-C*mc* F-4-35, Set 34/X.

17. See, for example, GB-L*cm* MS 1144, an important, albeit incomplete, set of first violin and bass (the second violin and the viola parts are lost) more or less from the same time as our British Library set. A fragment of Purcell's D minor Aire from the Second Musick in King Arthur is copied without clefs and key signatures onto a curved freely sketched staff on the blank folio 1r. The copied passage has one measure missing from its viola part and it seems that the copyist realized that there is "something wrong" in the part writing of the air and decided to copy the parts into a score in order to find a proper solution. Indeed, the fragment looks as if it was used for trial and error.

Chapter 2

1. LP English Medieval Christmas Carols, the Primavera Singers of the New York Pro Musica Antiqua, Counterpoint CPT-521.

2. Program Notes, New York Pro Musica: Florentine Medieval and Renaissance Music, 12 November 1965, University Musical Society, University of Michigan. http://ums.aadl.org/ums/programs_19651112e.

3. Program Notes, New York Pro Musica: Florentine Medieval and Renaissance Music, 14 February 1964, University Musical Society, University of Michigan. http://ums.aadl.org/ums/programs_19640214b.

4. Diego Ortiz: Recercadas del Tratado de Glosas (1553) Primera versión integral, Colección de Música Antigua Española/XIV, Casademunt, Gálvez, Savall (LP Hispavox, HHS 7, 1970); Diego Ortiz: Recercadas, Atrium Musicae De Madrid, Paniagua

(Harmonia Mundi France HM 2.393, 1979); Diego Ortiz: Recercadas del Trattado de Glosas 1553, Savall, Koopman, Duftschmid, Lislevand, Pandolfo, Lawrence-King (CD Astrée (Auvidis) E 8717, 1990)

5. The authors mentioned here are often grouped together as those whose treatises deal with ornamentation in melodic instruments like the viol, violin, recorder, or cornetto. Other authors, even if fewer, addressed similar topics in relation to so-called perfect instruments like the lute (Galilei) and the keyboard (Diruta).

6. I use scare quotes (to refer to "Proper" works, as opposed to examples taken from treatises) since the Work concept (to use Goehr's term) matured only significantly later. Nonetheless, there seems to be vast differences in the (original) use, character, and patterns of circulations between the two types of musical materials.

7. Some of his terminology is confusing. Ortiz calls the technique of embellishing a written melody "sobre el Libro," a term that usually denotes the improvisation of a counterpoint to a written melody. Moreover, Ortiz calls the unembellished melody to be improvised "sobre el Libro," by the term "canto llano" (plainsong), even though he explicitly mentions the relevance of his technique to "all the parts" of a polyphonic piece rather than just to plainsong ("y en todas las partes que quisiere glosar haga desta manera"). The cadential formulae embellished by Ortiz are also more characteristic of polyphony rather than of plainsong.

8. Similarly, the ascending minor sixth and the ascending octave, sometimes found in the repertoire, need not be checked as they are equivalent to the descending third and the unison respectively.

9. Some intervals may work with both variants.

10. From ascending fifth to descending fifth (nine intervals in total), and the contrapuntal potential of the ascending fifth and fourth is essentially identical to that of the descending fourth and fifth respectively (which narrows the list down to seven essential scenarios).

Chapter 3

1. For example, the work with the Newberry Partbooks yielded Alamire's album *Madrigals for a Tudor King*, with the partbooks serving as the framework of that album's concept. Similarly, the book *Musica quinque vocum motteta materna lingua vocata* (Venice, 1543) yielded Musica Secrata and Celestial Sirens' album *Lucrezia Borgia's Daughter*. Countless other recordings are based on the Cantigas de Santa Maria, the Llibre Vermell de Montserrat, the Cancionero del Palacio, Codex Buranus, the Eton Choir Book, the Fitzwilliam Virginal book, and other important sources.

2. The prominence of recordings in the transmission of the late medieval dances is implied by the little tempo variance their recordings show.

3. Indeed, those who search for "Anonymous" in a streaming service would find a very prolific, and stylistically varied, composer.

4. GB-L*bl* Zweig MS 63, f.18v–19r.

5. This can be examined by all on folio 34r of the digitized autograph in url: http://www.bl.uk/manuscripts/FullDisplay.aspx?ref=Add_MS_30930.

6. A similar case may be seen with Margaret Laurie's correction of what she perceived as a mistake in the *Ayres* version of the music to "Distress'd Innocence" (Schab 2009: 642).

7. Bach's main autographs and copies, including the sources for the two concertos, are freely accessible on https://www.bach-digital.de/.

8. Brüggen's original sleeve notes in German elaborate on the decision to avoid the later versions in the Le Cène print: "Das Bläserkolorit in den 'Venezianischen' Konzerten sowie ihre Spezialeffekte . . . strahlen eine wohltuende Unbürgerlichkeit aus, die man in den spätern 'Amsterdamer' Versionen vergeblich sucht, in denen die Bläserpartien in brave Streicherstimmen umgewandelt wurden und wo nach Bedarf eine Viola hinzukam, um einen quasi 4stimmigen Streichersatz zu erhalten. Außerdem sind diese Arrangements matt und unmusikalisch. Gerade diese Eigenschaften treffen aber für Vivaldi nicht zu. Vermutlich sind sie im Auftrag aber ohne Aufsicht Vivaldis von einem Kopisten angefertight worden. Wir sahen deshalb keine Veranlassung, diese Version einzuspielen." RCA Seon RL 30392. In the booklet of the CD reissue of the recording (Sony Seon SBK62945), Brüggen's blunt criticism of the Le Cène print is silenced, and his choice of the earlier concertos is mentioned in passing: "On the present recording, Frans Brüggen returns to the original, far more colourful Venetian versions of the concertos, restoring the first two to recorder."

9. Concentus Musicus Wien, Nikolaus Harnoncourt, *Concentus In Concert: Holland Festival*, LP Telefunken SAW 9626-M (1974).

10. A third "La Notte," the Bassoon concerto RV501, is unrelated to the two concertos discussed here.

11. Probably suspecting that the flat sign is omitted because of the key signature with only one flat, some editors do add an editorial flat sign on the viola's e'. Antonio Vivaldi, *Six Flute Concertos, Op. 10 in Full Score: With Related Concertos for Other Wind Instruments*, ed. Eleanor Selfridge-Field (Mineola, NY: Dover, 2002); Antonio Vivaldi, *Concerto in Sol minore F. VI no 13,* Vol. 455, ed. Gian Francesco Malipiero (Milan: Ricordi, 1949).

12. The clearest argument for interchanging the two readings appears in Michala Petri's recording of Op. 10 with the Academy of St. Martin-in-the-Fields and directed by Iona Brown. In that recording, the violas' e' appears as an e'♮ in measure 16 but as an e'♭ in measure 18.

13. See earlier discussion of autograph GB-L*bl* Add. MS 30,930 and of Sonata Z. 809.

Chapter 4

1. At the time of writing this book, the Toccata features among Frescobaldi's top five "tracks" on Spotify.

2. Jian Wang, Camerata Salzburg, *The Baroque Album*, CD Deutsche Grammophon 00028947423621 (2003).

3. The English Concert, Trevor Pinnock, *Johann Sebastian Bach: 6 Brandenburg Concertos / 4 Orchestral Suites*, CD Archiv Production 423 492-2 (1988; Brandenburg Concertos originally released as LP 2742003 in 1982); the English Concert, Trevor Pinnock, *Johann Sebastian Bach: Konzerte für Cembalo und Streicher*, LP Archiv Production 2533 467 (1981).

4. Academy of Ancient Music, Richard Egarr, *Handel: Organ Concertos Op. 7*, CD Harmonia Mundi HMU 807447.48 (2009); Academy of Ancient Music, Richard Egarr, *Handel: Trio Sonatas Op. 2 & Op. 5*, CD Harmonia Mundi HMU 907467.68 (2009).

5. Their only engagement with English music earlier than Purcell for the *Trésor* was but two years later, in their edition of *Parthenia* in the sixth volume, and there they also seem to eliminate false relations that appear in the original print.

6. The Works of Henry Purcell, Vol. 6 (1895) and J. & W. Chester (1912).

7. University-library copies, often transmitting pencil markings made by students and lecturers, are valuable primary sources when researching into the reception of the printed text. During the preparation of this chapter, I found a library copy of Ferguson's edition with the c‴, rightly corrected by Ferguson, crossed out by an arrogant reader and replaced with an a″, thus taking a step back to Barclay Squire, if not to Pauer and Farrenc.

8. An added natural appears in several recordings, for example the Jacobean Consort's 1956 recording and the Purcell Quartet's 1988 recording.

9. In Purcell's work, the choral repetition of Sleep's air "Hush, No More" from *The Fairy Queen* (1692) slightly expands the verse as it is sung by the bass just before. Marais's Plainte in G minor (from the *Pieces en Trio* of 1692, the same year of *The Fairy Queen*) is built in ABB′ form, but the only difference between the first and second B sections is that one measure in the repetition is harmonically intensified. The premier dessus part is even given a repeat sign, so that the performer has no reason to suspect that the repetition is modified at all. The deuxième dessus and the bass parts are written as if through composed—the difference in one note only in each of these two parts was important enough to justify engraving the sixteen measures of the phrase again.

10. For example, Barclay Squire's implied rule that false relations must adhere to voice-leading rules or, to take a hypothetical example, one may conclude, according to one's own grasp of the style, that a false relations cadence will always appear prior to a diatonic cadence in the same key, and never on the final cadence of a movement.

11. While limited by their commitment to consistency and clarity, critical editors cannot rely so much on intuition, but they do have the luxury of using the critical commentary to express their doubts. Roger Fiske, in the commentary of his edition, concisely suggests a chain reaction of editorial interventions that result in an all-false-relations reading of the passage: "[Sonata] VIII [measure] 45 Vl. II [note] 1 F natural? (cf. Vl. I's C natural in 37) If so, perhaps [bassus and basso continuo] [note] 1 in [measure 41] should be F natural." Roger Fiske, ed., *Purcell: Sonatas of Three Parts Nos. 7–12* (London: Eulenburg, 1975), ix, 10–11.

12. GB-L*bl* Add. MS *30,930*, f. 59r INV

13. My claim that a score may look pre-Restoration is not dissimilar to Schumann's famous observation about the way scores by different composers also look different on paper. "Überdies, scheint mir, hat jeder Komponist seine eigentümlichen Notengestaltungen für das Auge: Beethoven sieht anders auf dem Papier als Mozart, etwa wie Jean Paulsche Prosa anders als Goethesche" (Schumann 1974: 11).

14. Michael Tilmouth, in the 1990 revision of the edition, made several changes to rhythmic notation but did not change anything in the treatment of accidentals. Thurston Dart, ed., *Fantazias and Other Instrumental Music*, The Works of Henry Purcell, Vol. 31 (London: Novello, 1959); Thurston Dart, ed., and Michael Tilmouth, rev., *Fantazias and Miscellaneous Instrumental Music*, The Works of Henry Purcell, Vol. 31 (London and Sevenoaks: Novello, 1990).

15. Purcell-Warlock, *Fantasias for Strings* (London: Boosey and Hawkes, 1943).

16. Anthony Ford, ed., *Henry Purcell: Fantazias and In Nomines* (London: Eulenburg, 1973).

17. Henry Purcell, *Fantasien für Streichinstrumente*, Vol. 2, ed. Herbert Just (Hannover: Adolph Nagel, 1935), 12–13.

18. CD *Henry Purcell: Fantasias*, Hesperion XX (Astrée E8536).

19. CD *Henry Purcell: Fantasias*, Les Voix Humaines (ATMA ACD22591); CD *Purcell: 15 Fantasien*, La Gamba, Ekkehard Weber (Ars Musici AM11352).

20. The two passages are not mentioned in the "Critical Commentary" in the Purcell Society Edition but are mentioned in Anthony Ford's introduction to his edition of the fantazias. Anthony Ford, ed., *Henry Purcell: Fantazias and In Nomines* (London: Eulenburg, 1973), vi.

21. The phenomenon of enharmonic misspelling was not unique to English consort music. Field explores its manifestations in Italian vocal music. For instrumental music, one can refer to Giovanni Paolo Cima's *essampi*—eleven transpositions of ten-measure phrase into all keys—from his *Partito de Ricercari* (Milan, 1606), in order to observe how enharmonic misspelling took different forms in other genres and places. By contrast, even in works that probably explore the merits of meantone temperament, such as Louis Couperin's Pavanne in F♯ minor (Bauyn MS, F-Pn Rés, Vm7 675, f. 73), composers had no reservations about explicitly notating E♯ and A♯, even when they were supposed to sound as an F or B♭ respectively. Christopher D. S. Field, "Jenkins and the Cosmography of Harmony," 9–13. Giovanni Paolo Cima, *Partito de Ricercari & Canzoni Alla Francese* (Milan: Tini & Lomazzo, 1606); modern edition in Clare G. Rayner, ed., *Giovanni Paolo Cima: Partito de Ricercari & Canzoni alla Francese (1606)*, Corpus of Early Keyboard Music, Vol. 20 (Neuhausen-Stuttgart: Hänssler, American Institute of Musicology, 1966).

22. For example, Thurston Dart's thesis, arguing that the upper parts of the fantazias were intended for violins and the lower parts for viols (Dart 1958–1959: 90–91).

Chapter 5

1. Such cases are more common than one would think. In fact, most of Bach's works for *Clavier* are interpreted as works for either the harpsichord or the clavichord on the basis of their implied instrumental idiom rather than on any direct evidence.

2. Acceptance of the fundamental notion that Bach, to take the most iconic example, would have accepted the transcription of his works to other instruments need not necessarily lead to the conclusion that he would have loved the modern piano or the synthesizer, but the frequent misuse of the fluidity of instrumentation does not shake its essential validity.

3. This is exactly what Francesco Geminiani did in his *Concerti Grossi . . . Composti delli Sei Sonate del Opera Terza D' Arcangelo Corelli* (London, 1735). When publishing the new concertos, the publisher John Walsh based the *concertino* part books on his own previous printing of Corelli's Op. 3.

4. On a personal note, I must stress that my appreciation of some non-historical arrangement is sincere. Tedi Papavrami's transcriptions of Scarlatti's keyboard sonatas are, for example, among the most original and imaginative arrangements I have encountered, even if Scarlatti, and most of his contemporaries, would not have encountered a keyboard sonata transcribed for solo violin, let alone involving techniques that would have been cultivated about a century later.

5. Daniel Barenboim, "I Was Reared on Bach," http://danielbarenboim.com/i-was-reared-on-bach.

6. Some historically informed ensembles arrange music in a way that is modern in the sense that it adopts a critical scholarship-inspired vantage point. Mala Punica's recording of chansons from the Modena Codex is a good example: it is hard to say if the "a" section of Caserta's ballade "Beauté parfait" would have been performed six times in a row in the fifteenth century. In Mala Punica's rendition it is performed thus; instrumentally, first by the tenor alone, then joined by the cantus, and

finally by the contratenor; and moving from a rhythmically simplified version toward the complicated rhythms as they appear in the manuscript. Whatever the historical validity of such complicated arrangement, it provides a historically informed statement *about* the rhythmic complexity of the Ars Subtilior chanson.

7. Hypotheses regarding composers' tastes are commonly invoked in order to justify the use of instruments invented after their lifetime. While it may be helpful to use concrete examples of recorded arrangements to demonstrate some of the points raised in this chapter, criticizing specific recordings of the past two decades belongs, in my opinion, in the record reviews section in the relevant journals. In light of the principals unfolded here, one may justly assume that I find many recent recordings too "loose" in the scholarship they exhibit. References to "canonic" recordings older than twenty years appear only occasionally in this chapter's discussion.

8. Robert Rawson, *Princess Anne's "Hoboys": New Perspectives on an Elusive Court Band* (forthcoming).

9. Sensitivity to the "sound" of the ensemble—a rather amorphous term that usually encapsulates timbre, volume, and balance—might play a different role for a composer than for an arranger. For a baroque composer writing a piece from scratch, timbre was but one consideration (and not even a primary one) among several others, including melody, counterpoint, harmony, form, and scoring. Arrangers, for whom all these primary issues were givens, had only to worry about the scoring and the way that scoring would sound. It would thus be fair to expect arrangements to reflect an awareness of and attention to issues of sound. Such, however, was not always the case.

10. In four-part writing, of course, this problem does not occur, since the tenor may add any missing note.

11. Alonso Mudarra, *Tres Libros de Musica en Cifras para Vihuela* (Seville, 1546), Fol. 13r–15r.

12. On Fol. 14v [erroneously paginated 13v] and 15r: "Des de aquí hasta açerca del final ay Algunas falsas tañiendo se bien no pareçen mal."

13. Performing the violin part on the flute, for example, requires frequent transposition in the octave where Rameau indicates. One also needs to decide, in case of double stops in the violin, which of the two notes to perform. Rameau does not give sufficient details about performing the viol part on a second violin.

14. This is, of course, not the only case of a baroque piece that survives in two or more scorings, but the fact that in Rameau's *Pièces de clavecin*, both were published at the same time, in the same publication medium, and with the same stamp of authority, makes the comparison clearer.

15. Jean-Philippe Rameau, *Pièces de clavecin en concerts, avec un violon ou une flûte, et une viole ou un deuxième violon* (Paris, 1741), [i]; Jean-Philippe Rameau, *Pièces de clavecin avec une méthode pour la mécanique des doigts . . .* (Paris, 1724), [ix]. It is worth noting that while Rameau referred his readers to a previously published table of ornaments, subsequent foreign editions did not always supply such references, as is the case with the Walsh edition of 1750 (see Sadler 2020: 458–461).

16. Jean-Philippe Rameau, *Pièces de clavecin avec une méthode*, [9].

17. In Hotteterre's book the same ornament appears as *coulement* in the context of notation for the flute.

18. Jean-Philippe Rameau, *Zoroastre: Tragedie, mise en musique* (Paris, n.d.), 98–99.

19. One should avoid mixing up the concept of an abstract model promoted here and the treatment of some works, especially by Johann Sebastian Bach, as "abstract"—usually

with the implicit agenda of downplaying the issue of performing them on modern instruments. See, for example, Glenn Gould's views as expressed in Bruno Monsaingeon's film *Glenn Gould Plays Bach: The Question of Instrument* (1979).

20. Hille Perl, "... per la viola da gamba," CD DHM 05472775152; Anner Bylsma and Bob van Asperen, "J. S. Bach: Sonatas for Viola da Gamba," CD SK 45945.

21. Jean-Philippe Rameau, *Pièces de clavecin avec une méthode pour la mécanique des doigts . . .* (Paris, 1724), 15.

22. The copyist of the manuscript F-Pn VM2-376, who copied the movement into pages 23–24 of the manuscript score, was indeed surprised by this choice of instrument. It is visible that the copyist first wrote "1ʳ Viol." on the top staff, then "2ᵈ Viol." on the next, and then, realizing that the third and bottom staff is given to the second violin, had to go back to the first, wrote over the previous designation, somewhat inelegantly, "Flutes seule." and changed the "2ᵈ" to "1ʳ" on the second staff. https://gallica.bnf.fr/ark:/12148/btv1b10509015s/f31.image.

23. The most famous example of that is Pavan Lachrimae, which survives in three versions. While most scholars agree that the chronological order in which these versions were created was first the lute solo, then the song, and then the version for viol consort, it is impossible to suggest an authoritative earliest date for each version, save the publication dates of the song and the consort version—1600 and 1604 respectively.

24. Two peculiar variants in Wigthorp's arrangement, although they have implications on the rhetorical effect of the song, seem unrelated to the arrangement process, and may simply hint that he worked from a source other than the *Second Booke of Songs* (1600). One variant is the setting of the words "help now or never" is different—ending on b♭ in Dowland's book but climbing up to d″ in the arrangement; another is that the repetition of the phrase "alas I am condemned" is omitted in the arrangement, without any apparent reason.

25. Dowland modified the repetition of the final verse by doubling the length of the climactic d″ (on "and arise I never shall"). The repetition is reproduced in Example 5.14, measures 33–36. The first (and shorter) appearance of the climactic d″ is in measures 27–28, not reproduced here.

26. Both Gerard Lesne and Andreas Scholl revert from Wigthorp's modified spiritual lyrics; Musica Reservata reintroduced the omitted repetition of the final verse in the anonymous version. *Dowland: Ayres*, Gerard Lesne and Ensemble Orlando Gibbons, Naïve E8881 (2004); *Crystal Tears*, Andreas Scholl, Concerto di viole, Julian Behr, Harmonia Mundi HMC901993 (2008); *Metaphysical Tobacco: Songs and Dances by Dowland, East, Holborne*, Musica Reservata and Purcell Consort, Argo RG 572 (1968).

27. https://opacplus.bsb-muenchen.de/title/BV007861799; (Brown 1995); N. S. Lander, *Recorder Home Page: Iconography*. http://www.recorderhomepage.net/recorder-iconography/.

28. Solo piano arrangements of orchestral music are naturally limited. Arrangements for four hands had the advantages both of producing thicker and more complicated textures and of offering a *Hausmusik* experience for those who performed them.

29. For example, few musicians leave the harmony in the fourth bar of the Sarabande from Bach's Partita BWV 1004 untouched when transcribed for the keyboard or for ensemble. Fewer still agree about the specifics of its re-harmonization. Is it {IV₆–II ⁶₅–V of the IV}, as in Wilhelmj's arrangement? {II⁶₄–IV₆–VII⁶₅ of the IV}, as in Leonhardt's arrangement?

{II, of I and VII$^6_\sharp$ of the IV}, as in Gouin's arrangement? Ed. Gustav Leonhardt (Kassel: Bärenreiter, 2017); Ed. Pierre Gouin (Montreal: Les Éditions Outremontaises, 2014).

30. Some organ repertoires that composers intentionally kept simple, both harmonically and contrapuntally, may serve ensembles for other purposes. For example, the "intonazioni" by Andrea Gabrieli or Girolamo Cavazzoni exhibit neither interesting counterpoint nor interesting passagework—they are intended to establish a specific mode for the church choir. When arranged for four melodic instruments, however, they may serve as brilliant etudes. These pieces move, through stock passagework, from one firm chord to another (they are always firm primary chords within the given mode). When arranged for melodic instruments, the ensemble can move between chords in accurate timing (led by whoever takes each passagework) and tune on each chord, with each member getting a different function within a chord.

31. Years after I transcribed the fantasia for recorders, I found another transcription made by someone else (whom I did not know), and the first twenty-five bars of our respective transcriptions were identical, note-for-note.

32. Echo and "*pian e forte*" were central to Giovanni Gabrieli's experiments with the polychoral style.

33. A cursory survey of commercial recordings shows that many performers use substantial rubato, which blurs the asymmetry.

34. Robert Dowland's print was used as the source for the present arrangement. A modern tablature edition may be found in Robinson 1996.

Chapter 6

1. Besides its neoclassicist traits, Schoenberg's Suite usually marks its composer's adoption of strict twelve-tone technique.

2. The viola d'amore is briefly discussed in Berlioz 1844: 39–40 and, in passing, in Prout 1898: 50. Both authors cite the same famous romance from Act I of Meyerbeer's *Les Huguenots*, and both probably thought that the instrument merits mention because of that single piece.

3. De Falla performed the concerto in Paris in May 1927, a few months after Landowska's Barcelona premiere. A photo taken during the rehearsal for the Paris performance shows that, at least during rehearsal, the winds and strings faced the harpsichord, and the flute (Marcel Moyse) sat separately, and closer to the harpsichord. A detailed account of the genesis of the concerto, along with the aforementioned photo, can be found in Hess 2005: 159–166.

4. The recordings were made for this project by Idit Shemer on May 12, 2020. Shemer played a full chromatic scale on both traverso (Alain Weemaels after August Gresner, a′ = 415Hz) and a modern flute (Lillian Burkart, Professional, 14K, a′ = 440Hz). In the chromatic scale on the traverso she differentiated between enharmonic alternatives (for example, recording both g′♯ and a′♭. For the present study I chose seven notes (d′, f′, a′, d″, f″, a″, d‴) from each recording. Shemer recorded c. 4 seconds of each note, using a TASCAM DR-05 machine in home conditions. Spectrogram produced using Sonic Visualiser 3.1.1 (dBV^2 scale). Needless to say, different flute models and subtleties in the execution of each note may yield different spectrograms—a comprehensive study of the topic would require many recordings of several flutes played by several performers, and explore various dynamics and articulations. Within the scope of the present book, I can present but a cursory demonstration of the empirical research into the sound of early instruments.

5. The recordings were made by the author on May 20, 2020. I played a full chromatic scale on an alto recorder (P. v. d. Poel [after Denner], 1980, a′ = 415Hz). I recorded c. 4 seconds of each note, using a Zoom H2 machine in home conditions. Spectrogram produced using Sonic Visualiser 3.1.1 (dBV² scale).

6. Matejová (2020) considers her research into the subtleties of the traverso's harmonic structure as following the example of eighteenth-century author Charles De Lusse (1720–1774), who notates the instrument's harmonics in his *L'Art de la flûte traversière*.

7. See, for example, John Butt's recording of Kuhnau's Biblical Sonatas, where an organ, a harpsichord, and a clavichord perform alternately, and their respective volume levels are proportionate to one another. Therefore, the sonatas played on the clavichord sound significantly softer than those played on the organ and the harpsichord. *Johann Kuhnau: The Biblical Sonatas*, CD Harmonia Mundi USA, HMU 907133 (1995).

8. John Butt, Dunedin Consort, *Monteverdi: Vespers 1610*, Linn CKD 569 (2017).

9. Some of these orchestras, especially those based in London, drew on the same pool of musicians, so the similarity in their overall sound is not surprising.

10. The latter question is, of course, a mirror image of the question with which historically informed performers usually attack their colleagues who focus on later repertory: how can the gap between the romantic aesthetics reflected in the instrument's sound (timbre, temperament, tunning) on the one hand, and the early aesthetics reflected in the music on the other, be bridged?

11. If the performers play instruments tuned in a′ = 415Hz, then transposing the piece up by a semitone will set the piece in a key equivalent to F♯ minor (according to a′ = 440Hz).

12. The Tallis Scholars, Peter Phillips, *Taverner, Tye, Sheppard: Western Wind Masses*, Gimmel CDGIM027 (1993); Taverner Choir & Players, *Western Wind: Mass by John Taverner & Court Music for Henry VIII*, Avie AC2352 (2016); Circa 1500, *The Flower of All Ships*, CRD3448 (1987); Sirinu, *Court Jesters*, Griffin GRF-ED-4013 (1996).

13. The Boston Camerata, Anne Azéma, *Free America! Early Songs of Resistance And Rebellion*, HMM 902628 (2019).

References

Adams, Martin (1990). "Purcell's Laudate Ceciliam: An Essay in Stylistic Experimentation." In *Irish Musicological Studies, Vol. 1: Musicology in Ireland*, edited by Gerard Gillen and Harry White, 227–247. Blackrock: Irish Academic Press.

Adler, Samuel (2002). *The Study of Orchestration*. 3rd ed. New York and London: W. W. Norton.

Bach, C. P. E. (1974). *Essay on the True Art of Playing Keyboard Instruments*. Translated and edited by William J. Mitchell. London: Eulenburg Books.

Bagby, Benjamin (2011). "Between Music and Story-telling" [interview with Katarina Šter], http://sequentia.org/writings/music_story-telling.html.

Barenboim, Daniel. (n.d.) "I Was reared on Bach." http://danielbarenboim.com/i-was-reared-on-bach/.

Berlioz, Hector (1844). *Grand traité d'instrumentation et d'orchestration modernes*. Paris: Schonenberger.

Boulez, Pierre (1987). "Timbre and Composition—Timbre and Language." *Contemporary Music Review* 2, no. 1: 161–171.

Brett, Philip (1961–1962). "The English Consort Song, 1570–1625." *Proceedings of the Royal Musical Association* 88: 73–88.

Brover-Lubovsky, Bella (2008). *Tonal Space in the Music of Antonio Vivaldi*. Bloomington and Indianapolis: Indiana University Press.

Brown, Howard Mayer (1995). "The Recorder in the Middle Ages and the Renaissance." In *The Cambridge Companion to the Recorder*, edited by John Mansfield Thomson, 1–25. Cambridge: Cambridge University Press.

Butt, John (2002). *Playing with History: The Historical Approach to Musical Performance*. Cambridge: Cambridge University Press.

Butt, John (2005). "The Seventeenth-Century Musical 'Work.'" In *The Cambridge History of Seventeenth Century Music*, edited by Tim Carter and John Butt, 27–54. Cambridge: Cambridge University Press.

Caldwell, John (1985). *Editing Early Music*. Oxford: Clarendon Press.

Caselli, Gabriele, Giovanni Cecchi, Mirko Malacarne, and Giulio Masetti (2020). "Analysis of Violin Combination Tones and Their Contribution to Tartini's Third Tone." *Savart* 1, no. 9. Retrieved from https://SavartJournal.org/articles/29/article.pdf.

Cypess, Rebecca (2020). "Arrangement Practices in the Bach Tradition, Then and Now: Historical Precedent for Modern Practice." *Journal of Musicological Research* 39, no. 2–3: 187–212.

Dart, Thurston (1958–1959). "Purcell's Chamber Music." *Proceedings of the Royal Musical Association* 85: 81–93.

Dart, Thurston (1967). *The Interpretation of Music*. 4th ed. London: Hutchinson University Library.

Dirksen, Pieter (1997). *The Keyboard Music of Jan Pieterszoon Sweelinck: Its Style, Significance and Influence*. Utrecht: VNM.

Dolan, Emily I. (2013). *The Orchestral Revolution: Haydn and the Technologies of Timbre*. Cambridge: Cambridge University Press.

Elders, Willem (2013). *Josquin des Prez and His Musical Legacy: An Introductory Guide.* Leuven: Leuven University Press.

Everist, Mark (2013). "Singers, Scholars and the Performance of Medieval Polyphony." *Early Music* 41, no. 1: 44–48.

Ferand, Ernest Thomas (1961). *Improvisation in Nine Centuries of Western Music: An Anthology with a Historical Introduction.* Köln: Arno Volk.

Field, Christopher D. S. (1996). "Jenkins and the Cosmography of Harmony." In *John Jenkins and His Time: Studies in English Consort Music*, edited by Andrew Ashbee and Peter Holman, 1–74. Oxford: Clarendon Press.

Gale, Michael (2013). "John Dowland, Celebrity Lute Teacher." *Early Music* 41, no. 2: 219–237.

Gale, Michael, and Tim Crawford (2004). "John Dowland's 'Lachrimae' at Home and abroad." *The Lute* 44: 1–35.

Gavito, Cory M. (2015). "Oral Transmission and the Production of Guitar Tablature Books in Seventeenth-Century Italy." *Recercare* 27, no. 1/2: 185–208.

Girdlestone, C. M. (1958). "Rameau's Self-Borrowings." *Music & Letters* 39, no. 1: 52–56

Godwin, Joscelyn (1974). "Playing from Original Notation." *Early Music* 2, no. 1: 15–19.

Gollin, James (2001), *Pied Piper: The Many Lives of Noah Greenberg.* Hillsdale, NY: Pendragon Press.

Greig, Donald (2015). "Sightlines and Tramlines: The Orlando Consort at 25." *Early Music* 43, no. 1: 129–144.

Grier, James (1996). *The Critical Editing of Music: History, Method and Practice.* Cambridge: Cambridge University Press.

Haskell, Harry (1988). *The Early Music Revival: A History.* London: Thames and Hudson.

Haynes, Bruce (2007). *The End of Early Music: A Period Performer's History of Music for the Twenty-First Century.* Oxford: Oxford University Press.

Herissone, Rebecca (2000). *Music Theory in Seventeenth-Century England.* Oxford: Oxford University Press.

Hess, Carol A. (2005). *Sacred Passions: The Life and Music of Manuel de Falla.* Oxford and New York: Oxford University Press.

Hoffmann, Bettina (2004). "Dal concerto alto al concerto basso: accordature delle viole da gamba nell'Italia del Cinquecento." *Recercare* 16: 23–67.

Hogwood, Christopher (2003). "Creating the Corpus: The 'Complete Keyboard Music' of Henry Purcell." In *The Keyboard in Baroque Europe*, edited by Christopher Hogwood, 67–89. Cambridge: Cambridge University Press.

Holman, Peter (1994). *Henry Purcell.* Oxford and New York: Oxford University Press.

Holman, Peter (2001), "Compositional Choices in Henry Purcell's Three Parts upon a Ground." *Early Music* 29, no. 2: 251–261.

Hotteterre, Jacques-Martin (1968). *Rudiments of the Flute, Recorder and Oboe.* Translated by Paul Marshall Douglas. New York: Dover.

Kelly, Thomas Forrest (2011). *Early Music: A Very Short Introduction.* Oxford and New York: Oxford University Press.

Kroll, Mark (2012), "On a Pedestal and under the Microscope: The Arrangements of Beethoven Symphonies by Liszt and Hummel." In *Franz Liszt und seine Bedeutung in der europäischen Musikkultur*, edited by Markéta Štefková, 123–144. Bratislava: Ústav hudobnej vedy SAV, 123–144.

Kuijken, Barthold (2013). *The Notation Is Not the Music: Reflections on Early Music Practice and Performance.* Bloomington and Indianapolis: Indiana University Press.

Lander, N. S. (n.d.) "Recorder Home Page: Iconography." http://www.recorderhomep age.net/recorder-iconography/.

Lebrecht, Norman. "The Revolution Is Over." *Standpoint* (November 2014). https://standpointmag.co.uk/music-november-14-revolution-is-over-norman-lebrecht-christopher-hogwood/.

Lee, Annabelle (2016). "Social Media and the Early Music Industry." *Early Music Performer* 39: 18–25.

Mariani, Angela (2017). *Improvisation and Inventio in the Performance of Medieval Music: A Practical Approach.* Oxford and New York: Oxford University Press.

Matejová, Dorota (2020). "The Limits of Traverso: Exploring the Sound Possibilities of Traverso through Contemporary Music." Research Presentation, The Hague. Also published in https://www.researchcatalogue.net/view/728937/728938.

Milsom, John (2017). "Oyez!: Fresh Thoughts about the 'Cries of London' Repertory." In *Beyond Boundaries: Rethinking Music Circulation in Early Modern England*, edited by Linda Phyllis Austern, Candace Bailey, and Amanda Eubanks Winkler, 67–78. Bloomington and Indianapolis: Indiana University Press.

Morris, Stephen (2004). "William Young's Fantasias a3, by Another Name, Still Sound as Sweet." *Journal of the Viola da Gamba Society of America* 41: 5–35.

Mozart, Wolfgang Amadeus (1962). *Briefe und Aufzeichnungen, Bd. I 1755–1776.* Kassel: Bärenreiter.

Ortiz, Diego (1553). *Tratado de glosas sobre clausulas y otros generos de puntos enla musica de violones.* Rome.

Pinnock, Andrew (1995). "Fairest Isle™: Land of the Scholar-Kings." *Early Music* 23, no. 4 4: 651–665.

Pinnock, Trevor (2013). "Reflections of a 'Pioneer.'" *Early Music* 41, no. 1: 17–21.

Prout, Ebenezer (1898). *The Orchestra: Volume I: Technique of the Instruments.* London: Augner.

Purcell, Henry (1694). "A Brief Introduction to the Art of Descant." In *An Introduction to the Skill of Musick.* 12th ed., edited by John Playford, 85–144. London.

Rameau, Jean-Philippe (1724), *Pièces de clavecin avec une méthode pour la mécanique des doigts . . ..* Paris.

Rifkin, Joshua (2014). "Time Travel and Its Discontents: Historical Performance, Historical Reconstruction, and Culture Tourism." *Journal of the Alamire Foundation* 6, no. 1: 112–120.

Ring, Layton (1996). "'The Missing Bar' in Purcell's 3 Parts upon a Ground." *Consort* 52, no. 2: 92–95.

Robbins, Brian (2000). "Andrew Carwood & David Skinner: Interview." *Goldberg* 13: 40–51.

Robinson, John H. (1996). "The Complete Lute Solos of Gregory Howet." In a supplement to *Lute News: The Lute Society Newsletter* 39, no. 40.

Rose, Stephen (2013). "Towards the Digital Future." *Early Music* 41, no. 1: 129–130.

Rosenwald, Lawrence (2000). "Poetics as Technique." In *A Performer's Guide to Medieval Music*, edited by Ross Duffin, 264–292. Bloomington: Indiana University Press.

Rowland-Jones, Anthony (1995). "The Recorder's Medieval and Renaissance Repertoire: A Commentary." In *The Cambridge Companion to the Recorder*, edited by John Mansfield Thomson, 26–50. Cambridge: Cambridge University Press.

Rubinoff, Kailan R. (2009). "Cracking the Dutch Early Music Movement: The Repercussions of the 1969 Notenkrakersactie." *Twentieth-Century Music* 6, no. 1: 3–22.

Sadler, Graham (2020). "Rameau's Contacts with Britain." In *Musical Exchange between Britain and Europe, 1500–1800: Essays in Honour of Peter Holman*, edited by John Cunningham and Bryan White, 449–464. Woodbridge and Rochester, NY: Boydell Press.

Sadler, Sadler (1979). "Rameau's Harpsichord Transcriptions from 'Les Indes Galantes.'" *Early Music* 7, no. 1: 18–24.

Savall, Jordi (1992). "Performing Early Spanish Music." *Early Music* 20, no. 4: 649–653.

Schab, Alon (2009). "Distress'd Sources?: A Critical Consideration of the Authority of Purcell's Ayres for the Theatre." *Early Music* 37, no. 4: 633–645.

Schab, Alon (2010). "Revisiting the Known and Unknown Misprints in Purcell's Dioclesian." *Music & Letters* 91, no. 3: 343–356.

Schenkman, Walter (1978). "Cassadó's Frescobaldi: A Case of Mistaken Identity or Outright Hoax." *American String Teacher* 28, no. 2: 26–30.

Schubert, Peter (1994). "Authentic Analysis." *Journal of Musicology* 12, no. 1: 3–18.

Schulenberg, David (1992). *The Keyboard Music of J. S. Bach.* New York: Schirmer Books.

Schumann, Robert (1974). *Gesammelte Schriften über Musik und Musiker: Eine Auswahl.* Leipzig: Reclam.

Shay, Robert, and Robert Thompson (2000). *Purcell Manuscripts: The Principal Musical Sources.* Cambridge: Cambridge University Press.

Sherman, Bernard D. (1997). *Inside Early Music: Conversations with Performers.* New York and Oxford: Oxford University Press.

Shull, Jonathan (2006). "Locating the Past in the Present: Living Traditions and the Performance of Early Music." *Ethnomusicology Forum* 15, no. 1: 87–111.

Silbiger, Alexander (1991). "Is the Italian Keyboard Intavolatura a Tablature?" *Recercare* 3: 81–103.

Simpson, Christopher (1659). *The Division Violist: or An Introduction to the Playing upon a Ground.* London.

Skowroneck, Martin, and Tilman Skowroneck (2002). " 'The Harpsichord of Nicholas Lefebvre 1755': The Story of a Forgery without Intent to Defraud." *Galpin Society Journal* 55: 4–14.

Stevens, Denis (1980). *Musicology: A Practical Guide.* London: MacDonald.

Stravinsky, Igor, and Robert Craft (1979). *Conversations with Igor Stravinsky.* London: Faber.

Tai, Hwan-Ching, and Dai-Ting Chung (2012). "Stradivari Violins Exhibit Formant Frequencies Resembling Vowels Produced by Females." *Savart* 1, no. 2. https://www.savartjournal.org/index.php/sj/article/view/16/pdf.

Talbot, Michael (1978). *Vivaldi.* London and Melbourne: J. M. Dent.

Tarling, Judy (2020). "Working with Peter Holman: From a Seat in The Parley of Instruments." In *Musical Exchange between Britain and Europe, 1500–1800: Essays in Honour of Peter Holman*, edited by John Cunningham and Bryan White, 481–483. Woodbridge and Rochester, NY: Boydell Press.

Tatlow, Ruth (2013). "Theoretical Hope: A Vision for the Application of Historically Informed Theory." *Understanding Bach* 8: 33–60.

Upton, Elizabeth (2012). "Concepts of Authenticity in Early Music and Popular Music Communities." *Ethnomusicology Review* 17. https://ethnomusicologyreview.ucla.edu/journal/volume/17/piece/591.

Wegman, Rob C. (2014). "What Is Counterpoint?" In *Improvising Early Music*, edited by Dirk Moelants, 9–68. Collected Writings of the Orpheus Institute, Vol. 11. Leuven: Leuven University Press, 9–68.

Westrup, J. A. (1937). *Purcell.* London: J. M. Dent.

Wind, Thiemo. (n.d.) "Eyck, Jacob van." *Grove Music Online. Oxford Music Online.* Oxford University Press. http://www.oxfordmusiconline.com/subscriber/article/grove/music/09151.

Wind, Thiemo (2004). " 'Fantasia & Echo': Jacob van Eyck's Ultimate Mastery." Translated by Maria van der Heijde-Zomerdijk. *American Recorder* 45, no. 1: 18–24.

Zeichner, Craig (2000). "Early Music Discussion Groups." *Goldberg* 13: 6.

Index